Emerging Market Multinationals

Emerging market multinationals are becoming leaders in their industries, able to compete on equal terms with firms from advanced economies, but their paths toward global leadership are not always smooth. This book examines the specific challenges faced by emerging market multinationals as they seek to develop their international operations and proposes actionable solutions for them. The authors seamlessly combine academic analyses with a rich selection of real-world cases to provide a clear framework for understanding some of the barriers that prevent firms from emerging economies from succeeding abroad and show readers what actions can be taken to achieve sustained international growth. With clear, concise arguments and examples that bring the discussion to life, this insightful book will appeal to managers and students alike.

ALVARO CUERVO-CAZURRA is Professor of International Business and Strategy at Northeastern University, Boston. He is an expert on global strategy, with a special interest in emerging market multinationals. He co-edited *Understanding Multinationals from Emerging Markets* (Cambridge University Press, 2014). For more information, please visit www.cuervo-cazurra.com.

WILLIAM NEWBURRY is the SunTrust Bank Professor and Chair of the Department of Management and International Business at Florida International University. His current research interests focus on how multinational corporations manage and interact with subsidiaries and other local stakeholders.

SEUNG HO PARK is Parkland Chair Professor of Strategy at China Europe International Business School. He was the founding president of Samsung Economic Research Institute, China, and Managing Director of Skolkovo-EY Institute for Emerging Market Studies. His current research focuses on the growth strategies of local companies, the competitive dynamics between multinationals and local companies, and the roles of multinationals in emerging markets.

Emerging Market Multinationals

Managing Operational Challenges for Sustained International Growth

ALVARO CUERVO-CAZURRA, WILLIAM NEWBURRY, AND SEUNG HO PARK

CAMBRIDGE
UNIVERSITY PRESS

CAMBRIDGE
UNIVERSITY PRESS

University Printing House, Cambridge CB2 8BS, United Kingdom

One Liberty Plaza, 20th Floor, New York, NY 10006, USA

477 Williamstown Road, Port Melbourne, VIC 3207, Australia

4843/24, 2nd Floor, Ansari Road, Daryaganj, Delhi - 110002, India

79 Anson Road, #06-04/06, Singapore 079906

Cambridge University Press is part of the University of Cambridge.

It furthers the University's mission by disseminating knowledge in the pursuit of education, learning and research at the highest international levels of excellence.

www.cambridge.org
Information on this title: www.cambridge.org/9781107073142

First published 2016

A catalogue record for this publication is available from the British Library

Library of Congress Cataloging in Publication data
Cuervo-Cazurra, Alvaro, author. | Newburry, William, 1964–
author. | Park, Seung-ho, 1960– author.
Emerging market multinationals : managing operational challenges for
sustained international growth / Alvaro Cuervo-Cazurra,
William Newburry, Seung Ho Park.
New York : Cambridge University Press, 2016.
LCCN 2015042445 | ISBN 9781107073142 (hardback)
LCSH: International business enterprises. | Entrepreneurship. |
International cooperation.
LCC HD62.4 .C84 2016 | DDC 338.8/891724–dc23
LC record available at http://lccn.loc.gov/2015042445

ISBN 978-1-107-07314-2 Hardback
ISBN 978-1-107-42152-3 Paperback

To the memory of
Carmen Cazurra
Lily & Lee Cavanagh and Donald & Elaine Hoffman
Chun Sik Park

Contents

Figures

Tables

Foreword

By now, companies from emerging markets have come to account for 25 percent of the Fortune Global 500, up from 2 percent in 1995. And it has been forecast – by academics as well as consultants – that their share will approach 50 percent by 2025. But whether that happens or not, companies from emerging markets have clearly already developed a significant presence on the list of the world's largest companies. This is presumably not unrelated to the recent surge of interest in them.

What tends to be underemphasized in such discussions, though, is that companies from emerging economies are still significantly less internationalized, in general, than their counterparts from advanced economies. Stick to the Fortune Global 500 list for concreteness. To an (even) greater extent than companies from advanced economies, companies from emerging ones have done well by doing well at home; that is, they are not quite as internationalized in terms of sales. They also tend to report lower levels of R&D-to-sales and advertising-to-sales ratios, although this is due in part to differences in sectoral mix (energy and natural resource companies loom particularly large in the emerging economy list). And companies from emerging economies also tend to be (even) more ethnocentric in terms of their top management and governance.

These patterns in the data do not seem to have weighed much on writings celebrating the arrival of emerging economy multinationals, although the dearth of data often constrains them to overrelying on the same handful of success stories. This book is different. It engages seriously with the operational challenges that underpin the data presented earlier – and that continue to confront emerging economy companies as they multinationalize. Despite its brevity, it draws on a broader range of company examples, considers a broader range of countries of origin, and is significantly less skewed toward depicting just success stories than other recent moves on the same topic. Conceptually, it dovetails with my calculations that there is significantly less distance (defined broadly to include cultural, administrative, and economic differences), on average, between emerging economies than between them and advanced economies, as well as the strategic implications of attempts to model the interactions between competitors from emerging economies and advanced ones. And it manages to assemble a wealth of insights in a compact, easy-to-follow way with its life-cycle view of the challenges encountered in the process of international expansion: country and entry mode selection, establishment, operation and integration, and further expansion.

For all these reasons, I recommend this book as a serious attempt to grapple with the challenges that companies from emerging economies face in their multinationalization journey – and to scout some of the ways forward.

Pankaj Ghemawat
Global Professor of Management and Strategy and Director, Center for the Globalization of Education and Management, Stern School of Business, New York University, and Anselmo Rubiralta Professor of Global Strategy, IESE Business School, Barcelona

Preface

We have been fascinated by emerging market multinationals, and interested in understanding them better, for a long time. In our travels in emerging markets, we observed that emerging market firms were dramatically increasing in size and scope and in some cases expanding beyond their countries at a rapid rate. At the same time, existing recommendations about how to successfully invest in foreign markets did not seem applicable; established theories and models of international expansion were developed by analyzing firms headquartered in advanced economies and did not seem to fit the operating conditions of emerging markets. We thought we needed to go deeper into understanding how such conditions affected the internationalization of emerging market multinationals because we had experienced and observed such differences. All three of us had spent decades analyzing firms in emerging markets.

Sam had direct experience in Asia and Eastern Europe, Alvaro had focused his interests on Latin America, and Bill straddled two continents, having first gained experience in Asia before adding a Latin American focus. We had published extensively on the internationalization of firms, especially emerging market multinationals, but most of these publications were academic. We thought it was time for a managerial book that would sum up our experiences and thoughts and reach a wider audience.

This book started its life as a research project for the Skolkovo-Ernst & Young Institute for Emerging Market Studies (IEMS). In 2012, Sam was the managing director of the Institute and Alvaro and Bill were nonresident senior research fellows. At the 2012 annual meeting, we had animated discussions about the rise of emerging markets and their multinationals and marveled at how some were not only catching up with established competitors from advanced economies but, in some cases, also becoming global leaders. At the time, Sam had just completed his book *Rough Diamonds: The Four Traits of Successful Breakout Firms in BRIC Countries* (Jossey-Bass, 2013), in which he described the rise of these new global competitors and provided some fascinating stories from his conversations with managers. Later, Alvaro co-edited the book *Understanding Multinationals from Emerging Markets* (Cambridge University Press, 2014), in which he analyzed theoretical explanations for the emergence and expansion of emerging country multinationals, while Bill co-edited *Internationalization, Innovation and Sustainability of MNCs in Latin America* (2013) on the internationalization of Latin American firms, which provided additional insights. In our discussions, we realized that most analyses of emerging market multinationals focused on the process of internationalization and how these firms were catching up with advanced country competitors. However, from our exchanges with managers, we noticed that many of these firms faced challenges in their international expansion that had rarely been analyzed.

So, in 2013, we decided to join forces and write a book that would focus exclusively on the internationalization challenges faced by emerging market multinationals. In our consulting experience, we had several interactions with managers of emerging market multinationals and learned how they dealt with these challenges. A well thought-out framework could add additional value beyond our consulting work and reach a wider audience. This book is the result. We hope that it will be both interesting and useful to managers and help them make better decisions that will enable their firms to take full advantage of the opportunities available in foreign countries.

The book benefited from the help of Paula Parish at Cambridge University Press, who generously allowed us flexibility with the message of the book and the schedule. We are also indebted to many managers of emerging market firms who participated in the project. They candidly shared their experiences of the challenges they faced and provided us with the insights that form the basis of our arguments. Some of the background information was collected by a set of excellent research assistants, which include Caroline Paige, Caitlyn McBride, and Vittorio Ligresti at Northeastern University, Ying Liu and Jose Mauricio Geleilate at Florida International University, and Ji Hong at China Europe International Business School. We also thank Dong Chen at Loyola Marymount University and Armando Borda at Esan University for earlier inputs into the project. Finally, we benefited from the financial support of various sources, which include the Skolkovo-Ernst & Young IEMS; the Center for Emerging Markets, the Robert Morrison Fellowship, and the Patrick F. and Helen C. Walsh Research Professorship at Northeastern University; the SunTrust Bank Professorship at Florida International University; and the CEIBS Research Grant, the Parkland Professorship, and the Research Center for Emerging Market Studies at China Europe International Business School. And, of course, the support of our families and friends, Annique, Sebastian, Tristan, Ja Young, Alexandra, and Amelia, was invaluable for getting this project done, in many cases at the expense of time with them. Thank you to all.

Abbreviations

ARCOR	Grupo Arcor
BCG	Boston Consulting Group
BRF	Brasil Foods
BRIC	Brazil, Russia, India, and China
BSNL	Bharat Sanchar Nigam Limited
CEO	chief executive officer
CFIUS	Committee on Foreign Investment in the United States
CFO	chief financial officer
CIA	Central Intelligence Agency
CIFA	Compagnia Italiana Forme Acciaio (Italian Steel Formation Company)
CIS	Commonwealth of Independent States
CITGO	Citgo Petroleum Corporation
CIVETS	Colombia, Indonesia, Vietnam, Egypt, Turkey, and South Africa
CMMI	capability maturity model integration
CNOOC	China National Offshore Oil Corporation
CNPC	China National Petroleum Corporation
COFCO	China National Cereals, Oils and Foodstuffs Corporation
CRT	cathode ray tubes
CSR	corporate social responsibility
CTP	Concern Tractor Plants
DOT	Department of Transportation
DP	Dubai Port World
E&P	exploration and production
EMNCs	emerging market multinational corporations

ENPT	Entreprise Nationale de Travaux aux Puits (National Enterprise to Work Well)
EU	European Union
EY	Ernst & Young
FA	Football Association
FAW	First Automobile Works
FDI	foreign direct investment
FIFA	Fédération Internationale de Football Association (International Federation of Association Football)
GAZ	Gorkovsky Avtomobilny Zavod (Gorky Automobile Plant)
GCP	Global Customer Portal
HAI	Haier Asia International
HPEC	Hong Kong Prosperous Clean Energy Company
HQ	headquarters
HSE	health, safety, and environment
IBM	International Business Machines
IMF	International Monetary Fund
IP	intellectual property
ISAN	Impuesto sobre Automóviles Nuevos (Tax on New Automobiles)
ISO	International Organization for Standardization
IT	information technology
LDV	LDV Group (formerly Leyland DAF Vans)
MINT	Mexico, Indonesia, Nigeria, and Turkey
MIT	Massachusetts Institute of Technology
MNCs	multinational corporations
MTS	Мобильные ТелеСистемы (Mobile TeleSystems)
NBA	National Basketball Association
NTD	New Technology Developer
OFCs	offshore financial centers
OFDI	outward foreign direct investment
PC	personal computer
PDVSA	Petróleos de Venezuela S.A. (Petroleum of Venezuela)

PMI	postmerger integration process
P&O	Peninsular and Oriental Steam Navigation Company
PRC	People's Republic of China
R&D	research and development
SAIC	Shanghai Automotive Industry Corporation
SOE	state-owned enterprise
TCL	TCL Corporation
TTE	TCL-Thomson Electronics
TV	television
UAE	United Arab Emirates
UNCTAD	United Nations Conference on Trade and Development
UNGC	United Nations Global Compact
USWA	United Steelworkers of America
VAT	value-added tax
ZTE	ZTE Corporation

1 Introduction

The rise of EMNCS

1.1 INTRODUCTION

Emerging market multinational corporations (EMNCs) can become successful global players across a wide spectrum of industries, as demonstrated by companies such as the Brazilian airplane manufacturer Embraer, the Mexican bakery Bimbo, the Russian information technology (IT) firm Kaspersky Labs, the Indian conglomerate Tata Group, the South African brewer SABMiller, and the Chinese computer manufacturer Lenovo. This has resulted in a plethora of publications that discuss how such companies can challenge established multinationals from advanced economies and the distinct sources of competitive advantage they develop to achieve this.[1]

However, the paths EMNCs take toward global leadership have not always been smooth. Although many have benefited from the lessons learned from the mistakes made by their predecessors in advanced economies and the advice of academics and consultants on how to select and operate across countries, many also face new challenges that have been largely ignored in previous studies. These new challenges emerge from the conditions of EMNCs' countries of origin, for example, lack of supporting institutions or weak innovation systems,[2] and from firm characteristics that are more prevalent among multinationals from emerging countries, such as family or state ownership.[3]

A large number of authors have analyzed topics that reflect on different aspects of EMNC behaviors. A first set has focused on providing managers of advanced economy multinational corporations (MNCs) with guidance on how to operate more profitably in the challenging conditions of emerging markets. This line of research tends to concentrate on how managers can use and modify capabilities developed in advanced economies in the differing contexts of emerging markets.[4] A second set has focused on understanding how EMNCs represent new competition to MNCs from advanced economies. This line of inquiry tends to present case studies of leading EMNCs and discuss the different business models they have developed.[5] A third set analyzes how the actual behavior of EMNCs differs from current theoretical expectations.[6]

Rather than focusing on how EMNCs emerge as new competitors, and praising their advantages, in this book we take a contrasting and more critical stance, analyzing the challenges that these firms face and drawing lessons from past mistakes. We do, of course, marvel at many of these firms' accomplishments in the last few decades; however, these achievements present a skewed picture of the reality of these firms. Everybody praises the success stories without realizing that, in many cases, firms have struggled in countless unacknowledged ways.

We have written this book to address a void in our understanding of the internationalization of EMNCs by identifying the specific challenges they face and providing solutions to them. We analyze case studies of EMNCs that are expanding abroad, identifying the issues they face in the process of internationalization and providing analytical frameworks and solutions managers can use to address and overcome these difficulties.

1.2 EMERGING MARKET MULTINATIONALS

Before we analyze these challenges, we need to establish what these companies are and how they differ from the well-known multinationals from advanced economies that have been the focus of most existing literature. EMNCs are firms from emerging markets that have value-added activities outside their country of origin. For the purpose of this study, we consider emerging markets as those countries not classified as advanced economies by the International Monetary Fund (IMF).[7] As for value-added activities, we consider not only production facilities but also sales offices, research laboratories, design centers, purchasing offices, or any other activity controlled by the firm abroad that can help it create value. Although some EMNCs operate in many countries, we do not specify a minimum number of countries to qualify an EMNC as a multinational; investment in just one foreign country is sufficient.

EMNCs have increased their presence significantly over the last few decades, which has resulted in a large number of studies analyzing their advantages. However, many of these studies may have overplayed the importance of the rise of EMNCs. In fact, the rapid rise of EMNCs is not that unique. It is part of a general trend of rising outward foreign direct investment (OFDI) that has accompanied the increasing economic integration following the end of the Cold War and the implementation of pro-market reforms throughout the world.[8] Table 1.1 and Figure 1.1 provide a summary of the evolution of OFDI flows and stocks in the last few decades using data available from the United Nations Conference on Trade and Development (UNCTAD). It is noticeable that between 1970 and 2014, OFDI flows from emerging economies grew significantly (from US$0.04 billion to US$388.2 billion) and as a share of world flows grew from 0.28 to 27.3 percent in the same period. However, by 2014 emerging economies still only represented one-third of the OFDI flows from advanced economies, as the latter grew from US$14.1 billion in 1970 to US$1,034.6 billion in that year.

The conclusions from the analysis of OFDI change when we look at stocks rather than flows of OFDI. Between 1980 and 2014, OFDI stocks from emerging countries grew from US$56.8 billion to US$3,735.0 billion. However, as a percentage of the world total, they increased only from 10.16 to 14.74 percent. And the share of emerging country OFDI stock increased only slightly from 10.09 percent in 1980 to 11.13 percent in 2014 when we subtract OFDI from offshore financial centers, which, in many cases, are conduits for investment by firms from advanced economies even though they are classified as investments from emerging economies.

Table 1.1 *OFDI flows and stocks from emerging and advanced economies, selected years*

Emerging economies	**1970**	**1975**	**1980**	**1985**	**1990**	**1995**	**2000**	**2005**	**2010**	**2014**
OFDI flows (US$ million)	40	416	2,605	1,918	560	17,161	63,308	108,005	323,321	388,198
OFDI stocks (US$ million)	n.a.	n.a.	56,809	66,293	89,648	162,789	333,166	735,133	2,268,097	3,734,964
OFDI flows as percentage of world total	0.28	1.46	4.99	3.08	0.23	4.76	5.24	13.17	22.55	27.28
OFDI stocks as percentage of world total	n.a.	n.a.	10.16	7.35	3.97	4.06	4.51	6.19	10.88	14.74
Emerging economies minus OFCs	**1970**	**1975**	**1980**	**1985**	**1990**	**1995**	**2000**	**2005**	**2010**	**2014**
OFDI flows (US$ million)	40	389	2,280	1,620	2,173	11,067	18,840	79,879	241,252	300,360
OFDI stocks (US$ million)	n.a.	n.a.	56,406	65,661	87,258	143,199	227,391	538,599	1,726,155	2,818,963

OFDI flows as percentage of world total	0.28	1.37	4.37	2.61	0.90	3.07	1.56	9.74	16.83	21.11
OFDI stocks as percentage of world total	n.a.	n.a.	10.09	7.28	3.87	3.57	3.08	4.54	8.28	11.13
Advanced economies	**1970**	**1975**	**1980**	**1985**	**1990**	**1995**	**2000**	**2005**	**2010**	**2015**
OFDI flows (US$ million)	14,101	28,099	49,601	60,262	241,580	343,059	1,145,125	712,040	1,110,393	1,034,554
OFDI stocks (US$ million)	n.a.	n.a.	502,397	835,707	2,165,880	3,844,308	7,054,178	11,139,886	18,575,589	21,597,706
OFDI flows as percentage of world total	99.72	98.54	95.01	96.92	99.77	95.24	94.76	86.83	77.45	72.72
OFDI stocks as percentage of world total	n.a.	n.a.	89.84	92.65	96.03	95.94	95.49	93.81	89.12	85.26

Source: Computed using data from UNCTAD (2015) using the IMF (2013) classification of advanced economies and the IMF (2011) classification of offshore finance centers (OFCs). n.a.: not available.

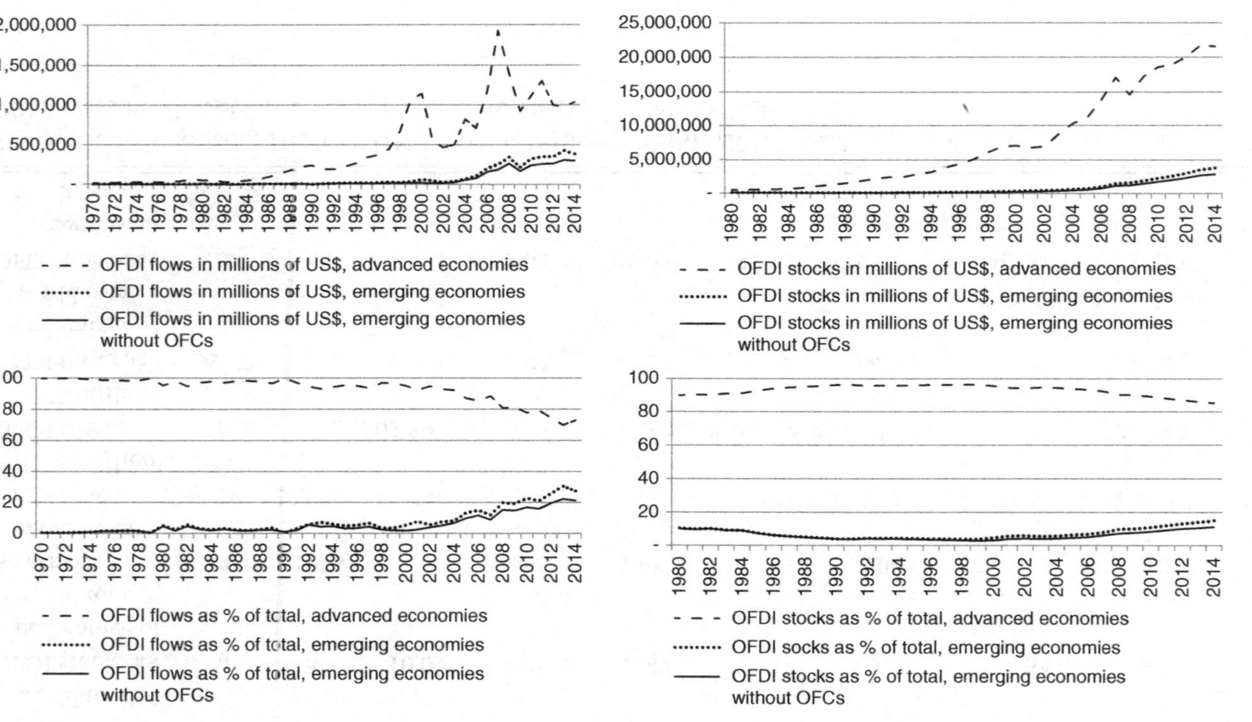

FIGURE 1.1 Evolution of OFDI from advanced and emerging economies

Although the OFDI figures are representative of the increase in the multinationalization of these firms, they provide a macro picture. We want to focus on the actual firms that have undertaken OFDI and concentrate on lists that identify EMNCs, the object of our study. Unfortunately, there is no one single list of EMNCs; classification varies by source as different criteria are used for inclusion. We have to review several lists.

The first is firms from emerging markets that appear in the Forbes Global 2000 list of the largest publicly traded companies. Although not all EMNCs are large publicly traded firms and not all large publicly traded firms from emerging markets are EMNCs, many leading EMNCs are large publicly traded firms. With these caveats in mind, Table 1.2 presents the largest 50 companies from emerging markets, included based on a mix of sales, profits, assets, and market value in 2015. The list presents some interesting surprises, as it has at the head many banks and insurance firms with limited international operations. Nevertheless, with these exceptions, many of the nonfinancial firms are true multinationals with operations in multiple countries, while some of the financial firms are also present in multiple countries. The distribution of the 475 firms from emerging markets among the 2,000 largest publicly traded firms (by country, 2015) reflects the size of the underlying economies: China (180), India (56), Russia (27), Brazil (24), Saudi Arabia (20), Malaysia (16), Thailand (16), Mexico (13), South Africa (13), United Arab Emirates (UAE) (13), Turkey (12), Qatar (9), Bermuda (8), Chile (8), Philippines (8), Indonesia (7), Poland (6), Colombia (5), Kuwait (5), Nigeria (4), Venezuela (4), Morocco (3), Vietnam (3), Bahrain, Lebanon, and Peru (2 each), and Argentina, Cyprus, Czech Republic, Egypt, Jordan, Kazakhstan, Oman, Pakistan, and Puerto Rico (1 each).

In 2006, the consulting company Boston Consulting Group (BCG) began compiling a list of firms from emerging markets that were viewed as challengers to established multinationals from advanced economies, based on a combination of size and subjective measures. Table 1.3 provides this list for 2014, which shows 100 global challengers dominated by firms from China (29) and India (19), followed by Brazil (13),

Table 1.2 *List of the 50 largest publicly traded firms from emerging markets among the global 2000 largest, 2015 (US$ billion)*

Global rank	Company	Country	Sales	Profits	Assets	Market value
1	ICBC	China	166.8	44.8	3,322.0	278.3
2	China Construction Bank	China	130.5	37.0	2,698.9	212.9
3	Agricultural Bank of China	China	129.2	29.1	2,574.8	189.9
4	Bank of China	China	120.3	27.5	2,458.3	199.1
8	PetroChina	China	333.4	17.4	387.7	334.6
20	China Mobile	China	104.1	17.7	209.0	271.5
24	Sinopec	China	427.6	7.7	233.9	121.0
28	Gazprom	Russia	158.0	24.1	356.0	62.5
32	Ping An Insurance Group	China	75.3	6.4	645.7	113.8
37	China Life Insurance	China	71.4	5.2	362.1	160.5
38	Bank of Communications	China	53.6	10.7	1,010.4	71.2
43	Itaú Unibanco Holding	Brazil	76.6	9.2	424.0	63.7
55	China Merchants Bank	China	45.5	9.1	762.7	64.0
59	Rosneft	Russia	129.0	9.0	150.0	51.1
61	Banco Bradesco	Brazil	66.7	6.5	403.1	51.4
73	Industrial Bank	China	39.4	7.6	650.8	57.9

79	China Minsheng Banking	China	40.0	7.2	647.2	51.7
84	Shanghai Pudong Development	China	38.2	7.6	676.3	49.2
94	China Citic Bank	China	38.3	6.6	667.1	49.7
103	CNOOC	China	44.6	9.8	106.8	64.4
109	LukOil	Russia	121.4	4.7	111.8	43.5
112	China State Construction Engineering	China	120.3	3.9	150.6	36.8
116	Saudi Basic Industries	Saudi Arabia	50.4	6.2	90.9	64.0
124	Sberbank	Russia	58.1	7.6	420.0	26.9
125	América Móvil	Mexico	63.7	3.5	85.2	74.5
127	China Shenhua Energy	China	39.6	6.0	85.8	63.8
130	SAIC Motor	China	99.5	4.4	62.1	47.1
133	Banco do Brasil	Brazil	68.8	5.0	482.9	23.6
143	Reliance Industries	India	71.7	3.7	76.6	42.9
144	China Telecom	China	52.7	2.9	90.5	53.9
145	China Everbright Bank	China	25.2	4.7	441.2	35.1
152	State Bank of India	India	40.8	2.3	400.6	33.0
155	China Communications Construction	China	58.5	2.3	101.6	41.2
160	China Railway Group	China	96.8	1.7	110.1	39.7
169	China Railway Construction	China	94.1	1.8	99.5	33.7

Table 1.2 (*cont.*)

Global rank	Company	Country	Sales	Profits	Assets	Market value
173	China Pacific Insurance	China	35.5	1.8	133.0	48.4
183	Oil & Natural Gas	India	28.7	4.4	59.3	43.7
185	China Unicom	China	46.2	2.0	88.0	39.8
198	Ecopetrol	Colombia	34.4	3.8	59.8	33.6
208	People's Insurance Company	China	55.7	2.1	126.0	21.8
209	Surgutneftegas	Russia	26.6	8.8	74.6	24.2
225	PTT PCL	Thailand	87.3	1.7	54.7	29.1
234	Dalian Wanda Commercial Properties	China	17.7	4.0	91.0	28.1
251	China Vanke	China	24.1	2.6	81.9	24.3
263	Tata Motors	India	42.3	2.7	37.4	28.8
269	Alibaba	China	11.5	4.4	43.6	201.7
273	Huaxia Bank	China	16.2	2.9	290.6	19.2
284	ICICI Bank	India	14.2	1.9	124.8	30.0
304	Tencent Holdings	China	12.8	3.9	27.6	181.1

Source: Forbes (2015).

Table 1.3 *Global challengers from emerging markets by country, 2014*

Country	Companies
Argentina	Tenaris
Brazil	Brasil Foods, Camargo Correa Group, Embraer, Gerdau, Iochpe-Maxion, JBS, Marcopolo, Natura Cosméticos, Odebrecht Group, Petrobras, Tigre, Votorantim Group, WEG
Chile	Concha y Toro, Fallabella, Latam Airlines Group
China	Alibaba Group, Aviation Industry Corporation of China, China Communications Construction Company, China National Chemical Corporation (ChemChina), China Minmetals, China Shenhua Energy, China Shipbuilding Industry Corporation, China International Marine Containers, CITIC Group, China National Offshore Oil Corporation, China Railway Construction Corporation, Fuyao Glass Industry Group, Geely International, Goldwind, Haier Group, Johnson Electric, Mindray Medical International, PetroChina, Shanghai Electric Group, Sinochem, Sinoh ydro, Sinoma International Engineering, Sinopec, Tencent Holdings, Trina Solar, China UnionPay, Wanxiang Group, Zoomlion, ZTE
Colombia	Grupo Empresarial Antioqueño
Egypt	El Sewedy Electric
India	Apollo Tyres, Bajaj Auto, Bharti Airtel, Crompton Greaves, Dr. Reedy's Laboratories, Godrej Consumer Products, Hindalco Industries, Infosys, Larsen & Toubro, Lupin Pharmaceuticals, Mahindra & Mahindra, Motherson Sumi Industries, Reliance Industries, Sun Pharmaceutical Industries, Tata Consultancy Services, Tata Motors, UPL, Vendata Resources, Wipro
Indonesia	Golden Agri-Resources, Indofood
Malaysia	AirAsia, Petronas
Mexico	Alfa, América Movil, Femsa, Gruma, Mabe, Mexichem
Philippines	Jollibee Foods

Table 1.3 (*cont.*)

Country	Companies
Quatar	Qatar Airways
Russia	EuroChem Mineral and Chemical, Gazprom, Lukoil, Severstal
Saudi Arabia	Saudi Basic Industries
South Africa	Aspen Pharmacare, Bidvest Group, MTN Group, Sasol
Thailand	Charoen Pokphand Group, IndoramaVentures, PTT, Thai Beverage, Thai Union Group
Turkey	Koc Holding, Sabanci Holding, Turkish Airlines, Yildiz Holding
UAE	Emirates Global Aluminum, Etihad Airways, Etisalat

Source: BCG (2014).

Mexico (6), Thailand (5), Turkey (4), South Africa (4), Russia (4), Chile (3), UAE (3), Indonesia and Malaysia (2 each), and Argentina, Colombia, Egypt, Philippines, Qatar, and Saudi Arabia (1 each). However, the usefulness of this list for identifying all leading EMNCs is limited given that BCG excludes what it terms "graduates" from the list, that is, firms that become widely dispersed multinationals. In 2014, graduates included the Brazilian miner Vale, the Chinese telecom-equipment maker Huawei, the Chinese PC maker Lenovo, the Chinese supply chain company Li & Fung, the Indian steel producer Tata Steel, the Indonesian agribusiness company Wilmar International, the Mexican construction materials company Cemex, the Mexican baker Grupo Bimbo, the Saudi Arabian oil company Saudi Aramco, the South African miner Anglo American, the South African brewer SABMiller, and the UAE airline Emirates.

Another alternative list of EMNCs appears in UNCTAD, which ranks the largest nonfinancial transnational firms based on foreign assets. However, this source classifies countries the IMF (2013) considers advanced – Hong Kong, South Korea, Taiwan, and Singapore – as emerging. We omitted firms from these countries from the remaining firms in the UNCTAD list shown in Table 1.4. This list is more

Table 1.4 *Largest EMNCs by foreign assets, 2012*

Corporation	Home economy	Industry	Assets (US$ million)		Sales (US$ million)		Employment	
			Foreign	Total	Foreign	Total	Foreign	Total
CITIC Group	China	Diversified	78,602	565,884	9,561	55,487	25,285	125,215
Petronas – Petroliam Nasional Bhd	Malaysia	Petroleum expl./ref./distr.	49,072	163,275	71,939	94,543	5,244	46,145
Vale SA	Brazil	Mining and quarrying	45,721	131,478	38,326	47,694	15,680	85,305
China Ocean Shipping (Group) Co.	China	Transport and storage	43,452	56,126	19,139	29,101	4,400	130,000
China National Offshore Oil Corp.	China	Petroleum expl./ref./distr.	34,276	129,834	21,887	83,537	3,387	102,562
América Móvil SAB de CV	Mexico	Telecommunications	32,008	75,697	37,395	58,950	67,525	158,719
Lukoil OAO	Russia	Petroleum and natural gas	31,174	98,961	113,801	139,171	18,144	120,300
Cemex S.A.B. de C.V.	Mexico	Nonmetallic mineral products	30,730	36,808	11,717	14,986	35,387	45,087
Petróleos de Venezuela S.A. (PDVSA)	Venezuela	Petroleum expl./ref./distr.	27,462	218,424	46,899	123,223	4,877	126,945

Table 1.4 (*cont.*)

Corporation	Home economy	Industry	Assets (US$ million)		Sales (US$ million)		Employment	
			Foreign	Total	Foreign	Total	Foreign	Total
Sabic – Saudi Basic Industries Corp.	Saudi Arabia	Petroleum expl./ref./distr.	23,540	90,089	33,377	50,422	25,391	40,000
Gazprom JSC	Russia	Petroleum and natural gas	23,425	396,454	92,016	153,863	27,400	431,200
Tata Motors Ltd.	India	Automobiles	21,575	31,281	26,519	34,765	20,379	62,716
Ooredoo QSC	Qatar	Telecommunications	20,304	26,104	7,601	9,303	15,289	17,130
China National Petroleum Corporation (CNPC)	China	Petroleum expl./ref./distr.	19,284	541,083	11,296	425,720	31,442	1,656,465
Abu Dhabi National Energy Co PJSC	UAE	Utilities (electricity, gas, water)	18,198	33,377	5,660	7,566	2,547	3,300
Genting Bhd	Malaysia	Other consumer services	17,719	21,940	3,411	5,599	43,559	58,000
Petroleo Brasileiro SA	Brazil	Petroleum expl./ref./distr.	16,927	331,078	14,071	144,275	7,640	85,065
Gerdau SA	Brazil	Metal and metal products	15,684	26,072	11,677	19,475	19,211	41,869

MTN Group Ltd.	South Africa	Telecommunications	15,263	21,409	10,651	16,486	19,690	27,000
Bharti Airtel Limited	India	Telecommunications	15,153	30,783	4,442	14,796	10,514	24,725
Tata Steel Ltd.	India	Metal and metal products	14,994	27,027	17,658	24,803	37,638	80,534
Sinochem Group	China	Petroleum expl./ref./distr.	14,704	45,488	55,555	71,891	9,828	48,414
YTL Corporation Bhd	Malaysia	Utilities (electricity, gas, water)	13,010	16,154	4,920	6,499	6,405	9,000
Steinhoff International Holdings Ltd.	South Africa	Other consumer goods	12,453	16,090	8,008	10,374	49,632	79,900
Lenovo Group Ltd.	China	Electrical and electronic equipment	11,962	16,882	19,335	33,873	8,092	35,026
Fomento Economico Mexicano SAB	Mexico	Food, beverages, and tobacco	11,919	22,752	6,292	18,125	35,560	182,260
Hindalco Industries Ltd.	India	Diversified	11,325	22,186	11,249	14,765	11,618	20,238
Gold Fields Ltd.	South Africa	Metal and metal products	10,931	11,200	3,078	3,528	18,030	44,230
Oil and Natural Gas Corp. Ltd.	India	Petroleum expl./ref./distr.	10,930	46,630	3,233	29,901	3,908	32,923

Table 1.4 (*cont.*)

Corporation	Home economy	Industry	Assets (US$ million)		Sales (US$ million)		Employment	
			Foreign	Total	Foreign	Total	Foreign	Total
Sonatrach	Algeria	Petroleum and natural gas	10,358	103,584	71,722	75,608	5,061	50,608
Etisalat – Emirates Telecom Corp.	UAE	Telecommunications	9,834	21,821	2,546	8,972	7,280	42,000
Sasol Limited	South Africa	Chemicals	9,486	24,638	11,008	21,855	5,600	34,916
San Miguel Corp.	Philippines	Food, beverages, and tobacco	9,437	25,298	2,017	16,601	2,838	18,275
Zain	Kuwait	Telecommunications	9,412	10,438	3,398	4,585	5,344	6,541
JBS SA	Brazil	Food, beverages, and tobacco	8,804	24,307	29,577	38,813	78,842	140,000
Ternium SA	Argentina	Metal and metal products	8,412	10,867	5,919	8,608	10,955	16,600
China Mobile Limited	China	Telecommunications	8,349	166,972	4,445	88,906	0	182,487
Naspers Ltd.	South Africa	Other consumer services	7,769	8,811	1,576	4,649	15,413	19,000

Tata Consultancy Services	India	Other services	7,247	9,616	10,602	11,598	20,546	276,196
Grupo Bimbo SAB de CV	Mexico	Food, beverages, and tobacco	7,209	10,491	7,164	13,168	48,592	122,986
Orascom Construction Industries SAE	Egypt	Construction	7,146	11,271	4,281	5,510	47,548	75,000
China Electronics Corporation (CEC)	China	Electronics	7,784	29,047	6,841	25,527	34,825	129,948
Dubai Port (DP) World Limited	UAE	Transport and storage	6,877	16,434	1,009	3,121	14,560	28,000
Sime Darby Bhd	Malaysia	Diversified	6,628	15,068	10,680	15,318	27,638	108,675
Turkcell Iletisim Hizmetleri AS	Turkey	Telecommunications	6,461	10,428	532	5,839	4,190	13,901
Severstal Group Holdings	Russia	Metal and metal products	5,954	15,707	2,344	14,104	11,557	67,297
China National Cereals, Oils and Foodstuffs Corporation (COFCO) Ltd.	China	Food, beverages, and tobacco	5,952	41,264	0	31,752	45,330	106,642
Embraer	Brazil	Aircraft	5,707	9,465	5,371	6,245	3,246	18,032
Medi-Clinic Corp. Ltd.	South Africa	Other consumer services	5,343	6,154	1,693	2,892	8,548	23,475

Table 1.4 (*cont.*)

Corporation	Home economy	Industry	Assets (US$ million)		Sales (US$ million)		Employment	
			Foreign	Total	Foreign	Total	Foreign	Total
Mechel OAO	Russia	Metal and metal products	5,186	17,695	5,711	11,275	8,715	90,465
Sinopec – China Petrochemical Corp.	China	Petroleum expl./ref./distr.	5,030	201,027	110,734	441,991	1,000	376,201
China Minmetals Corp.	China	Metal and metal products	4,885	39,225	8,239	51,482	62,100	126,036
Suzlon Energy Ltd.	India	Diversified	3,990	5,337	3,186	3,451	9,064	13,000
Netcare Ltd.	South Africa	Other consumer services	3,892	5,325	1,314	3,131	8,578	28,032
Sappi Ltd.	South Africa	Wood and paper products	3,866	6,168	4,788	6,347	9,563	14,039
Enka Insaat ve Sanayi AS	Turkey	Construction and real estate	3,804	8,209	1,365	5,722	10,042	21,290
China Railway Construction Corp. Ltd.	China	Construction	3,761	76,282	2,682	74,543	21,932	224,523

Source: UNCTAD (2014). We excluded firms from Korea, Hong Kong, Singapore, and Taiwan from this list because these countries are considered advanced in the IMF (2013) classification.

accurate than others because it uses a combination of foreign assets, sales, and employees to categorize companies as EMNCs or transnationals and so provides a very different view of EMNCs. The list is still dominated by China (12), which is followed by South Africa (8), India (7), Brazil (5), Malaysia, Mexico, and Russia (4 each), UAE (3), Turkey (2), and Algeria, Argentina, Egypt, Kuwait, Philippines, Qatar, Saudi Arabia, and Venezuela (1 each).

All these different classifications show how difficult it is to identify EMNCs. There is no list to provide us that information, and if it did exist, it would probably be size based. But identifying the largest or leading EMNCs is not the objective of this book because we are not aiming to explain how they achieved their size. Instead, we want to understand the challenges these firms as well as small EMNCs faced when they moved out of their home countries and entered other emerging and advanced markets. Moreover, the challenges we want to identify are faced by both well-run and poorly run EMNCs.

Gathering information about this is not easy. Few managers are willing to talk openly about the problems faced by their firms, which is understandable, bad publicity can be misconstrued. Nevertheless, it is as important to understand and analyze the success of firms as it is to understand and analyze their difficulties. To do this, we relied on secondary accounts from the press, case studies, and academic analyses. We also interviewed managers of firms in emerging markets and key informants who were willing to discuss the challenges faced, on the condition they remained anonymous. We also conducted case studies that focused on the internationalization of EMNCs and the specific problems they faced abroad.

1.3 CONCLUSIONS

EMNCs have become major contenders and, in some cases, leaders in their industries. This is a recent phenomenon that is attracting a great deal of attention in the literature. However, despite the success of these firms, there is still much for their managers to do to accomplish their goals. International expansion has not been a smooth path for EMNCs, and surprisingly, these "bumps in the road" have received little attention. This is partly due to some hyperbolic analyses of these firms and a lack of critical assessment, but it is also due to the challenge of finding information on the difficulties these firms face. In this book, we provide an analysis of these challenges and discuss solutions to them that managers may find relevant and useful when they take their firms abroad.

Notes

1. This includes both consulting reports (e.g., BCG, 2014), newspaper articles (e.g., Economist, 2008), and edited academic books (e.g., Cuervo-Cazurra and Ramamurti, 2014; Ramamurti & Singh, 2009; Sauvant, 2008; Williamson, Ramamurti, Fleury and Fleury, 2013) in addition to the usual interest in academic journals (e.g., see the special issues edited by Aulakh, 2007; Luo & Tung, 2007; Cuervo-Cazurra, 2012; and Gammeltoft, Barnard and Madhok, 2010).
2. See Khanna and Palepu (2010) for a discussion of the conditions of emerging markets, in particular what they call institutional voids, and how these affect the behavior of firms in and coming from emerging markets.
3. See Ramamurti (2012) and Cuervo-Cazurra (2012) and the chapters in Cuervo-Cazurra and Ramamurti (2014) for a review of the unique traits of EMNCs.
4. Among these, one finds Yadong Luo's *Multinational Enterprises in Emerging Markets* (Copenhagen Business School Press, 2002), Nenad Pacek and Daniel Thorniley's *Emerging Markets: Lessons for Business Success and the Outlook for Different Markets* (Profile Books, 2004), Tarun Khanna and Krishna G. Palepu's *Winning in Emerging Markets: A Roadmap for Strategy and Execution* (Harvard Business Press, 2010), Jim O'Neill's *The Growth Map: Economic Opportunity in the BRICs and Beyond* (Penguin, 2011), Harvard Business Review's *Harvard Business Review on Thriving in Emerging Markets* (Harvard Business School Publishing, 2011), and Anil K. Gupta, Toshiro Wakayama, and U. Srinivasa Rangan's *Global Strategies for Emerging Asia* (Jossey Bass, 2012).
5. In this line of inquiry, one finds Ming Zeng and Peter Williamson's *Dragons at Your Door* (Harvard Business Press, 2007), Antoine van Agtmael's *The*

Emerging Markets Century: How a New Breed of World-Class Companies Is Overtaking the World (Free Press, 2007), Jean Paul Laçon's *Chinese Multinationals* (World Scientific, 2009), Lourdes Casanova's *Global Latinas: Latin America's Emerging Multinationals* (Insead Business Press, 2009), Arthur Yeung, Katherine Xin, Waldemar Pfoertsch, and Shengjun Liu's *The Globalization of Chinese Companies: Strategies for Conquering International Markets* (Wiley, 2011), Afonso Fleury and Maria Tereza Leme Fleury's *Brazilian Multinationals: Competences for Internationalization* (Cambridge University Press, 2011), Andrei Panibratov's *Russian Multinationals: From Regional Supremacy to Global Lead* (Routledge, 2012), Mauro Guillen and Esteban Garcia-Canal's *Emerging Markets Rule: Growth Strategies of the New Global Giants* (McGraw Hill, 2012), Amitava Chattopadhyay, Rajeev Batra, and Aysegul Ozsomer's *The New Emerging Market Multinationals: Four Strategies for Disrupting Markets and Building Brands* (McGraw Hill, 2012), and Javier Santiso's *The Decade of the Multilatinas* (Cambridge University Press, 2013).

6. Among these, one finds Alvaro Cuervo-Cazurra and Ravi Ramamurti's *Understanding Multinationals from Emerging Markets* (Cambridge University Press, 2014), Andrea Goldstein's *Multinational Companies from Emerging Economies: Composition, Conceptualization and Direction in the Global Economy* (Palgrave Macmillan, 2007), Karl P. Sauvant's *The Rise of Transnational Corporations from Emerging Markets: Threat or Opportunity?* (Edward Elgar, 2008), and Karl P. Sauvant, Wolfgang A. Maschek, and Geraldine A. McAllister's *Foreign Direct Investments from Emerging Markets: The Challenges Ahead* (Palgrave Macmillan, 2010).
7. The countries considered advanced by the IMF were the following (IMF, 2013): Australia, Austria, Belgium, Canada, Cyprus, Czech Republic, Denmark, Estonia, Finland, France, Germany, Greece, Hong Kong, Iceland, Ireland, Israel, Italy, Japan, Korea, Latvia, Luxembourg, Malta, Netherlands, New Zealand, Norway, Portugal, San Marino, Singapore, Slovak Republic, Slovenia, Spain, Sweden, Switzerland, Taiwan, United Kingdom (UK), and United States (US).
8. For a review of globalization and the spread of pro-market reforms, see Yergin and Stanislaw (1998).

2 Understanding the challenges of internationalization

2.1 INTRODUCTION

Expanding across borders can be a highly beneficial growth strategy for a company. It can find new markets for its products, new sources of raw materials, cheaper labor, or more sophisticated technology. For this reason, increasing numbers of firms are moving out of the confines of their home markets to export products and services, import production factors, and invest abroad to control access to customers or suppliers.[1] Even if managers were not aware that the firm's products could have a market abroad, they may have been contacted by customers or entrepreneurs looking to distribute new products and convinced that the positive prospects in the new country would lead the company toward foreign markets.[2]

However, expansion across borders is also challenging.[3] Success at home does not always result in success abroad, no matter how well liked the products are at home and how desirable they seem to be to customers abroad. Venturing abroad entails serving customers with different preferences, facing new and, in some cases, stronger competitors, and having to deal with cultural, economic, technological, social, legal, and political differences between countries. These will affect the overseas success not only of emerging market multinational corporations (EMNCs) but also of highly successful firms from advanced economies. For example, the US retailer Walmart entered the German market in 1997 but was unable to operate profitably there and decided to exit in 2006. Although Walmart was the largest retailer in the world and had a highly sophisticated logistics system, it could not understand the preferences of German consumers and was unable to counter the strengths of low-cost local competitors.[4] Moreover, failure in the German market was not a unique occurrence for Walmart; it was also unable to understand Korean consumers and had to exit that market as well. And failure abroad was not restricted to Walmart; the first foreign venture of the US retailer Target into Canada in 2013 was also a failure, this time because of difficulties in the management of its supply chain and an inability to face domestic rivals, which led to its exit in 2015.[5]

EMNCs face many of the same challenges as multinational corporations (MNCs) from advanced economies, but they also have to deal with additional challenges that are unique to the conditions of their country of origin and affect not only their operations at home but also their international expansion.[6] For example, they typically come from countries where a large portion of the population has a low level of income, and they operate in countries with underdeveloped institutions,[7] which affect how they create an advantage at home and how they can transfer this advantage and operate abroad.

2.2 A PROCESS APPROACH TO THE CHALLENGES OF INTERNATIONALIZATION

We adopt a process view to analyze the challenges EMNCs face in their international expansion. Although this process is not unique to EMNCs, and some of the challenges discussed are also experienced by firms from advanced economies, companies from emerging countries hit a barrage of challenges when they expand abroad. To facilitate the identification and analysis of these challenges, and the solutions to them, we compartmentalize and separate them into two sets based on a series of decisions the firm takes as it expands abroad.

Figure 2.1 summarizes this process framework.[8] The first set contains three decisions EMNCs have to make as they seek to enter and start operating in a foreign country[9]: choice of host country, selection of the specific mode used to enter the host country, and establishment of a viable operation there. The second set contains decisions managers have to make once a new operation is established in the host country and begins to coordinate with activities undertaken in other

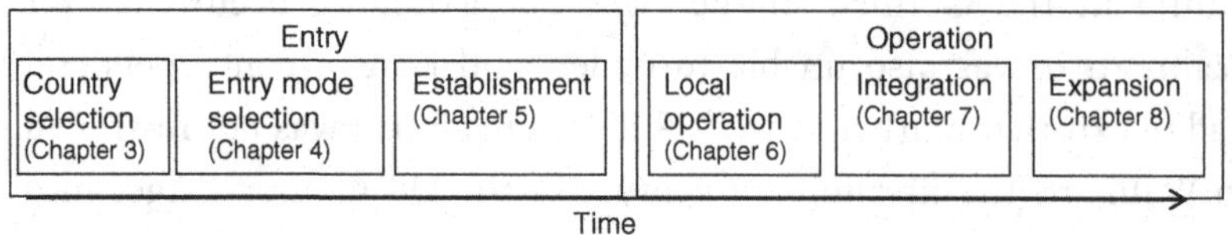

FIGURE 2.1 Chain of decisions in the internationalization process of the firm

countries: management of the local operation, integration of the local operation with other operations in the company, and expansion of the local operation within the host country and across other industries or countries.

This process view identifies the manager of the firm as the decision maker who proactively determines the internationalization of the firm, the location and type of operations, integration, and expansion. In Table 2.1, we summarize the sequence of decisions that the manager has to take into account at each of the stages of international expansion. We present this as a sequential process, with decisions at one stage forming the foundation for subsequent decisions.

First, in country selection, which we analyze in Chapter 3, the manager has to identify the reason behind taking the company abroad and determine either how the company's existing competitive advantage can be used abroad or what new comparative advantages can be gained by entering a foreign market. Once this is done, the manager has to analyze how to transfer advantage across borders. Challenges that the manager faces here may be that the company's existing competitive advantage is not appropriate for the country selected or that the company is unable to access and transfer advantage across borders.

Second, in the selection of entry mode, which we analyze in Chapter 4, the manager has to identify the complementary resources needed to expand across borders in order for the firm to be able to compete and operate in the host country and then select the mode that best enables the company to obtain them. Potential challenges the manager confronts here may be that the company cannot access

Table 2.1 *Types of challenges in internationalization and their consequences*

Action	Decisions	Challenges
Country selection (Chapter 3)	Identify the objective of foreign expansion Identify the advantage that drives the foreign expansion Select the country to enter Transfer the advantage across borders	The company cannot transfer advantage across borders The industry is not viable in the host country The country selected is not appropriate for the company
Entry mode (Chapter 4)	Identify the complementary resources needed to expand across borders Identify the complementary resources needed to compete abroad Identify the complementary resources needed to operate abroad Select the entry mode that best helps obtain the complementary resources needed	The company lacks complementary resources to operate across borders The company lacks complementary resources to compete in the industry in the host country The company lacks complementary resources to operate within host-country institutions The entry mode used is not appropriate for obtaining the complementary resources needed
Establishment (Chapter 5)	Identify the resources that create disadvantages abroad Avoid or diminish the resources that create disadvantages abroad	The company transfers resources that create disadvantages abroad The government discriminates against companies from the

Table 2.1 (*cont.*)

Action	Decisions	Challenges
	Have foreign operation fully functional and competitive	country of origin of the firm Consumers discriminate against companies from the country of origin of the firm
Local operation (Chapter 6)	Identify and develop relationships with important local stakeholders, particularly those less prevalent in the home-country environment, such as unions Identify host-country institutional and social expectations and how to meet them	The company has inexperienced managers and employees The company lacks experience with unions in the host country The company has limited reputation with customers and society
Integration (Chapter 7)	Identify the mandate of the local operation Identify the relationship of the local operation with headquarters (HQ) Identify effective means of transferring knowledge Establish effective corporate governance structures for the subsidiary	The company lacks scalable organizational structures that will allow the firm to integrate operations Corporate governance of HQ such as being state-owned, family-owned, and/or part of a business group creates challenges for effective corporate governance
Expansion (Chapter 8)	Identify new business opportunities in the local country	The company faces network management issues needed to facilitate expansion

Table 2.1 (*cont.*)

Action	Decisions	Challenges
	Identify advantages that can be used to benefit from new business opportunities Identify new business opportunities outside the country that can be served from the local operation Identify advantages that can be used to set up new business opportunities outside the country in coordination with other subsidiaries	The company lacks learning capabilities to integrate location-based knowledge into the overall organization Expansion requires developing additional firm capabilities to facilitate a more extensive operation The company's growth increases stakeholder demands of the company

these complementary resources and as a result cannot operate in the host country.

Third, to establish an operation in the host country, which we analyze in Chapter 5, the manager has to identify any disadvantages caused by resources the company transfers to the host country. Once those disadvantages are identified, they will have to be addressed swiftly. The challenge the manager faces here is that disadvantages may not just be transferred; they can also emerge suddenly and limit the firm's ability to set up a fully functioning operation in the host country.

Fourth, once the company has a fully functional operation in the host country, the manager has to solidify relationships with customers, employees, and other stakeholders to ensure that the transferred competitive advantage lasts. We analyze this in Chapter 6. This entails strengthening and protecting competitive advantage from local competitors, as well as identifying and satisfying emerging social and institutional demands. Some of the major challenges the manager faces here involve overcoming a relative lack of managerial talent and other qualified labor, building experience – particularly in dealing with unions and legal issues – and overcoming a lack of firm reputation in the host country.

Fifth, the manager has to identify how to integrate the local operation within the mandate of HQ and with other subsidiaries in the network of the multinational, which we analyze in Chapter 7. The manager can strengthen and change such relationships by establishing and refining effective corporate governance and control standards. The challenge the manager faces here is that the mandate from HQ may not match the abilities of the local operation or that the local operation is unable to integrate with other subsidiaries to support its global advantage. Knowledge transfer between the local operation and HQ or other subsidiaries becomes a key issue during this stage.

Sixth, once the local operation is fully competitive and integrated with the network of subsidiaries in the multinational, the manager may decide to continue growing the operation, finding new business opportunities, deploying new sources of advantage to make the most of them, and developing appropriate activities, which we analyze in Chapter 8. Business opportunities can occur in the host country, and the company can grow within the industry or diversify into new industries. Business opportunities may also occur in other countries, and the manager can decide whether the firm should pursue these. The challenges the manager faces here are that the subsidiary, in conjunction with the parent company and other subsidiaries in the EMNC network, needs to ensure an effective management of the network to enable expansion or that the local operation cannot build the capabilities and advantages needed to benefit from new opportunities.

2.3 CONCLUSIONS

We take a process view to analyze the sequence of decisions managers have to make to address the challenges EMNCs face abroad. Although the overall process framework can be used to analyze the challenges of multinationals in general, we focus on the specific challenges faced by MNCs in emerging economies.

In the following chapters, we analyze each of the six steps identified in Table 2.1 in turn, exploring how EMNCs deal with these issues. We pay particular attention to how the country of origin of these companies affects the decisions and challenges the firms face, because the country of origin is the principal factor that sets EMNCs apart from multinationals from advanced countries. Thus, although some of the challenges described may be familiar to managers of advanced economy multinationals, there are nuances that only managers of EMNCs experience.

Notes

1. A discussion of the motives behind the expansion of firms appears in Dunning (1993) and in Cuervo-Cazurra, Narula, and Un (2015).
2. See the innovation-related models (Bilkey and Tesar, 1977; Cavusgil, 1980; Czinkota, 1982; Reid, 1981) for a discussion of how managers change their attitudes toward foreign markets.
3. This idea was initially discussed as the cost of doing business abroad (Hymer, 1976) and later as the liability of foreignness (Zaheer, 1995). For reviews of the different components of these challenges, see Cuervo-Cazurra, Maloney, and Manrakhan (2007).
4. See Economist (2006a).
5. See Economist (2015).
6. See Cuervo-Cazurra and Ramamurti (2014) for a detailed analysis of how the underdeveloped economic and institutional conditions of the country of EMNCs affect their international expansion and Cuervo-Cazurra and Genc (2008) for an explanation of how experience with these conditions can help the company expand abroad.
7. See Khanna and Palepu (2010) for a discussion of the conditions of emerging countries.
8. There are several process models that explain the internationalization of the firm: the incremental internationalization or Uppsala model (Johanson and Vahlne, 1977, 2003, 2009; Johanson and Wiedersheim-Paul, 1975), the innovation-related model (Bilkey and Tesar, 1977; Cavusgil, 1980;

Czinkota, 1982; Reid, 1981), the life-cycle model (Vernon, 1966), and extensions of these models such as the born-global firms model (Knight and Cavusgil, 2004; Oviatt and McDougal, 1994) and the network model (Ghoshal and Barlett, 1990; Johanson and Mattsson, 1988). We rely on their process view and a discussion of a sequence of actions to take as the manager decides to take the firm international, chooses countries in which to expand, chooses modes to enter, and then chooses actions to improve the local operations and coordinate across borders. However, our focus is not on the particular sequence of steps but rather on the challenges faced in each step.

9. This analysis is based on Cuervo-Cazurra, Maloney, and Marakhan (2007) and Cuervo-Cazurra and Un (2007).

3 Country selection

3.1 INTRODUCTION

Most countries have the potential to offer benefits to a budding multinational. There are always opportunities to expand abroad and serve new customers who may have similar needs and desires as a firm's customers at home. Such expansions can be very beneficial as the firm can obtain higher returns on previous investments in technology and knowledge. There are also opportunities to expand abroad to obtain inputs in better conditions than those available at home, because they are either available at a lower cost or more sophisticated in other countries. These superior inputs can help the firm improve its operations at home.

The challenge for managers of emerging market multinational corporations (EMNCs) is not really identifying such foreign opportunities. Country indicators and tools are widely available, and many consulting firms offer services that can help managers assess conditions and identify opportunities for foreign expansion. The global mobility of managers also enables them to spot new business opportunities. The greater challenge is to identify which particular country is the most appropriate for the company, that is, whether the company can build advantages over competitors and serve customers there or obtain inputs that will improve its home operations.

Identifying an appropriate country for foreign investment requires, first and foremost, a deep analysis of the firm and its reasons for expanding outside the home country. Understanding the logic for moving across borders can help narrow down the list of potential countries and, more important, determine whether foreign expansion is a potentially value-creating strategy. Moving abroad just because everyone in the industry is doing so is not a good enough reason for doing the same; in this case, the manager is merely following others rather than deciding what is best for the firm. In some cases, deciding not to expand across borders may be the better strategy, never mind what everyone else is doing.

In this chapter, we focus on analyzing the reasons for expanding abroad, distinguishing between expanding to sell more and expanding to buy better.[1] Expanding to sell more requires transferring and using in another country competitive advantages created by the firm in its home country. Expanding to buy better requires accessing and transferring comparative advantages of a foreign country to the home country and using them there. The main challenge managers face in making these decisions is facilitating the transfer of advantages across countries. This is a delicate situation because managers tend to assume that because the firm is very good at home, or because the foreign country provides excellent inputs, advantages can be transferred easily. Unfortunately, in some cases the transfer is either not possible or can only occur in a limited manner, reducing the potential success of the foreign operation. Our opening case, about the Mexican diversified conglomerate Salinas Group and the Chinese car company FAW Group Corporation (FAW), provides a good example of this. Despite a clear market opportunity in producing and selling low-priced Chinese cars in Mexico, FAW could neither transfer its competitive advantage to Mexico nor benefit from the comparative advantage of Mexico as a platform for serving the US and Canadian markets.

3.2 OPENING CASE: SALINAS GROUP AND FAW: SELLING CHINESE CARS IN MEXICO

The joint venture between the Mexican conglomerate Salinas and the Chinese car manufacturer FAW illustrates the challenges of transferring advantage across countries.[2] In 2009, Grupo Salinas was one of the largest business groups, or conglomerates, in Mexico, with around 45,000 employees working in Argentina, Brazil, El Salvador, Guatemala, Honduras, Mexico, Panama, Peru, and the United States and with sales of 63 billion pesos (about US$5 billion). It was composed of four segments: media (Azteca TV), retail and finance (Grupo Elektra), telecommunications (Iusacell), and social responsibility.

The retailer Elektra served low-income consumers by offering finance via weekly or biweekly payment schemes. In 2003, as it sought to increase the variety of goods in its stores, it started selling tires and quickly became the third largest dealer in Mexico. Its success in selling tires led to the importation of Chinese motorbikes, under the name Italika, which became a very profitable and successful venture. By 2007, Italika motorcycles accounted for 56 percent of all motorbikes sold in Mexico.

In 2007, Ricardo Salinas Pliego, chief executive officer (CEO) of Grupo Salinas, wanted to replicate the success of Italika and decided to look for a Chinese partner that could produce low-priced cars to sell to the low-income market in Mexico that was not being served by other brands. Grupo Salinas started a formal search and partnered with FAW, one of the largest vehicle manufacturers in China. At the time, FAW had 140,000 employees and produced 1.4 million cars annually. It exported cars to 70 countries and, in addition to producing under its own brand, had joint ventures with Audi, Hyundai, Mazda, Toyota, and Volkswagen.

Grupo Salinas and FAW signed a memorandum of understanding in 2007 to start marketing cars in Mexico by the first quarter of 2008. Initially, the vehicles were to be imported from China, and after three years, they would be produced in Mexico. This would enable Grupo Salinas to avoid the punitive 50 percent import duties imposed on Chinese cars, which would render them uncompetitive and unprofitable. FAW would start by importing vehicles and pricing them below the average sales price of those sold by its competitors in Mexico, financed by a weekly payment system that included vehicle maintenance and insurance.

Grupo Salinas and FAW planned to build a plant in Zinapécuaro in the state of Michoacán to manufacture at low prices, using domestic automotive components, and export to other neighboring countries. It would create about 2,000 direct and 14,000 indirect jobs and was hailed as the largest Chinese investment in Mexico. The assembly line had an initial investment of US$150 million for a planned annual production capacity of 100,000 cars and an investment of US$100 million to create a distribution and service network. The plant was supposed to begin car production by 2010 so that it could meet the rising demand in the country and export to Latin America, beginning with destinations where Grupo Salinas was already present. FAW had a keen interest in exploring the possibility of selling in the US and Canadian markets from Mexico.

The firms built a network of dealers with sales floors and service centers. They did not use franchises so that the process could be completely controlled from the time they assembled the car until it was sold and returned to service, obtaining customer feedback along the way. The creation of specialized points of sale for the cars, brand-certified workshops, and access to original spare parts were part of FAW's strategy.

However, despite the good prospects, the operation was unsuccessful. Although the cars were priced competitively and the financing was attractive, Mexican consumers shunned the Chinese-made cars, as they were suspicious of the reliability of the Chinese brand. Additionally, the 2008 recession that started in the United States and spread globally had a negative impact on the demand for cars in Mexico. Fearful consumers stopped buying cars, and new vehicle sales in December fell nearly 20 percent, closing the year with a reduction of 6.8 percent. The causes of the decline were multiple, including the lack of credit, job insecurity, and a general rise in car prices, as well as the constant increase in gasoline prices, taxes (value-added tax [VAT], Impuesto sobre Automóviles Nuevos [ISAN], and *tenencia*, annual fees for having a vehicle), and payment services such as verification, plates, and insurance against theft and accidents. In 2008, automobile credit fell by 12 percent. Financial institutions were not only reluctant to provide credit, but also imposed additional restrictions on lending money. Mexico's federal government gave the automobile industry a rescue package to stay afloat during the crisis. On top of this, there was more bad news: FAW's cars did not meet Department of Transportation (DOT) safety and pollution standards in the United States, a market that it wanted to serve from Mexico. All these factors led to a delay in investment in the assembly plant. In 2010, the company quietly shelved its plans to complete it and stopped selling Chinese cars in Mexico.

3.3 SELECTING THE COUNTRY TO EXPAND: TRANSFERRING COMPETITIVE AND COMPARATIVE ADVANTAGE

The alliance between Salinas and FAW reflects the challenges entailed in the transfer of the advantage across borders. There was a clear business opportunity in Mexico to sell low-priced cars to large, unfulfilled market segments, and the two partners had complementary capabilities. FAW produced reliable, low-cost cars adapted to the conditions of emerging markets, and Grupo Salinas had a deep knowledge of the Mexican market and an established support infrastructure. Nevertheless, the two companies were unable to benefit from these opportunities. The reputation of FAW among Chinese consumers did not transfer to Mexico, where consumers viewed Chinese-made cars with suspicion. And plans to use Mexico as a production base to serve the US and Canadian markets failed because the quality standards of the cars did not meet the safety specifications of those markets. Despite all the acknowledged potential of the operation, the advantages did not materialize as expected, and the companies ended up shutting the operation down and absorbing the losses of the investment in the distribution network and initial construction.

This is the challenge we analyze in this chapter: how, despite the good prospects of a foreign venture, the failure to transfer advantage across borders limits the success of a promising international expansion. Let us analyze it now in detail, but before we embark on this, we need to clarify a few concepts and ideas.

Country analysis. The usual start of a foreign expansion entails the analysis of opportunities in foreign countries. Many countries provide opportunities that can help a company, and an analysis of countries can be done easily by an initial assessment of publicly available data. A consulting company can provide a manager with a summary of the key characteristics of several countries, with sophisticated graphs and ample data to support an entry decision. This option tends to be accompanied by legal requirements for data needed to justify decisions to the board, especially decisions about the magnitude of investment in a foreign country.

Alternatively, the manager can conduct an independent analysis, using freely available databases, and select data that will be most interesting to the company. Table 3.1 lists some of the databases that provide detailed free country-level information and that incidentally become the basis for many consultant reports. All these databases can be used to get a sense of what a country looks like, as well as differences across countries, using standardized measures. They provide an overview of general trends, and they are particularly useful when managers do not have deep knowledge of foreign countries.[3]

Competitive and comparative advantages. However, an analysis of statistics about several countries is only a first step toward the internationalization of the company. The key decision the manager has to take is not so much identifying which country provides the best opportunities in general but rather identifying which country provides the best opportunities for the company the manager is running. This requires an analysis of the firm's conditions, in particular its competitive advantage, to identify how the firm can use and improve its advantage by becoming a multinational.

A crucial first step in identifying the competitive advantage of a firm in global competition is to clarify the difference between competitive and comparative advantage. Although these concepts are related, and both help the company compete globally, they are very different. Competitive advantage is the advantage that the company

Table 3.1 *Country analysis databases*

Topic	Databases
Multitopic	United Nations (http://data.un.org/), World Bank (http://data.worldbank.org/), International Monetary Fund (IMF) (www.imf.org/external/data.htm), US Central Intelligence Agency (CIA) Factbook (www.cia.gov/library/publications/the-world-factbook/)
Economics	Heritage Foundation (www.heritage.org/index/), Fraser Institute (www.freetheworld.com/datasets_efw.html)
Technology	World Intellectual Property Organization (www.wipo.int/patentscope/en/data/), International Telecommunications Union (www.itu.int/en/ITU-D/Statistics/Pages/stat/default.aspx)
Finance	Bank for International Settlements (www.bis.org/statistics/index.htm)
Politics and governance	Center for Systemic Peace (www.systemicpeace.org/polity/polity4.htm), Comparative Study of Electoral Systems (www.cses.org/), Freedom House (https://freedomhouse.org/report-types/freedom-world#.VVhoOPlViko),
Governance	Worldwide Governance Indicators (http://info.worldbank.org/governance/wgi/index.aspx#home), Doing Business (www.doingbusiness.org/rankings), Transparency International (www.transparency.org/research/cpi/overview)
Conflict	Uppsala University Conflict Data Program (www.ucdp.uu.se/gpdatabase/search.php), Correlates of War Project (www.correlatesofwar.org/)
Culture and society	World Values Survey (www.worldvaluessurvey.org/WVSContents.jsp)
Society	United Nations Development Programme (http://hdr.undp.org/en/data)
Labor	International Labor Organization (www.ilo.org/global/statistics-and-databases/lang--en/index.htm)

Table 3.1 (*cont.*)

Topic	Databases
Natural resources	World Resources Institute (www.wri.org/resources/data_sets), NASA (http://sedac.ciesin.columbia.edu/data/collection/epi/#data)
Trade and foreign direct investment (FDI)	World Trade Organization (www.wto.org/english/res_e/statis_e/Statis_e.htm), United Nations Trade Statistics (http://unstats.un.org/unsd/trade/default.asp), United Nations Conference on Trade and Development (UNCTAD) (http://unctad.org/en/Pages/Statistics.aspx)

has over existing competitors in serving the needs of particular customers. This advantage is specific to the company and depends on how its resources satisfy the needs of customers compared to those of its competitors.[4] Identifying competitive advantage requires the manager to assess what resources and activities help the firm generate value for current customers in a different and better way than its existing competitors. This can be done initially in the home country and domestic market.

There are multiple potential sources of advantage: for example, a wider distribution network, better design, more sophisticated technology, a more motivated workforce, or greater proximity to customers. The company might have several of these advantages when compared to particular competitors. For example, it might have a wider distribution network than one competitor, better design than another, and more sophisticated technology compared to a third, and these may also vary depending on the customer analyzed. Thus, the identification of competitive advantage is a more complex exercise than is usually assumed, because the firm rarely has one source of advantage against all competitors but rather different sources against different competitors when serving particular customers. Some of these sources of advantage may not be commonly considered but could be important, such as being more conveniently located for some customers.

Comparative advantage, however, is the advantage that a location has over other locations in supplying resources that companies need. It can be identified by comparing the conditions of the supporting infrastructure and inputs that a location provides firms and what additional advantages the firm would gain if it is located in one country, or a region or city within the country, when compared to other potential locations. This advantage tends to be available to all companies locating in the same place, as they have access to better transport infrastructure, less costly labor, more sophisticated university graduates, more predictable application of regulations, and so on.

The distinction between competitive and comparative advantage is important because it helps managers identify the basis on which the firm can compete globally. A company operating in its home country competes against domestic firms on the basis of its competitive advantage, because the comparative advantage is available to all other domestic competitors as well. Companies in the same country, or city within the country, have access to similar sources of comparative advantage, for example, a highly educated workforce, low-cost labor, or abundant and inexpensive capital.

However, a company that operates globally competes on the basis of a combination of its competitive advantages and the comparative advantages of the locations in which it operates.[5] In some countries, a company may be able to export abroad on the basis of the comparative advantage of its home country, even if it does not have a competitive advantage abroad. For example, the firm could rely instead on lower labor costs or abundant energy to help it provide better products abroad, as long as this type of comparative advantage compensates for the costs of transportation. However, this sort of advantage will erode if other firms operating from the same location replicate this strategy, whether these are other domestic firms or foreign firms with established operations in that location.

If the manager decides to invest and operate in another country, that is, make a company a multinational, the firm needs to transfer its competitive advantage across countries to succeed there. Operating in another country means that the firm will face local competitors that have access to the comparative advantage of the host country. However, it also means that the benefit the foreign firm gains from the comparative advantage in its home country will be limited because it no longer operates from there. So, to be able to compete abroad, it needs to use its competitive advantage.

Eventually, as the firm becomes a multinational with operations in multiple countries, it combines multiple sources of competitive advantage from its own operations with the comparative advantages available in different locations to serve customers globally against multiple competitors.[6]

Objective of international expansion: sell more or buy better? Whether competitive or comparative advantage can be transferred across borders and what challenges the firm will face if such a transfer does not happen depend on the objective of the international expansion.

The first question that managers need to be able to answer when considering international expansion is why they want to take their company abroad. Operating in the home country is almost always easier because the company is already established there, has a reputation among consumers, has an established network of suppliers and distributors, and has a good understanding of its competitors and government regulations, among other benefits, all of which build and support its advantage. As a result, expansion at home usually causes few problems, as long as the business model is scalable. However, moving abroad entails many difficulties arising from differences across countries and requires a purposeful understanding of the logic behind such expansion.

The two main objectives that drive investments abroad are to sell more and to buy better. Both are driven by advantages, competitive in the first case and comparative in the second. The idea behind taking the company abroad to sell more[7] is that the company is successful at home, selling products or providing services that customers like. The manager realizes that there is a bigger market outside the home country that could be served by existing facilities or knowledge. In effect, the company aims to benefit from economies of scale on its existing competitive advantage; it has already invested in the development of a competitive advantage and intends to make more intensive use of it in other countries.

Alternatively, the manager can decide to take the company abroad to buy better.[8] In this case, the company will benefit from the comparative advantage of a different location. Other countries can offer lower-cost, higher-quality, or more abundant inputs than those available in the home country. By expanding abroad, the company can use these inputs in its existing operations and so reduce the cost and improve the quality of its products. In this way, the company will benefit from the comparative advantages of other locations and strengthen its competitive advantage at home.

However, in some cases the manager may not be able to proactively select the internationalization path of the firm and instead may be forced by competitors or important customers to take the firm abroad. For example, as foreign competitors enter the company's home country, the manager may decide to retaliate and enter their home countries to maintain a flexible competitive response to their actions. Or domestic competitors may have expanded to a foreign country, and the manager may decide to follow them there to reduce their opportunities and potential improvement in their competitive advantage.[9] Alternatively, important customers may decide to expand abroad and want the firm to follow them as a supplier. The firm will do so to avoid losing their business in the home country. In all these cases, decisions about internationalization and specific locations are taken or strongly influenced by people other than the manager. In this book, we will not discuss these cases but concentrate instead on more proactive internationalization, when the manager takes a company abroad either to sell more or to buy better. In the next section, we analyze these two motives separately because they have very different implications for how the company transfers its advantage abroad and the challenges it faces.

3.4 EXPAND ABROAD TO SELL MORE: TRANSFERRING COMPETITIVE ADVANTAGE

One of the main motives for companies to move abroad is to sell more. This motive underlines most theories and models of international management. Under this logic, the manager realizes that success in the home country could be replicated in other countries. However, the assumption that because the firm has been successful at home it will also be successful abroad can lead managers to look for countries that offer good business prospects rather than doing a complete analysis of how the company achieved its competitive advantage at home and whether that advantage can be successfully transferred abroad. Of course, the manager's instinct may prove correct, and the failure to carry out an analysis of the competitive advantage may not matter much. However, it is always better to be mindful of current sources of advantage. Whether or not a country offers good business opportunities is one criterion for country selection, but a more important consideration is whether the company will be able to transfer its existing competitive advantage abroad to take advantage of those opportunities.

The examples that follow illustrate two situations where the transfer of competitive advantage may not happen. In the first case, the firm is unable to transfer its advantage because the conditions underlying the home advantage do not apply abroad; we call this the inability to transfer advantage. In the second, the firm is not able to transfer its advantage because the industry in which it operates is not viable in the host country; we call this the inability to create value.

Inability to transfer competitive advantage. Sometimes the company is unable to transfer its advantage abroad. For example, in 2012, the Brazilian mining company Vale found that the ultralarge ships it had designed and built to transport iron ore from Brazil to China to compete with its Australian-based competitors could not be used because they were not accepted in Chinese ports.[10]

Vale started life as a state-owned firm in 1942 to facilitate the economic development of Brazil. However, following its privatization and the opening of Brazil in the 1990s, it had grown to become one of the three leading iron ore producers in the world, helped in part by the large Chinese demand for raw materials. It competed with the Australian miner BHP Billiton and the Anglo-Australian company Rio in the supply of iron ore to China but had a logistic disadvantage: it took ships 45 days to reach China from Brazil but only ten days to reach China from Australia. To compensate for the additional cost of transportation, in 2008 Vale ordered the construction of a new category of ultralarge iron ore transporting ship, the Valemax, which at over 380,000 deadweight tons and 1,180 feet in length was much larger than other dry-bulk ship classes, such as the Capesize (170,000–220,000 deadweight tons; 1,050 feet) for trips around the Cape of Good Hope in South Africa or the Panamax (70,000 deadweight tons; 754 feet) for trips through the Panama Canal. Vale ordered the construction of 35 ships, 24 from Chinese and 11 from South Korean shipyards, at a cost of over US$100 million each. The state-controlled Export-Import Bank of China and the Bank of China provided half the finance for the Chinese ships (US$1.3 billion), but the work was carried out by private firms. The construction of the Valemax ships put Vale in direct competition with the dry-bulk shipping lines it used to contract to transport the iron ore Vale produced. In December 2011, one Valemax, the *Bergé Everest*, unloaded 350,000 tons of iron ore in 55 hours, a world record, in the Chinese port of Dalian.

However, in early 2012, the Chinese Transport Ministry banned the Valemax ships from unloading in Chinese ports because of concerns about the ships' safety. In December 2011, one Valemax, the *Vale Beijing*, had developed a 60-cm crack in its hull while loading in Brazil. Nevertheless, this seemed to be an isolated incident, as other Valemax had unloaded at ports in Japan, the Philippines, Italy, and the Netherlands without problems. The Chinese ban appeared to have emerged following pressure from Chinese competitors. The Chinese Shipowners' Association viewed the Valemax ships as "a matter of monopoly and unfair competition, which not only harms the shipping interest of mainland China, but also that of South Korea, Japan and Taiwan area."[11] The chairman of the association was also chairman of the state-controlled shipping line Cosco, China's largest shipping line by capacity, which had suffered losses in 2011 due to the slowing global economy and overcapacity in the sector. The Chinese ban wiped out the advantage the large ships gave Vale over its Australian and Indian competitors. Vale was forced to use transit centers in Africa and Asia, where it transferred the Valemax cargo to smaller ships that were allowed into Chinese ports. To facilitate this, it built a trans-shipment operation in Malaysia through which it could mix different iron ore grades and avoid selling high-grade ore at a discount to Chinese steel mills.

Although one Valemax was allowed to unload 220,000 tons of iron ore at the port of Lianyungang in Jiangsu Province in April 2013, the ban was not lifted until October 2014, after Vale had agreed to sell four of its ships to Cosco, which ordered the building of an additional ten and then agreed to charter all 14 ships from Cosco for 25 years. Vale developed similar charter agreements with other shipping companies for 15 of the 31 Valemax it owned, and the Chinese conglomerate China Merchants Group agreed to build another ten Valemax and charter them to Vale for 25 years.

There are several reasons why a firm that has a well-honed advantage in its home country is unable to transfer it abroad. First, a company may not be able to transfer its resources: many resources cannot be moved because they are physically tied to a location. For example, a firm whose advantage depends on a wide proprietary distribution system may not be able to transfer this to another country. In other cases, resources or products may be physically able to move across borders, but regulations in the country of origin may prevent their transfer abroad. For example, companies in the defense industry need government permission before they can sell their products to firms from certain countries.

Second, a resource that the firm uses in its home operation may fail to create value for customers abroad. This can happen when customers do not associate the resource with value. For example, an established and well-liked brand name may provide consumer recognition and value in the home market but mean nothing to customers in the host country, as the case of the Chinese automobiles built by FAW in Mexico illustrates.

A third reason for the failure to transfer competitive advantage is imitation. For example, a company may have some distinctly designed products that support its sales at home but discovers when it enters a new country that local competitors have copied or independently developed similar designs that render this particular source of advantage (uniqueness) obsolete.

The inability to transfer advantage across borders results in a lack of profits and even revenues in the host country. Customers in the host country may not be prepared to pay a premium for products if they do not perceive them to provide additional value beyond what is already offered by domestic competitors. They may be deterred by the switching costs of purchasing products from another firm, especially one that is unknown and does not seem to offer something different from what is already available. In some cases, domestic competitors may react aggressively to the entry of the firm and block it from offering its products and services to customers, in effect preventing it from selling, as the case of Vale's Valemax ships illustrates.

To work out why a company cannot transfer its advantages, the manager first needs to understand which particular activities or resources enable the firm to achieve an advantage over its competitors in its home country. Once these sources of competitive advantage are identified, the manager can assess whether the basis of the advantage can be transferred to another country. Will customers in the host country find that the resources transferred, or the products made from them, add value for them? Will competitors in the host country find ways to imitate or substitute the source of advantage? This requires a deeper analysis than the usual analysis of industry characteristics.[12] It means evaluating existing competitors in the country, analyzing their sources of advantage, and determining whether the firm offers something different.

Inability to create value. Other times a firm cannot create value in the host country because the industry is not viable there. For example, while alcoholic drinks can be purchased easily in Muslim countries like Turkey, the sale and consumption of alcohol are banned in Saudi Arabia.[13] Expatriates, many of whom live in special quarters, can obtain alcoholic drinks, sometimes via diplomatic bags that are not checked at customs, but the unwritten rule is that they are consumed only at home. The ban on alcoholic drinks has resulted in smuggling from neighboring Gulf states like Bahrain or Jordan, where beer and spirits are produced, and the illegal manufacture of alcohol from grapes or dates. People found guilty of selling alcohol are punished with jail sentences and lashes – in 2001, four Britons were sentenced to an average of two years in prison and 400 lashes.

However, the ban on alcoholic beverages has opened the way for sales of nonalcoholic beer. In 2003, Heineken purchased Egypt's only brewer, Al Ahram Beverages Company, which enabled it to avoid the 300 percent tariffs that its alcoholic imported beers faced. At the same time, the purchase allowed Heineken to brew nonalcoholic beer, certified as halal, in a range of flavors, like pineapple or mango. Ahram produced nonalcoholic beer (29 percent of 2001 sales of US$105 million), regular beer (52 percent), spirits and wine (11 percent), and soft drinks (8 percent). Heineken's distribution expertise helped the Egyptian brand to be distributed widely, including to Arab countries like Jordan and Morocco and countries with Muslim majorities, like Nigeria and Indonesia. The acquisition gave Heineken a monopoly in Egypt and access to a large number of countries with which Egypt had free trade agreements. By 2013, the Middle East accounted for almost a third of sales of nonalcoholic beer in the world.

Religious restrictions enforced by government regulations, like the sale of alcoholic drinks in Saudi Arabia, can prevent the transfer of advantage, but there are other factors, like the weather, to consider.

Products designed for cold countries will not find a market in countries with very different conditions, no matter how good the products are or how easy it is to transfer them across countries.

Identifying this kind of difficulty is relatively easy. A lack of competitors, whether foreign or domestic, may indicate that the industry is not viable in a particular country. For example, it was not until 1999 that Bhutan allowed television (TV) broadcasting, first allowing the Bhutan Broadcasting Service (BBS) and half a year later allowing global TV broadcasting.[14] Additional analyses of the industry may reveal religious, cultural, regulatory, or geographic reasons that will limit the potential for firms to sell their products there.

3.5 EXPAND ABROAD TO BUY BETTER: ACCESSING COMPARATIVE ADVANTAGE

Expanding abroad to buy better requires accessing the comparative advantage of the host country and transferring it to the home country. In this case, the manager needs to identify the foreign country in which the comparative advantage resides and obtain access to it before the advantage can be transferred to the home operation. Unfortunately, the access and transfer of the comparative advantage are not always successful. We discuss these two difficulties now.

Inability to access comparative advantage. It is commonly assumed that because it is location based, comparative advantage is accessible to firms that move to that location. This prompts firms to invest in countries with low labor costs or abundant natural resources. However, it is not always possible to access comparative advantage. For example, the Brazilian mining firm Vale faced a legal nightmare in its development of one of the world's largest high-grade iron deposits in Simandou in Guinea.[15] In 2010, it purchased the development rights to half the concession but became embroiled in a legal battle over the rights to these deposits with the Anglo-Australian mining company Rio, BSG Resources (BSGR) which was owned by the Israeli diamond billionaire Beny Steinmetz, the government of Guinea, and arbitration panels and courts in the United States. The story of this imbroglio started in 1997, when Rio was granted exploration rights to the area, where it found large high-grade iron ore deposits in 2002. The following year, it received development rights to the area. Developing the Simandou deposit and building the railway and port to facilitate export of the ore cost about US$20 billion.

However, in 2008, the government of Guinea, led by a long-time dictator, stripped Rio of half the rights and gave them to BSGR, arguing that Rio had not fulfilled its development schedule. In April 2010, Vale purchased 51 percent of the BSGR rights for US$2.5 billion, with an immediate payment of US$500 million and the balance due once production targets were met. In July 2010, Rio signed an agreement with the Chinese mining company Chinalco to develop its half of Simandou.

Before the end of that year, however, following the death of Guinea's dictator and an unsuccessful coup, a new president was elected. After taking power, he reviewed previous deals and allegations that the former mining minister had received US$200 million to take half of Rio's rights and transfer them to BSGR. In April 2013, Vale stopped payments to BSGR as the corruption probe widened. The US authorities detained a former BSGR intermediary who had allegedly offered the widow of the late dictator US$6 million to destroy documents about the bribes BSGR had paid to secure the rights, and Swiss authorities questioned Beny Steinmetz, who was a resident in Switzerland. In April 2014, the Guinean government completed its review of the deal and concluded that BSGR had obtained its development rights through bribery and recommended cancellation of the joint venture between Vale and BSGR. The inquiry concluded that BSGR would be excluded from future development but exonerated Vale, which had not engaged in bribery. Rio filed a complaint against Vale, BSGR, and Beny Steinmetz. Vale filed against BSGR to recover the payments it had made and prepared to bid for the rights it had been stripped of. Vale's CEO Murilo Ferreira indicated that the company could recover its investment: "We believe we are entitled to a credit on the acquisition that we made and also on the investments made there."[16] BSGR fought the allegations and filed for arbitration. In November 2014, a court in Florida seized assets belonging to the widow of the dictator, which had been purchased with money from bribes.

If the company cannot access a comparative advantage in the host country, it will not succeed despite the initial good prospects of the country. It is not always easy to access the comparative advantage of location-dependent resources, and access might have to be paid for.[17] For example, entering a country that has lower labor costs requires the firm to hire employees, but the best, most productive employees are likely to be working for other companies already. This means the firm will have to pay people more to attract them to the firm or invest in additional training to improve the skills of other potential employees. Firms that move to another country because of the abundant natural resources found there will have to pay the owners of those resources.

Identifying barriers to accessing comparative advantage can be done by analyzing who holds the rights to resources and what conditions are needed to secure access to them. However, as the case of Vale illustrates, identification is not always straightforward; despite the due diligence done by Vale on the ownership of the development rights at Simandou, it was stripped of its rights because its joint venture partner had engaged in bribery. In some cases, there may be regulations that limit foreign firms' investment in the country and their portion of stock ownership in a particular industry.

Inability to transfer comparative advantage. The firm that moves abroad to buy better has to contend with the problem that it may be unable to transfer the comparative advantage back home. For example, in 2009, the Chinese automobile firm SAIC Motor Corporation Limited (SAIC) faced accusations of transferring sensitive technology from its acquired Korean firm SsangYong back to China.[18]

In 2004, SAIC purchased 51 percent of SsangYong for US$500 million. It was the first Chinese firm to control a foreign automobile firm, and the acquisition offered SAIC the opportunity to move out of China and control the fourth largest Korean automaker, which had a strong position in sport utility vehicles (SUVs) at a time when there was growing demand for this class of car in China. Unfortunately, the acquisition was plagued by challenges from the beginning. Labor unions were strongly opposed to the acquisition, and in 2006 a walkout cost the firm 10,200 vehicles in production losses. There were few apparent synergies and widespread concerns that SAIC would transfer production lines back to China. However, Philip Murtaugh, SAIC's vice-president and SsangYong's representative director, dismissed criticism. "[Critics say] SAIC is stealing their technology and they are just gonna take the products. They are gonna move manufacturing to China. That's all crap. [...] SAIC owns 51 percent of SsangYong and SAIC is spending a lot of money to help ensure SsangYong's long-term viability."

Nevertheless, in November 2009 the Seoul Central District Prosecutors' Office indicted seven senior engineers at SsangYong for transferring advanced technology on gasoline-electric hybrid cars as well as diesel engine and transmission technologies. The hybrid car technology had been developed between 2004 and 2008 and was half-funded by the Korean government. The transfer of subsidized technology required government permission that SsangYong did not obtain. The government alleged that, as the majority owner, SAIC had pressured SsangYong engineers to share the technology. The accusations compounded SAIC's refusal to support SsangYong financially in 2009, which led to a two-month labor conflict, the layoff of assembly workers, and eventually the bankruptcy of SsangYong. In 2010, SsangYong was purchased by the Indian firm Mahindra & Mahindra, India's largest SUV producer, with the view of expanding into fast-growing emerging markets like South Africa and Russia, where SsangYong had a large presence, and helping the Korean firm enter the growing SUV Indian market.

The inability to transfer advantage constrains the firm from achieving its objective. Even if the firm has access to resources in the host country, it may not be able to transfer them back to home operations because the resources are location bound. For example, the advantage may reside in a set of host-country conditions that limit its transferability such as in the case of location-based tacit knowledge. The government can also limit the transfer of the comparative advantage across borders, for example, by forcing the foreign firm to use the comparative advantage in the host country or requiring the processing of raw materials into semifinished products, like processing bauxite into aluminum or processing fish into canned fish, in the host country. Requirements like these may eventually limit the benefit to be gained from access to the comparative advantage. Alternatively, the government may even prohibit the transfer of the advantage across borders to avoid the loss of technology from the country.

The manager may face challenges identifying this difficulty. In many cases, managers assume that once the firm has access to the host-country resources, because it has secured the appropriate rights, it can transfer them back to the home country. Unfortunately, this is not always the case, and the manager should check the regulations governing cross-border technology transfer if the firm enters the country intending to access and bring back more sophisticated technology.

3.6 SOLUTIONS: MATCHING COMPETITIVE AND COMPARATIVE ADVANTAGES AND TRANSFER ABILITY

The solution to these challenges is a full identification of competitive and comparative advantages and the conditions that enable their transfer across borders. In most cases, managers understand the basis for the competitive advantage in the home country, as they battle with competitors and serve customers daily. However, when considering foreign expansion, they need to take into account that customers and competitors abroad differ and that some of the sources of the competitive advantage at home, such as reputation, brand name, proximity to customers, distribution channels, or supply chain, do not travel well across countries. Similarly, the identification of comparative advantage in a foreign country tends to be accompanied by the assumption that the company can always access the advantage. However, this is not always the case, as the comparative advantage has owners and in some cases its transfer across borders is restricted.

We propose two sets of staged questions that managers should address when making decisions about moving their company abroad. The ability to address these questions will ensure a greater likelihood that the country managers choose will enable the company to achieve its objectives, whether they are taking their firm abroad to sell more or to buy better. Table 3.2 summarizes the stages in the decision-making process, which we discuss now.

Transferring competitive advantage across borders. If the manager decides to go abroad to sell more, the first question to address is why? Yes, the manager needs to identify the countries that offer the best potential opportunities for increasing sales. However, before investing abroad, the manager needs to think about whether the firm needs to invest in the foreign country to achieve the objective of selling more. An increase in sales can be achieved through exporting, which is an easier option because it reduces exposure to the challenges of operating in another country and can be much more easily reversed if the firm encounters problems because it does not have physical operations to dispose of in the host country. In some situations, exports may not be feasible, for example, because transport costs are prohibitive or because tariffs render exports unprofitable, and the firm may have to invest if it is to sell in the host country.

Once the need for investing abroad to sell more is identified, and before selecting a particular country, the manager has to identify the company's sources of advantage in the home country. This also entails identifying the customers served by the advantage and the competitors over whom the advantage is held. This exercise in identification

Table 3.2 *Solutions for addressing the challenges of country selection*

Issues	Expanding abroad to sell more	Expanding abroad to buy better
Identify investment opportunity	Identify the reason for expanding abroad to sell more	Identify the reason for expanding abroad to buy better
	Identify the need to invest in the country instead of using exports	Identify the need to invest in the country instead of using imports
Identify country opportunity	Identify the countries that provide the best potential opportunity for selling more	Identify the countries that provide the best potential opportunity for buying better
	Identify the conditions and needs of customers	Identify the conditions of the desired factor of production
	Identify the conditions and advantage of competitors and the regulations in the industry against and for foreign competitors	Identify the owners of the desired factors of production and the regulations against and for foreign firms wanting to access the desired factor of production
Identify advantage	Identify the sources of competitive advantage of the firm in the home country against particular competitors and for serving the needs of particular customers	Identify the conditions of the factor of production that you are interested in buying in comparison to their conditions at home or in other countries in which the firm operates

Table 3.2 (*cont.*)

Issues	Expanding abroad to sell more	Expanding abroad to buy better
Identify transfer of advantage across borders	Identify how you are able to separate the resources that provide the advantage from other resources in the home country Identify how you can transfer them abroad	Identify how you can access the desired factor of production in the host country, whether they can be separated from other conditions in the host country Identify how you can transfer it to the home country
Match advantage and opportunity	Identify how you can achieve an advantage abroad to serve particular customers and against specific competitors	Identify how you can use the desired factor of production in the home country to serve particular customers and against specific competitors
Select country	Identify the country that will best facilitate the transfer of an advantage abroad	Identify the country that will best facilitate the transfer of the desired factor of production home

sets the stage for identifying the transferability of the advantage across borders. If the advantage is based on resources that cannot be transferred, there is little point in trying to invest in another country: the company will be just like any new domestic competitor having to establish an advantage from scratch. However, managers cannot assume that because resources can be moved across borders, the advantage associated with them will also move. Customers' preferences and competitors' strengths differ.

So the next step is to match the opportunities in the host country with the advantage that the company will be transferring. Will the resources transferred enable the company to serve customers in the host country better than the competitors that are already there? In doing this analysis, the manager needs to be aware that some resources that do not provide an advantage in the home country may become sources of advantage and create value for customers abroad. This can happen if competitors in the host country are not up to par with competitors at home. For example, the company may have achieved efficiencies in its operations that are on par with competitors at home but that are above the efficiency levels of host-country competitors, thus achieving an advantage from a source that was not a source of advantage at home.

Once the opportunity and advantages are matched, the final stage in these analyses is to identify which country is most likely to enable the company to transfer and create an advantage there.

Transferring comparative advantage across borders. If the manager decides to invest abroad to buy better, the first question to answer is, once again, why? There may be many countries that have comparative advantages in particular factors and drive the desire to buy better, but this does not mean the manager should invest there. The manager needs to assess whether the company could obtain the comparative advantage through imports, rather than investment, and by controlling the supply of inputs. Importing is a simpler and, in some cases, cheaper option than investing to supply from abroad, once the costs of the investment are taken into account. But, in some cases, importing is not an option available to the firm, for example, because there are no host-country suppliers that can provide the firm with the desired inputs.

If the manager decides that investment is necessary, the next step is to analyze the conditions of multiple host countries and how their comparative advantages compare to those of the home country. This also requires finding out whether there are regulations against foreign companies investing in the host country.

After these analyses, the manager can compare factors of production in the host country with those in the home country, bearing in mind that there is a cost associated with accessing factors of production. This access cost is an important factor in assessing the ability of the company to transfer comparative advantage across borders. The question is not so much to make sure that factors of production in the host country are in better condition than those at home but whether the company can separate that particular factor of production from the host country and transfer it to the home country.

If the transfer is possible, the next step is to analyze how that particular factor of production will be used in the home country and how it will help the company improve its competitive advantage over its existing competitors in serving customers' needs.

This analysis ends with selection of the country that is most likely to enable the firm to integrate the comparative advantage of the host country with its competitive advantage at home.

3.7 CLOSING CASE: THE CEMEX WAY

The Mexican cement producer Cemex has developed a process – the Cemex Way– that ensures the transfer and integration of competitive advantage across countries.[19] The company started life in 1906, and by the 1980s it was one of several cement producers in Mexico. Cemex began acquiring firms at home and abroad and in a couple of decades had become the third largest cement firm in the world and the only one from an emerging country. By 2013, it had sales of US$15.2 billion, had 43,000 employees, and was present in over 50 countries.

Before its international expansion, Cemex had developed a set of core competencies that would shape its later trajectory, including strong operational capabilities based on engineering and information technologies and a culture of transparency. It had also mastered the art of acquisition and integration within Mexico, having grown through acquisitions over the years. In 1992, Cemex acquired a majority stake in two Spanish cement companies, giving it a majority market share in one of Europe's largest cement markets, enabling it to respond to the

Swiss company Holcim's growing market share in Mexico, and providing it with lower cost of capital by operating in an investment-grade country. However, it soon discovered that by introducing its current Mexico-based best practices to the Spanish operation, it was able to reduce costs and increase plant efficiency to a much greater extent, with annual savings/benefits of US$120 million and an increase in operating margins from 7 to 24 percent. This acquisition, because of its size and the fact that it was in a foreign country, forced Cemex to formalize and codify its postmerger integration (PMI) process, which was known internally as the Cemex Way.

Cemex's move into Spain was followed soon after by acquisitions in Venezuela, Colombia, and the Caribbean in the mid-1990s and the Philippines and Indonesia in the late 1990s. These acquisitions exploited Cemex's core capabilities, which now combined learning from the company's operations in Mexico and Spain. The PMI process also underwent a significant change during this period. Attempts to impose the same management processes and systems used in Mexico on the newly acquired Colombian firm resulted in an exodus of local talent. Cemex learned that, as well as transferring best practices that had been standardized throughout the company, it needed to make a concerted effort to learn best practices from acquired companies, integrating them when appropriate.

The Cemex Way was the core set of best practices with which Cemex conducted business throughout all its locations. More a corporate philosophy than a tangible process, the Cemex Way was driven by five guidelines: (1) manage the global knowledge base efficiently, (2) identify and disseminate best practices, (3) standardize business processes, (4) implement key information and Internet-based technologies, and (5) foster innovation.

The Cemex Way was arguably what made Cemex's PMI process so unique. While typically 20 percent of an acquired company's practices were retained, instead of eliminating the 80 percent in one swift move, Cemex Way teams cataloged and stored those practices in a centralized database. They were then benchmarked against internal and external practices. Processes that were deemed "superior" (typically two to three per standardization group or 15–30 new practices per acquisition) became enterprise standards and part of the Cemex Way. Furthermore, in just eight years, Cemex was able to bring down the duration of the PMI process from 25 months for the Spanish acquisitions to fewer than five months for Texas-based Southdown.

A key feature of the PMI process was the strong reliance that Cemex placed on middle-level managers both to diffuse the company's standard practices and to identify existing capabilities in the acquired firms that might contribute to Cemex's current capability platform. PMI teams were formed ad hoc for each acquisition. Functional experts in each area (finance, production, logistics, etc.) were selected from Cemex operations around the world. These managers were then relieved from their day-to-day responsibilities and sent, for periods varying from a few weeks to several months, to the countries where the newly acquired company operated. Because these managers were teaching the newly acquired firm's managers the jobs they were doing at home, they were not only the best teachers but also the most likely Cemex employees to identify which of the standard practices of the acquired firm could be adapted and integrated into the Cemex Way. What is more, because they were regarded as the best and brightest within Cemex, these managers had the legitimacy to propose and advocate changes in the firm's operation standards in a way no other managers could.

3.8 CONCLUSIONS

The internationalization of a firm can offer great opportunities, from access to more customers in new markets to accessing better inputs and factors of production. However, to benefit from these opportunities, the manager needs to identify and transfer competitive and comparative advantage across countries, to sell more or buy better, respectively. Managers sometimes face challenges because their firms are unable to transfer their advantages across borders. This can happen when the sources of their competitive advantage do not create value for customers in the host country or have been imitated by local competitors, as the cases of FAW's cars in Mexico or Vale's Valemax ships in China illustrate. It can also happen when the sources of comparative advantage cannot be accessed and transferred across borders, as the cases of Vale's Simandou project in Guinea and SAIC's acquisition in South Korea illustrated. These challenges threaten the success of the foreign expansion from the start, as the firm that cannot transfer advantage will not be able to fulfill its objectives, no matter how well it manages the foreign operation.

Nevertheless, EMNCs can develop ways to identify and successfully transfer advantages across countries, benefiting from the mix of the competitive and comparative advantages of the home and host operations to achieve global success, as the case of Cemex illustrates. Here the firm integrated ideas from the home and host countries and refined them in a way that facilitated the integration of new operations quickly and the identification of new capabilities that could then be diffused to other firm operations, including those in the home country. This process was created and refined over time as the company faced the challenge of integrating increasingly larger and more complex operations, but crucially, it was the openness of managers in the home country that facilitated its success. Unlike other firms that impose the perceived "better way" of doing things from home, Cemex's managers were open minded and willing to apply the PMI process to home operations and allow good practices from other countries to be incorporated into the best practices that were later applied to all operations.

Notes

1. For a more detailed discussion of the differences between these motives for internationalization and others, see Cuervo-Cazurra, Narula, and Un (2015).
2. This case is an abridged and modified version of Cuervo-Cazurra and Montoya (2014).

3. See Ghemawat (2001) and Khanna, Palepu, and Sihna (2005) for a discussion of differences across countries and how to use them in the internationalization of the firm.
4. For a discussion of competitive advantage and how to identify it, see Porter (1980, 1985) and Barney (1991, 1999).
5. Kogut (1985a, 1985b) and Ghemawat (2007) provide an explanation of the use of comparative advantage in multinationals.
6. See Bartlett and Ghoshal (1989), Prahalad and Doz (1987), and Doz, Santos, and Williamson (2001) for a detailed discussion of the advantage of multinationals with widely dispersed operations.
7. This motive is known in the literature as market seeking (Dunning, 1993). See Cuervo-Cazurra, Narula, and Un (2015) for a more detailed discussion of the sell more and buy better motives.
8. This motive groups other motives discussed in the literature as natural resource seeking, factor seeking, and strategic asset seeking (Dunning, 1993).
9. This is usually the logic for international expansion in oligopolistic industries (Knickerbocker, 1973).
10. Information on this case comes from Grant & Pearson (2014), Hook & Wright (2012), Hook (2013), Hornby (2014), Murphy (2012), and Jamasmie (2014).
11. Murphy (2012).
12. See Porter (1980, 1985) for the industry analysis framework of the five forces.
13. Information on this case comes from Allam (2003), BBCNews (2001), Economist (2013b), and Hawwari (2001).
14. See BBCNews (2004).
15. Information on this case comes from Antonioli (2014), Burgis (2014), and Van Voris & Riseborough (2014).
16. Wilson, Burgis, and Leahy (2014).
17. See Narula (2012) for a discussion.
18. Information on this case comes from Chen et al. (2009), Chosun Nilbo (2009), Fontanella-Khan & Song (2010), Park (2009), and Song (2007).
19. This is an abridged and modified version of Lessard and Reavis (2009). Additional information from Economist (2001, 2013a), Lessard and Lucea (2009), and Uranga (2011).

4 Entry mode selection

4.1 INTRODUCTION

Once the manager has selected the country that provides the best opportunities and identified the sources of advantage to be transferred and the mechanisms that ensure the transfer happens, the next step is to select the mode of entry that best enables the firm to access the complementary resources that it is not transferring across countries to be able to have a fully functioning operation in the host country. We look at how to do this in this chapter. Complementary resources are resources that support the resources that are a source of advantage but that are not sources of advantage in themselves. For example, a firm's source of advantage may be its technology, and the marketing function may be merely a complement, enabling the firm to sell the technology to its customers. However, if the company lacks complementary resources, it is disadvantaged, because this deficiency will detract from the advantage created by other resources as the company does not have a fully functioning operation abroad. In our previous example, if the firm has a poor marketing function, it may serve its customers poorly and detract from the advantage provided by the technology as customers look for other products that, although not as technologically sophisticated, are better adapted to their needs.

One additional challenge with complementary resources is that because they are not perceived as a source of advantage, their analysis is often neglected. The usual assumption regarding complementary resources is that they can be obtained from external vendors when the need arises. However, in some cases, complementary resources are not readily available, and the lack of them can call the overall success of the foreign expansion into question. This appeared to be the case behind the acquisition of the French firm Thomson by the Chinese electronics firm TCL Corporation (TCL).

4.2 OPENING CASE: TCL ACQUISITION OF THOMSON

In November 2003, TCL International Holdings combined with the French firm Thomson and became the world's largest producer of television (TV) sets, making 18 million a year, 6 million more units than Sony. Thomson owned 33 percent and TCL 67 percent of the combined firm, which became known as TCL-Thomson Electronics (TTE). Unfortunately, this provided the Chinese firm with the wrong complementary resources in a rapidly changing industry.[1]

TCL was created in China in 1981 as TKK Electrical Home Appliances to make magnetic tape for the growing Chinese music market. In 1985, it moved to telephone equipment and changed its name to TCL Communications Equipment, becoming the largest seller of phones by 1989. In the 1990s, it diversified into TVs, mobile phones, computers, and electrical switches and acquired the Hong Kong TV maker Lu Co, becoming the second largest TV manufacturer, producing under its own brands in China and for other brands outside China.

Thomson was a French electronics manufacturer that could trace its history back to the nineteenth century. It grew via acquisitions, was nationalized in 1982, and then privatized in 1999. In 1988, it purchased General Electric's consumer electronics business and its RCA brand. However, by the 2000s, it had run into trouble because it produced in high-cost countries. To address this, it closed factories in the United States, transferred production to China, and moved into new services such as TV studio equipment and software.

The joint venture seemed beneficial to both companies at the time. The deal provided TCL with size, a global presence (especially in Europe and the United States), well-established brand names such as RCA and Thomson that could be used to price products higher, and the ability to circumvent antidumping rules in the United States and Europe. In 2002, TCL had purchased the bankrupt German TV manufacturer Schneider Electronics to avoid antidumping complaints in Europe. According to TCL's chairman, Li Dongsheng, the deal "fulfills our objective of being one of the top five players in multimedia electronics devices in the global marketplace."[2] As for Thomson, the joint venture enabled it to access China's inexpensive production bases. Both Thomson and TCL made traditional TVs with cathode ray tubes (CRTs), even though these were being replaced by new flat-screen displays. Combining was viewed as providing both companies with the economies of scale needed to withstand the profit squeeze. They reorganized the use of their brands across the globe, using RCA in the United States, Thomson in Europe, and TCL in Asia and other emerging countries.

TCL ran profitable operations in China, where it had a well-known brand, and in other emerging countries, into which it imported unassembled TVs below the level at which they would face punitive tariffs and completed assembly there. However, in Europe, it was unable to turn around the operation, and it continued to suffer losses. In 2006, it lost €159 million on sales of €328 million. To address this, in 2006, TTE closed most of its European operations, including a Polish factory, the regional headquarters (HQ) in France, and an expensive distribution network with six marketing and sales subsidiaries. It then decided to stop investing in the development of the RCA and Thomson brands and concentrate on producing TVs for other firms. Unfortunately, the industry was quickly moving away from CRT and toward flat-screen products. Nevertheless, Li Dongsheng was confident the company could compete, saying that "flat-panel TV is gaining popularity in major TV markets. Being the leader in the cathode ray tube TV segment, TTE would capitalize on its advantages in the CRT TV segment and try its utmost best to improve its position in the flat-screen TV market."[3] Despite the cost-cutting effort, in May 2007, TTE declared the joint venture insolvent, closing a chapter that had seen parent firm TCL's revenue drop 10 percent to HK$29.1 billion and losses increase fivefold to HK$1.53 billion.

4.3 SELECTING THE ENTRY MODE TO ACCESS COMPLEMENTARY RESOURCES

The acquisition of Thomson by TCL illustrates the challenges of selecting the correct mode of entry to host countries that provides the firm with the right complementary resources. TCL wanted to improve its global presence and needed well-established brands and distribution channels. With Thomson, it acquired a company that provided all these assets but also several others assets it did not need, such as managerial and manufacturing facilities in high-cost European countries. What is more, TCL did not have experience in managing far-flung operations or integrating large acquisitions. The result was that although the acquisition made sense on paper, the firm had acquired superfluous complementary resources in operations and still lacked those it needed to manage a large multinational.

When considering investment in another country, managers can choose between three main modes of entry: acquisition, alliances, and internal development. Acquisition is the purchase or part purchase of a company in the host country. Alliance is a collaboration with a host-country firm, either through the creation of a new firm of which the foreign and domestic firms share ownership or through distribution or representation agreements or franchises. Internal development is the independent creation of a new operation in the host country by the firm. Entry mode selection has a long tradition of multiple factors to be taken into account.[4] However, in our discussion, the main questions that underlie the selection of the method are what are the complementary resources the company needs in the host country and which is the best method to obtain them.

If the company can transfer all the resources it needs to operate to the host country, it can replicate its business model there and achieve full control over how it is managed, selecting in effect a form of internal development. However, in many cases, the firm cannot transfer resources across countries, either because the resources are location bound and cannot be moved or because they are not valuable in a country that has different operating and competitive conditions. In these cases, the manager is forced to select alternative modes of entry, such as alliances or acquisitions. The selection between the two is relatively straightforward: if the firm can obtain the complementary resources it desires in the market, it would do better buying only the resources it needs. Otherwise, it may need to establish an alliance with a domestic company if these resources are not available or purchase a domestic company if alliance partners are not available, disposing of unneeded resources obtained with the purchase of the acquired firm.

4.4 COMPLEMENTARY RESOURCES AND INTERNATIONAL EXPANSION

As we indicated earlier, the lack of complementary resources creates challenges abroad as the firm is unable to establish a fully functioning operation. Unlike exporting, in which the firm serves foreign markets from its home facilities, when the firm invests abroad, it has to replicate part of its value-added chain in the host country to be able to compete and serve customers there. As we have seen, when investing, the first step is to make sure that the resources that provide the firm with an advantage are transferred and that the advantage is realized in the host country. Now let us turn our attention to how the manager can find the complementary resources that will enable the firm to have a fully functioning operation abroad.

We have identified four types of complementary resources needed for a fully functioning operation abroad. Three are complementary resources that the firm needs to be able to become a multinational and operate abroad: (1) complementary resources that enable management of the larger scale and complexity of a multinational; the lack of these results in what we call liability of expansion; (2) complementary resources that enable the company to compete in the industry in the host country; their lack will result in a liability of newness; and (3) complementary resources that enable the company to operate within the institutions and relationships in the host country; their lack creates a liability of foreignness.

The fourth type of complementary resource is resources needed by customers in the host country to be able to use the firm's products. In the home country, these complementary resources may be widespread among customers, but this might not be the case in the host country. The lack of this fourth type of resource creates liability of infrastructure. We review each of these liabilities in turn.

Liability of expansion. A firm that becomes a multinational will need to have additional managerial capabilities and structure to be able to coordinate the associated added complexity and size. A company that lacks these complementary resources suffers from the liability of expansion.

For example, the international expansion of the Filipino fast-food chain Jollibee was hampered by the lack of a structure to manage the complexity of its growing international operations.[5] In 1975, the Tan family started Jollibee as an ice cream parlor. In 1978, Tony Tan Caktiong (known as TTC) transformed a few ice cream parlors into fast-food restaurants. He borrowed ideas from MacDonald's, using a red-and-yellow color palette in the restaurants and adopting a mascot, a smiling tuxedo-wearing bee, Jollibee. The company made hamburgers that catered to Filipino taste buds, with seemingly usual offerings of pineapple-topped burgers and spaghetti with hot dogs. It adopted a five F's code of friendliness, flavorful food, fun atmosphere, flexible catering to customer desires, and focus on families. When MacDonald's entered the Philippines in 1981, Jollibee focused on improving service and further adapting the offering to the local taste to fend off the much larger and experienced competitor, achieving dominance in its home market. The management team was composed of mostly family members with the exception of a few positions such as finance and marketing, which were headed by nonfamily professionals. In 1993, Jollibee became a publicly traded company, but the Tan family maintained majority ownership and control. It diversified its fast-food brands by acquiring Greenwich Pizza Corporation in 1994, establishing joint ventures with Delifrance in 1995 and with the Chinese restaurant Chowking, which it acquired in 1999. Despite this, Jollibee restaurants were the main source of revenues. The family expanded Jollibee rapidly using franchises.

As the company grew and became successful in fending off McDonald's in the Philippines, foreign entrepreneurs asked TTC for franchise rights abroad. However, the initial foreign forays were not always successful. In 1985, a friend of a Filipino franchisee started Jollibee's first foreign operation, opening restaurants in Singapore. However, soon after opening, the relationship between the Singaporean manager and Jollibee declined, and in 1986, Jollibee severed the relationship and closed the restaurant. Despite this setback, Jollibee continued its foreign expansion, creating a joint venture with a family friend in Taiwan in 1986. A rapid initial growth in sales was followed by a rapid decline and conflicts between the partners. In 1988, when rent rose rapidly, Jollibee closed the operation and exited. In the meantime, Jollibee established another joint venture in Brunei in 1987. Unlike in Singapore and Taiwan, the local partner allowed Jollibee to run the operation, and by 1993 it had successfully grown to four restaurants. In 1989, Jollibee started operating in Indonesia with the help of a family friend. The initial operation faced strong local competition and conflicts with the local partners, leading Jollibee to sell the operation to a new franchisee.

In 1993, TTC realized that to continue growing, Jollibee needed to provide its international operations better support, given that the majority of its managers were focused on the much larger and successful Filipino operation. In 1994, TTC brought in Tony Kitchner from Pizza Hut Asia Pacific as the Vice-President for International Operations. Kitchner reported to TTC and obtained autonomy and support to establish the International Division of Jollibee. Kitchner decided to upgrade the image of the international operations to be able to select better partners in foreign markets and operate more like a multinational than like a local company. To achieve this, he established a dress code, the first in the company, with managers expected to wear ties; renovated the offices of the International Division at headquarters; and hired external and internal managers who had international experience. "We had to look and act like a multinational, not like a local chain. You can't have someone in a short-sleeved open-neck shirt asking a wealthy businessman to invest millions,"[6] a manager noted. He expanded his staff from three to 12, with external managers with experience in finance, product development, marketing, and quality control. He faced challenges in attracting internal candidates because internal managers were not interested in working in the international division and their superiors did not allow them to move to the new division.

With the new team in place, Kitchner focused on achieving a rapid international growth, to make Jollibee a leading global player in fast food. To accomplish this, he selected countries in which the company faced limited competition and in which there was a relatively large Filipino community, and in two years, between 1994 and 1996, they entered Dubai, Kuwait, Saudi Arabia, Guam, Bahrain, Malaysia, Hong Kong, and Vietnam. Focusing on countries with limited competition enabled the firm to establish a presence as a foreign player before others and benefit from first-mover advantages. Focusing on countries with a large Filipino community enabled Jollibbee access to a market that was aware of the company and appreciated its food. For example, the first US restaurant was located in Daly City, California, in 1998, and later locations included Long Beach and San Francisco, all of which had large Filipino populations. The company later modified this pattern and expanded into mainstream areas, adapting the recipes to US tastes, with little success. Jose Miñana, head of the US operations, reflected on this by noting that "that's when we realized and learned our lesson that, hold on, we're a totally unknown brand here, no matter how good we are back home."[7] After this, the company closed underperforming stores, returned to its original recipes, and focused on areas with a large

Filipino presence. In 2015, it opened its first Canadian store in Toronto.

As the case of Jollibee illustrates, the lack of resources to coordinate the larger size and complexity that accompany the internationalization of the firm, especially managers and staff who can coordinate the expansion of operations and manage dispersed operations, can become a challenge. This is a problem that tends to affect most companies at the beginning of their global expansion. Even if the firm has become large in its home country and has enough financial resources to support investments abroad, in many cases it does not have the organizational structure and managerial capabilities needed to coordinate the new complexities that come with being a multinational. The existing coordination and managerial structures were not developed in anticipation of foreign markets and in many cases become strained as the firm invests abroad, especially if it embarks on a rapid foreign expansion.

The essence of this challenge comes from the lack of managers and coordination structures needed to manage complexity rather than size. Once a firm reaches a certain size, adding one or several operations in the home market can be easily done with existing structures. However, adding an operation in a foreign country is a qualitatively different challenge, as the managers have not dealt with the significant increase in complexity that comes from managing an operation in a host country that has a different language, customs, legal system, industry regulations, and so on.

The consequence of the liability of expansion is an increase in inefficiencies in the management of operations in the host country and, in some cases, home operations as well. The structures designed to manage the home operation become stretched to manage the additional complexity of host-country operations. In the case of scarce managerial talent in particular, this distracts attention from the main business, as the top managers attend to the demands of the host country. For example, as our earlier case showed, TCL faced additional problems because its management had to devote attention to solving the problems of the European operations instead of paying attention to how the industry was moving from CRT to flat-screen TVs.

The liability of expansion can be identified preemptively before the firm embarks on its foreign investments or before it starts a sequence of rapid foreign investments that result in the need to manage a dispersed company. To assess this need, the manager can carry out an internal analysis of the company's organizational and managerial structure and identify not only whether it will be feasible to add more activities but also whether activities in other countries could be performed using existing managers and information-processing structures or whether new managers and a more sophisticated coordination structure will be needed.

Liability of newness. A firm that becomes a multinational and invests in a foreign country will find itself operating in an industry that, while sharing many technical and technological features with the industry in the home country, will differ in many other aspects, such as the competitors already operating there, the industry structure, distribution channels, supplier networks, and regulations. This creates a liability of newness, in which the foreign firm becomes a new entrant in the industry, an unknown, that has to establish relationships with suppliers and customers and has to deal with incumbent firms that are already well positioned in the industry.

For example, the Peruvian soft drinks firm AJE[8] had to resort to creative marketing to compensate for the lack of a brand image in Asian markets and compete against much larger and well-known US firms Coca-Cola and PepsiCo. The family-owned AJE Group started operations in 1988 in Ayacucho in Peru. At the time, the country was experiencing violence from the Shining Path Maoist rebels, who attacked trucks with Pepsi and Coca-Cola products coming from the capital. The family started making a cola drink, called Kola Real, from their house and sold it in recycled beer bottles at a low price. In the 1990s, they expanded across Peru as violence subsided, selling at lower prices than competitors, relying on entrepreneurs to distribute to remote locations instead of creating their own distribution network, producing their own syrup to reduce costs further, and relying on word of mouth instead of spending on marketing. Although its larger competitors in some cases reduced prices to counter their low-price strategy, these price cuts were temporary, and AJE continued to prosper. In 1999, it began its global expansion, starting in Latin America with Venezuela in 1999 and then entering Ecuador (2001), Mexico (2002), Costa Rica (2004), Guatemala, Nicaragua, and Honduras (2005), Colombia (2007), Panama (2009), Brazil (2011), and Bolivia (2013). In 2006, it expanded into Asia, entering Thailand and then India, Vietnam, and Indonesia (2010), and Reunion (2013). It also established a corporate office in Spain in 2006 to better manage the Latin American and Asian operations and exported and distributed its products in Cambodia, Malaysia, Myanmar, and Laos, as well as in African countries like Egypt and Nigeria. As a result, AJE grew its sales at an average of 22 percent per annum between 2000 and 2013, and by 2014, it had become the fifth largest soft drinks producer in Latin America and the twenty-first in the world, with sales of US$2 billion.

AJE's expansion in Indonesia illustrated its strategy as an unknown newcomer in an industry dominated by global giants. The company focused on selling low-priced cola in large containers, offering more value for their money to poor consumers. It did all the manufacturing and then relied on local distributors to move the products to minimarts, small eateries, and street stalls where low-income Indonesians made their purchases. "The consumption of soft drinks in emerging markets is a question of affordability, as well as availability,"[9] said Antonio Soto, head of AJE in Asia. If costs increased, the company did not raise prices but instead reduced the size of the units so that poor consumers could still purchase their soft drinks. It ran different marketing campaigns from its larger competitors. "We don't create our brand by having huge shelf displays for Big Cola in supermarkets,"[10] said Soto. The company used football sponsorship to increase its profile among consumers, establishing deals with FC Barcelona in Latin America and the English Football Association (FA) in Asia. As a result, some consumers in Indonesia perceived that the company came from the United Kingdom rather than Peru. As Soto explained, "The partnership with the FA has been critical for us in Asia in having something else to offer the consumer."[11] AJE ran competitions offering winners the opportunity to train with or watch English football players. "The FA England deal was good for both sides. They were looking at Asia at a great moment of its development. It's a good match. There are far more fans watching the England team in Asia than there are in England."[12]

As AJE illustrates, the foreign firm, as a new entrant in the industry, needs to obtain complementary resources to be able to compete successfully. Although it may bring its source of advantage to the host country, it needs additional resources such as production facilities, relationships with suppliers, relationships with distributors, and so on to have a fully functioning operation in the host country and enable its advantages to succeed. AJE's understanding of low-income consumers and its strategy of offering more value by selling lower-priced products in larger quantities helped it succeed in emerging countries. However, in each country, it had to obtain complementary resources that enabled it to compete, such as a distribution network that would reach its low-income target consumers, along with creating a brand image for consumers who did not know the firm's products.

A company facing a liability of newness will have lower revenues than expected. Even if the products are highly desired by consumers, the lack of a distribution system will limit sales, or a lack of adequate supplies will limit the ability of the firm to produce enough to meet demand. As the firm invests in the development of these complementary resources, it will initially have higher costs than established competitors that have already established relationships and a reputation in the marketplace or possess well-tuned operations. Nevertheless, over time, the new entrant can improve efficiency and reduce its costs to the level of established competitors and achieve similar or even better results if its sources of advantage are superior.

This liability of newness can be identified through an indirect analysis of incumbent competitors in the industry, studying what a company needs to replicate its value chain and achieve a level of operational efficiency similar to established firms. As the foreign firm will be bringing some of the resources that form part of the value chain, especially sources of advantage, the challenge is to identify the resources it is not bringing and will need to obtain to have a fully functioning operation in the host country.

Liability of foreignness. As the firm enters a foreign country, it also needs to obtain complementary resources that will enable it to understand how to operate within the new institutions and relationships in the host country. These complementary resources are independent of the particularities of the industry in which the firm operates. They are related to understanding the norms and rules of behavior of the host country, determined by culture, language, and religion, as well as general laws and regulations, that apply to all firms regardless of industry. Domestic firms have developed these resources as their managers and employees grew up in the country and learned how to interact with other individuals and companies and how to manage relationships. Managers of foreign firms have not experienced these location-based interactions and so suffer from what we call the liability of foreignness.

For example, some of the main challenges that the Brazilian motor manufacturer WEG faced in its Chinese operation were posed by problems of language and cultural relationships rather than the implementation of its technology in the factories.[13] WEG started operating in Jaragua do Sul in the State of Santa Catarina, Brazil, in 1961, producing electric motors. It expanded throughout Brazil and then abroad as the country opened up to allow foreign investment by its companies. In 1992, it acquired a firm in Belgium to serve Europe and established sales operations throughout Europe in the 1990s. In 2000, it purchased a factory in Mexico from the Swiss-Swedish ABB and two factories in Argentina. In the 2000s, it continued expanding in

Latin America and Europe, and in 2004, it bought a factory in China, its first production facility in Asia. It continued opening sales subsidiaries and establishing production facilities in selected countries, such as South Africa in 2010 and India in 2011. By 2013, WEG was the largest manufacturer of electric motors in Latin America, with an annual revenue of US$2.6 billion and 30,000 employees, and operated in 24 countries.

In 2004, WEG was looking for somewhere to establish a production site to serve Asia, as supplying from Brazil entailed very high logistics costs. It established its first Asian production facility in China, purchasing a state-owned firm in Nantong at a time when the Chinese government was promoting the sale of state-owned firms to domestic and foreign investors.

As Siegfried Kreutzfeld, managing director of WEG Motors, explained, "From the beginning, the implementation phase of the plant, the relationship between company and the government was very positive, so you build the foundation for future growth opportunities. However, it was not all rosy. We have been in China for about seven years and during this period we had to deal with different cultural challenges. This was a great shock and, over time, we had to adapt. What enabled this to happen was not technologies or machines, but key people. We had the technology and brought the machines. With people, the issue was very different. We had to hire about 20 Sino-Brazilian trainees (speaking, besides Chinese, Portuguese and English) and trained these people in WEG in Brazil. We found many Chinese with dual citizenship, who lived in Brazil but understood the Chinese culture well – mainly engineers. This was undoubtedly different from our local setting. We brought Brazilians from different areas – engineering, human resources, and accounting – who stayed there for about six months. We have a production manager on site in our factory – all are required to undergo this training. In addition, we sent Brazilian expatriates to take key management positions. Today, our CEO in China is a Chinese who speaks Portuguese and English. The Operations Director of the unit is a Brazilian who does not speak Chinese. In China, you must be able to speak Chinese if you are responsible for contacts and relations. This is called *guanxi* and is critical to the success of a foreign company. I've been to China many times and realized that close contacts with our partners are critical. It is important to have dinner with them and talk about generalities. Another issue that we discovered during these years is that the first relationship should be with the top person at the potential client, not among sales representatives. Our Director, Liu Cheng, is responsible for the first contact, then we send a Director from Brazil to China, and only then the relationship begins to progress, from the trust established in a very personal way. In China [...] salary is the religion. We had to change some features on the factory floor, e.g., inventory management, which did not exist in the company before its purchase by WEG. The employee was paid by quantity produced, i.e., by piece. The planning was based on ensuring the highest production, even if it was subsequently kept in stock. This, however, is not a plan. We had to work hard to change it. We established a canteen in the factory. Before that, the Chinese used to have lunch next to their machines. It took three years of hard work to get these changes implemented. The Chinese are internationalizing and are familiarizing themselves little by little with our cultural standards, which is very interesting. They do not lose *guanxi*, but other aspects are actually being absorbed."[14]

WEG's challenges of managing differences in institutional norms across countries were not limited to the Chinese operation, however. Despite the perception that countries in Latin America share cultural commonalities, there are still large differences in culture, language, and traditions. Harry Schmelzer, president of WEG Group, commented on the differences between Brazil and Mexico[15]: "When I got to Mexico for the first time and saw that you ate pork ribs and tacos and refried beans for breakfast, I was a bit scared," he said. "Lunch in Brazil is at midday and then you go back to work in the afternoon. You may have a glass of wine, but you watch your intake. In Mexico, you go to lunch at three and the day's over. It's tequila and then you're out of it."

A firm suffering from liability of foreignness will experience lower sales if it cannot interact with key decision makers or its own consumers in the host country. Some problems may arise from differences in languages, as the case of WEG illustrated. It can also arise from something as simple as the translation of a brand name. For example, the Iranian Paxam Company sells a detergent called "Barf" in Iran and the Middle East. "Barf" means snow in Farsi, but in English it is an informal term for vomit.[16] Differences in other institutions, like legal systems, can also create challenges. In civil-law countries, laws are codified and change slowly over time, whereas in common-law countries, laws are codified both as laws and as judicial interpretations of the law and can respond flexibly to new situations. Also, in some countries, the judicial system may not be well developed, and individuals tend to resort to personal relationships in lieu of contractual relationships. In some cases, the exchange of gifts helps build relationships[17]; however, such exchanges may be construed as bribery in the home country.

Identifying the liability of foreignness is easily done by analyzing differences in norms and rules of behavior across countries. There are many publications and consulting companies that offer advice on how to manage differences across cultures and adapt to cultural norms. Although cross-cultural training before visiting the foreign country is useful, there is a limit to how much one can learn at home. Unlike other differences that exist across countries, differences in institutional and norms of behavior reflect deeper unwritten assumptions about what constitutes acceptable and unacceptable behavior, assumptions that are rarely made clear. The manager needs to experience these norms and rules directly by visiting the country and trying to understand the reasons behind particular behaviors.

Liability of infrastructure. Finally, even when the firm has transferred or obtained all the complementary resources it needs to manage across borders, has a fully functioning operation abroad, and interacts within the institutional framework, it may still find that it cannot succeed because consumers lack the complementary resources needed to use its products. The firm's products developed in the home country tend to take the existence of complementary resources for granted, such as a reliable supply of electricity or clean facilities, which may not be the case in the host country. Some of these limitations in infrastructure may also exist in the home country in emerging countries, inducing the firm to invest in their development and thus become able to better adapt to the needs of consumers abroad. For example, the Brazilian brewer AmBev created bars in Brazil to ensure the quality of consumption of its beers.[18] AmBev was created in 1999 from the merger of the Brazilian brewers Brahma and Antarctica. It then merged with the Belgium-based brewer Interbrew in 2004 to form the Brazilian–Belgian brewer InBev, which in 2008 purchased the US brewer Anheuser-Busch to become Anheuser-Busch InBev, the largest brewer in the world by sales. In 2012, AmBev, the Brazilian subsidiary of Anheuser-Busch InBev, started creating branded bars in Brazil to ensure quality and consistency in the consumption of its beers. In 2011, AmBev launched a pilot operation in São Paulo with Nosso Bar ("Our Bar") and rolled it over in other areas. The idea for Nosso Bar arose from consumer complaints about the warm beer and dirty locales of bars in remote areas. The company operated as a quasi-franchise. Franchisees invested between US$14,400 and $24,000, could choose the name of the bar, and owned and ran it. AmBev provided a guidance manual and advice on location, training, marketing, furniture, and decoration. "The franchisee purchases materials and consumer goods at subsidized prices, because we have the possibility of buying from suppliers and offer lower prices," explained Ricardo Rolim, director of institutional relations. The manual was very specific. On page one, for example, it indicated that the bar had to have two rest rooms, male and female, and elsewhere it indicated the type of entertainment it was suitable to offer. By 2014, AmBev had 900 franchisees.

The liability of infrastructure arises from the lack of both tangible and intangible assets among customers, for example, the availability of refrigeration for products that are better consumed cold (tangible) and an understanding of how to use the products or services the firm supplies (intangible). The lack of these complementary resources among customers will limit the firm's ability to realize its sales potential. Although consumers may try the products once, a bad experience (not being able or not knowing how to use them properly) may discourage them from buying again. The problem may also lie in distribution channels. The firm may have to develop its own distribution channel to reach customers or be creative and allow local entrepreneurs to do so, as the case of AJE illustrates.

This liability of infrastructure can be identified by visiting the host country and potential customers and analyzing what additional assets they need to use the firm's products and how they use them. Identifying the tangible assets needed can be done easily, as it requires observation of whether consumers can or cannot use the products of the firm. However, identifying intangible assets can be more difficult, as it requires learning whether consumers know how to use the product correctly. Consumers in the host country may have some superficial knowledge of a product, for example, through advertisement of the brand name, which will disguise their need to be educated further about it. Moreover, consumers may be reluctant or embarrassed to share that they do not know how the product actually works, even if they know the brand. Or in some cases they may be using the product for the wrong purpose. For example, the Chinese white goods manufacturer Haier found out that some of its rural customers were using its washing machines to clean not only clothes but also potatoes, which resulted in the machine malfunctioning.[19]

4.5 SOLUTIONS: ENTRY MODE SELECTION TO OBTAIN COMPLEMENTARY RESOURCES

The solution for the lack of complementary resources needed to manage across borders, compete in the industry, and operate in the host country is to obtain them. This is where selecting the mode of entry comes into play. Which of the three alternative modes to choose (acquisition, alliance, or internal development) will depend on the availability of a particular complementary resource, its importance for the company, and the speed and cost of obtaining or developing it.[20]

We can divide the selection of entry mode into four stages based on the type of complementary resources the company needs to (1) manage across borders, (2) compete in the industry in the host country, (3) operate in the host country, and (4) sell to host-country consumers. Table 4.1 summarizes the four stages and the questions managers should address when choosing entry mode.

First, the company needs complementary resources to manage across countries because it will face additional complexity and scale. These complementary resources can be as simple as money to fund the investment, the need for spare capacity in its current production line to manufacture additional quantities to serve the host country, or the need for more managers who can coordinate operations.

The selection of entry mode will be driven by the types of resources needed to support the company's advantage. The company can obtain generic resources, that is, not specific to the firm, from outside. This applies to finance, for example, as the company can issue debt to obtain funds to support its foreign expansion. For resources that are more integral to the company, it can form alliances with other companies. For example, it can employ consultants to devise information systems that will help process the additional information and complexity involved in expanding operations. Finally, resources that are highly sensitive to the company's operations, such as management, will need to be developed internally.

In some cases, highly sensitive resources need to be developed quickly and can be complemented with externally acquired resources, for example, hiring external managers to help internal managers learn how to manage a multinational. However, although external managers will bring experience in dealing with the conditions of the

Table 4.1 *Solutions for addressing the challenges of entry mode selection*

Issues	Actions
Managing across borders	Identify the spare financial resources the firm has to invest abroad Identify the spare production capacity the firm has to serve foreign countries Identify the spare managerial capacity and structure the firm has to coordinate operations abroad Identify the best mode for obtaining additional financial resources, production capacity, and managerial capacity in terms of their cost, speed, and need
Competing in the host industry	Identify what parts of the firm's value chain have been transferred and which parts are missing abroad Identify the best mode for obtaining the missing parts of the value chain in terms of their cost, speed, and need
Operating in the host country	Identify what the institutions and rules of behavior of the host country are and what the firm knows and does not know about the institutions and rules of behavior of the host country Identify the best mode for obtaining missing institutional resources in terms of their cost, speed, and need
Selling to host-country customers	Identify what resources customers need to use the firm's product Identify whether the firm needs to redesign products to reduce the need for infrastructure resources Identify whether the firm needs to develop and provide such resources to ensure exclusivity Identify the best mode for providing the resources to customers in terms of their cost, speed, and need

foreign country, the company will also need internal managers who understand operations within the company. So, if the firm is planning to expand abroad, it needs to start developing managers who will eventually be able to run operations overseas.

Second, the company needs complementary resources to compete abroad, and the selection of entry mode will be driven by the types of resources that support the competitive advantage it is transferring from home. The company can purchase many resources in the open market, especially those that are not easily transferable across borders – like a plant, machinery, or office equipment – and hire individual employees to manage the operation. However, some of these resources may not be available as individual purchases, in which case the company may be forced to buy an ongoing operation or establish an alliance with a firm that controls the resources needed. This is usually the case for intangible resources such as reputation, connections with customers, and brand names. In contrast, resources on the input side, such as a network of suppliers or a logistics system, can be readily obtained in the open market by establishing contracts. Additionally, by purchasing individual resources, the company benefits from being able to design the local operation the way it wants, making the individual resources fit the sources of competitive advantage that have been transferred from the home operation, rather than having to fit the sources of advantage from the home operation to the characteristics of the company purchased or to the alliance partner in the host country. If individual resources are not available in the market, it is advisable to establish alliances with existing companies to obtain them or to purchase ongoing operations. With these two latter modes, managers need to take into account that it may take time to integrate the sources of advantage with ongoing operations, and the firm may be saddled with additional resources it does not need or want but for which it nevertheless has to pay.

Third, the company also needs resources to operate in the host country, and the selection of entry mode for obtaining those resources will depend on the extent of integration with existing operations.

Operating in another country requires intangible knowledge of its institutional conditions (cultural, social, legal, regulatory, etc.). In contrast to the resources needed to compete in the industry, which may share commonalities across countries, institutional conditions differ from country to country, and the resources to deal with institutions are never fully transferable from one country to another. The reason is not only that there are differences between countries in institutions but also and primarily because these are tacit and part of the assumptions developed as one learns to interact in the country. The firm therefore needs to select the entry mode that facilitates the learning of tacit knowledge for operating and interacting with external parties in the host country. Employing external managers and consultants and hiring local employees can achieve this and provide the firm with a quick way to incorporate tacit knowledge. However, while alliances can be useful to obtain this tacit knowledge, they also have a limitation: managers may tend to rely on their alliance partners when in doubt rather than learning about the norms themselves. Although in principle internal development is the best way to develop intangible knowledge, it takes time and may not be so helpful at the beginning of the operation. Hence, one way to address this is by staggering the method used, starting the operation with the help of local managers and consultants or even local partners. Once the operation is established and the company has obtained rapid access to institutional resources via consultants or partners, the company can change its mode to internal development to ensure that its managers understand how to operate in the host country. For example, the company can rotate employees from HQ to a subsidiary to facilitate the transfer of tacit knowledge and understanding of the conditions of the host country.

Fourth, developing the infrastructure to sell to customers in the host country is best done through internal development, because it will ensure that infrastructure resources work well with the company's products or services and can be designed to reduce the potential spillover onto competitors' products. The company can make customers use the infrastructure exclusively with its own products. For example, a manufacturer of frozen food or beverages can give small retailers the fridges needed to keep the products at the right temperature and ask the retailer to agree not to stock competitors' products in the fridges. This type of infrastructure will create an additional barrier to entry to competitors' products. These fridges can also carry the brand names of the company and act as an additional source of in-store advertising. In AmBev's case, the whole bar decoration served as an advertising platform for the company's products.

4.6 CLOSING CASE: LENOVO'S ACQUISITION OF IBM'S PERSONAL COMPUTER UNIT

A good example of how to obtain the complementary resources needed to achieve global status is the Chinese computer firm Lenovo's purchase of the personal computer (PC) business from the US firm International Business Machines (IBM) in 2004.[21] Lenovo started life as an offshoot of the Chinese Academy of Sciences, which in 1984 gave US$25,000 to 11 of its computer scientists to create the New Technology Developer (NTD) to market innovations. NTD started importing and selling computers to the government. In 1987, it marketed the Legend Chinese-character card, a piece of hardware it created that translated operating systems from English into Chinese. The card facilitated the sale of imported PCs, and in 1988 NTD established a joint venture with a small manufacturer, DAW, moving to Hong Kong to benefit from favorable policies for foreign investors and to avoid regulations in PC manufacturing, becoming known as Legend Computer Group Co.

In 1990 Legend started selling its Legend-branded PCs in China, focusing on the business segment. In 1993 it expanded by marketing PCs to consumers via a retail network, and in 1996 it introduced laptops and PCs using Intel's Pentium chips, expanding sales dramatically by benefiting from economies of scale. By focusing on innovations for the consumer market, such as Chinese voice recognition or a pad for writing in Chinese characters, while its competitors focused on the business segment, it became the leading PC firm in the Chinese market. As founder Liu Chuanzhi indicated, "We found that the computer market was visibly divided into high-end and low-end products. The high-end products were mainly made by large US corporations.... The low-end product market was basically taken by Taiwanese companies.... We felt that the technological capability at ICT [Institute of Computing Technology] was strong.... However, were we able to compete directly with the world's best in areas such as super-computers or mini-computers? Definitely not. But with our best Chinese team, we could compete in the low end of the high-end products."[22] By 1999, the combination of domestic sales, sales of imported PCs, and exports to Asia made it a leader in the Asian-Pacific market, with management focused on becoming a global leader as competition in the Chinese market intensified. However, it discovered that it could not use the name Legend because this was already trademarked in several countries. Hence, it created a new name for international operations: Lenovo, which was a combination of Le from Legend and Novo from new; this was available for trademark and easy to pronounce. To increase visibility, it became an official partner of the Olympic Games.

As part of its global expansion plan, in December 2004, Lenovo purchased the PC Division of the US computer firm IBM for US$1.75 billion, and IBM became a shareholder with 18.9 percent of the firm. The sale enabled IBM to exit the low-margin PC business and focus on the high-margin consulting services, as well as increase its exposure to the Chinese market via the ownership stake. IBM manager and later Lenovo's chief marketing officer Deepak Advani indicated, "We had to decide what the right long-term play for IBM was. PCs were more and more at the fringe, with IBM moving more and more into services. A potential acquisition by Lenovo was an option, as was spinning out the division to a private equity firm. IBM and Lenovo decided to do the deal."[23]

The acquisition enabled Lenovo to become a global player. Liu Chuanzhi said, "I am excited by this breakthrough in Lenovo's journey toward becoming an international company. ... From the beginning, however, our unwavering goal has been to create a truly international enterprise. From 2003 when we changed our international brand name, to 2004 ... to today's [merger] with IBM, I have been delighted to watch Lenovo become a truly world-class company."[24] Lenovo obtained the well-known IBM ThinkPad laptop and ThinkCentre desktop brands, a 30,000-strong sales force, could use the IBM logo on the acquired products for five years, and had IBM's global computer support for five years. As Advani reflected, "On paper this was pretty much a match made in heaven. [...] We had complementary products and client bases, and practically no channel conflict. We could use the broad product portfolio we sell in China and use global distribution and take products around the world."[25]

4.7 CONCLUSIONS

Firms need complementary resources to have successful operations abroad. No matter how powerful the company's sources of advantage are, if it lacks complementary resources, the company cannot realize its potential. Unfortunately, these complementary resources tend to receive insufficient attention because they are not themselves the source of advantage.

If a firm can bring all the resources it needs to a host country, it does not need complementary resources. However, this is rarely the case because even if it can bring all the tangible assets (machinery, technology, etc.) and has a fully functioning operation, it will need to develop intangible assets in the form of relationships with suppliers, distribution channels, and customers, as well as an understanding of the institutions and ways of doing business in the host country. So no matter how successful the firm is in its home country or how well it has standardized its geographic expansion within the home country, the expansion across borders will require additional complementary resources that the firm will need to obtain. The internal development of resources is the best strategy because it enables the firm to obtain the complementary resource in the manner it specifically needs for its operations. However, internal development not only takes longer but in some cases also moves the firm out of its area of expertise. Buying the resources in the marketplace or relying on external partners can be more appropriate, especially for complementary resources that do not form the basis of the firm's advantage. However, these kinds of acquisitions or alliances need to be more focused than most entry modes pursued by firms so that the company does not find itself buying resources it does not need. Instead of focusing on which companies have the desired resources, it is better to focus on which resources are needed and aim to obtain only those, buying parts of a company rather than the whole company or establishing limited partnerships that enable the firm to obtain the needed complementary resources.

The case of Lenovo illustrates the need for managers of emerging market multinational corporations (EMNCs) to understand their firms' requirements for complementary resources and make sure they get them. The company already had a well-established ability to produce quality computers, but it was not well known outside its home country, as it had mainly produced for other labels. In order to conquer global markets, it needed to develop a brand that would enhance its reputation. The acquisition of IBM's PC unit provided the firm with the brand it needed as well as design and distribution in the United States and established consumer relationships. This complemented its prowess in manufacturing and its well-established operations in low-cost China. Moreover, by purchasing only IBM's PC unit, Lenovo avoided having to acquire the whole firm, along with assets that it neither needed nor wanted. The right to use the brand enabled the firm not only to access the goodwill of IBM but also to associate its own brand with the quality and design of the computers, changing the perception of consumers in advanced countries about the firm and the quality of its products.

Notes

1. Developed using information from Economist (2006b), Lau (2006), Liu (2007), Ramstad (2003), and Tabliabue (2003).
2. Tagliabue (2003).
3. ICMR (2006).
4. See Newburry and Zeira (1997) for a review.
5. Information for this case comes from Ballon (2002), Bartlett (2001), Ebenkamp (2007), and Levinson (2014).
6. Bartlett (2001).
7. Levinson (2014).
8. Information from Bland (2014), Bland and Schipani (2014), and Nueno, Bazan, and Rodriguez (2011) Robertson (2008).
9. Bland and Schipani (2014).
10. Bland and Schipani (2014).
11. Bland and Schipani (2014).
12. Bland, and Schipani (2014).
13. Information comes from Barros de Castro (2011), Marsh (2007a, 2007b), and Weg (2014).
14. Author's translation of Barros de Castro (2011).
15. Downei (2010).
16. Gianaitasio (2009).
17. Donaldson (1996).
18. Derived from Lira (2013), Lucas (2012), and Sousa (2014).
19. Backaler (2010).
20. See Capron and Mitchell (2012) for a discussion of the selection among methods to grow a firm.
21. Information for this case comes from Ahrens and Zhou (2013), Quelch and Knoop (2006), and Tse and Couturier (2009).
22. Ahrens and Zhou (2013).
23. Quelch and Knoop (2006).
24. Tse and Couturier (2009).
25. Quelch and Knoop (2006).

5 Establishment

5.1 INTRODUCTION

In some instances, a company can create a disadvantage from the resources it transfers abroad. This can happen if the resources are not appropriate for operating in the host country or because the host country's government or consumers dislike them. This problem is particularly challenging for EMNCs, as individuals not only in advanced economies but also in other emerging countries can have a negative attitude toward emerging country firms and tend to associate them with less sophisticated products.

5.2 OPENING CASE: CHINA NATIONAL OFFSHORE OIL CORPORATION'S FAILED BID FOR UNOCAL

The Chinese oil firm China National Offshore Oil Corporation (CNOOC) found out the hard way that its state ownership and Chinese origin were a competitive disadvantage in the eyes of the US Congress when it tried to acquire the US oil firm Unocal in 2005.[1] CNOOC was a Chinese state-owned firm in charge of managing offshore oil and gas projects. It created CNOOC Ltd. as a Hong Kong–quoted subsidiary to undertake exploration and production (E&P) operations in collaboration with foreign firms. CNOOC controlled 70 percent of CNOOC Ltd., with the remaining shares were traded in New York and Hong Kong.

In December 2004, CNOOC Ltd.'s CEO considered acquiring the US independent petroleum firm Unocal Corporation. Unocal had been created in 1890 and over the decades had gained expertise in offshore E&P operations and a good success record in finding hydrocarbons. Unocal expertise and its large operations in Indonesia,

Thailand, Bangladesh, and Myanmar seemed a good complement for CNOCC expansion plans.

CNOOC Ltd.'s CEO discussed the possibility of acquiring Unocal with its CEO, but by the time he discussed this action with the CNOCC Ltd.'s board and made a formal offer, the operation turned into a competitive takeover. On April 4, 2005, the US petroleum giant Chevron made a bid for the purchase of Unocal, offering US$62 per share in 25 percent cash and 75 percent stock. On June 22, 2005, CNOOC Ltd. countered this with its offer of US$67 per share in cash. On June 22, 2005, Chevron increased its offer to US$63.01 in 40 percent cash and 60 percent stock.

However, despite the higher price and all-cash offer made by CNOOC Ltd. for Unocal, its bid ran into political opposition in the US Congress. The acquisition of a US firm by a foreign firm needed approval from the Committee on Foreign Investment in the United States (CFIUS), and there was opposition by members of both the Republican and Democratic parties. They expressed concern over the backing by the Chinese government of the acquisition would and whether the acquisition "advance China's energy agenda to the detriment of US national security objectives."[2] For example, the Democratic Senator Charles Schumer asked, "Would China allow an American company to take over a Chinese company? We know countless instances where it hasn't been allowed," while a letter sponsored by Democrat William Jefferson indicated, "We have no objection to market-based foreign companies buying US energy companies, but state-owned and financed companies buying American energy companies raises many national security questions."[3] And Michael Wessel, a member of a bipartisan panel that advised Congress, the US–China Economic and Security Review Commission, raised the issue of national security concerns, saying that "other parts of this deal have very wide repercussions in terms of the military. We should know, are they going to restrict access to the oil? Does Unocal have technologies that have military applications?"[4]

Fu Chengyu, CNOOC's chairman and chief executive, described the bid as a "good offer for Unocal. ... it is a good offer for America."[5] To reduce concerns, in a June 27 letter to members of Congress, he indicated that "we have also committed that substantially all of the oil and gas produced by Unocal in the U.S. will continue to be sold in the U.S. should a merger occur. It is important to note, Unocal's U.S. oil and gas production currently accounts for less than 1% of total U.S. oil and gas consumption. Furthermore, the combined company will enhance the development of resources currently held by Unocal in the Gulf of Mexico. [...] I would like to reiterate our commitment to retain the jobs of substantially all of Unocal's employees, including those in the U.S. We value them and the expertise they bring to U.S. operations."[6]

Despite this, the acquisition by CNOOC Ltd. continued to be subjected to strong opposition by US lawmakers, who delayed the regulatory inquiry by two months, giving Chevron time to increase its offer and get acceptance at Unocal's shareholders' meeting in August. This created pressure on CNOOC Ltd. to increase its own offer, with Charles Williamson, Unocal's CEO, telling Mr. Fu on July 15 "to make his best offer," indicating that "a sufficiently large increase in the proposed consideration could likely result in a conclusion of the process."[7]

By August 2, 2005, CNOOC Ltd. withdrew the bid. It had run into both a more sophisticated lobbying effort by Chevron and political angst among US lawmakers about the rise of China and the global ambitions of Chinese firms. As the president of the National Foreign Trade Council, William Reinsch, indicated, "We are in a time and place where every single one of these deals is going to go through extra scrutiny, because the deals give fodder to the view that China is the enemy, and we shouldn't be giving them anything because we are moving into an adversarial relationship with them."[8] Eight days later, Unocal's shareholders accepted Chevron's offer.

5.3 ESTABLISHMENT: DEALING WITH DISADVANTAGES

The case of CNOOC Ltd. illustrates how on some occasions EMNCs face disadvantages abroad. Despite CNOOC Ltd. offering a higher price and promising to keep the operations of Unocal in the United States, US politicians' negative perceptions of the firm's country of origin and its association with the Chinese government created a disadvantage that the company did not expect and that forced it to eventually withdraw its bid.

Once the EMNC has transferred the resources that provide it with an advantage and has obtained the complementary resources that enable it to have a fully functioning operation, it has to make sure that the operation is established at the same level as, if not better than, its competitors. However, on some occasions, the EMNC may face additional disadvantages that limit its competitiveness and success abroad. Some of these disadvantages arise from resources that it transfers to the host country that create problems there, even though such resources were not creating problems in the home country.

In this chapter, we discuss two situations in which resources transferred from the home country, where they created no problems, can become sources of disadvantage abroad. First, some firms may bring practices that have worked well in the home country but that create problems in the host country. We call this the disadvantage of transfer. Second, a firm's association with its country of origin becomes a source of disadvantage in the host country because individuals in the host country dislike foreign firms in general or the country of origin in particular and discriminate against the firm. We call this the disadvantage of foreignness.

Disadvantage of transfer. Some firms may transfer practices that worked well in the home country but that unfortunately generate problems in the host country because they clash with practices and behaviors there, creating a disadvantage of transfer. For example, the Chinese white goods maker Haier created problems in its initial manufacturing in the United States with the practices it transferred from China to incentivize workers.[9] Haier originated in the Qingdao General Refrigerator Factory. In 1984, a new manager, Zhang Ruimin, arrived at the state-owned firm and turned around its strategy to focus on quality. As the company improved, it was asked to take control of other ailing state-owned white goods firms in the area. It established an alliance with the German firm Liebherr, further improving the quality of its manufacturing process. In 1991, it adopted the name Haier, a derivation of its partner's name. In the 1990s, it continued diversifying into electronics and internationalized, establishing production plants abroad. By 2014, Haier was the largest white goods producer in the world, with sales of US$13.8 billion and 55,000 employees.

In 1999, Haier broke ground for a refrigerator manufacturing plant in Camden, South Carolina, in the United States, and started production there in 2001. This enabled it to improve the image of China and avoid being accused of dumping and stealing US jobs. Indeed, it received an incentive package that included a US$370,000 tax break and a 110-acre lot that belonged to the county. However, some of the management practices that it brought to the United States created problems. One of the practices developed by Haier in China was social humiliation. At the start of a shift, workers lined up, and the worker who had made the most mistakes the previous day (e.g., working slowly or scratching products) would stand on a set of large green footprints outlined on the factory floor to listen to a lecture on the importance of quality. This practice seemed to contribute to productivity at home, but when Haier implemented it in its factory in the United States, it backfired. It angered US workers, and they refused to put up with it, with some quitting rather than becoming subject to the embarrassment. The practice was dropped after Haier replaced Chinese managers with Americans.

This type of disadvantage of transfer originates in the way the firm develops resources and capabilities adapted to the particular conditions of the home country, taking into account the inputs available there as well as the prevailing social and cultural norms and regulations. The way in which the firm manages the resource becomes part of its practices and routines; it becomes embedded in the corporate culture of the firm and the assumptions of managers and employees.[10] However, in another country, inputs, social and cultural norms, and regulations will differ. In some cases, they may be incompatible with the practices that are transferred from the home country, creating problems, as the case of Haier illustrates.

The implementation of practices that conflict with the norms of the host country creates operational problems. As a result, the firm may be less efficient than initially expected because host-country employees and managers have problems adapting to the firm's practices. This may also generate higher turnover than expected as employees begin to realize that they cannot adapt to the corporate culture of the foreign firm. This problem is compounded when the firm comes from an emerging country and operates in a more advanced economy. In many such cases, host-country employees will view the practices and managers of the home country as inferior and put up additional resistance to adapting to them.

Identifying instances where transferred practices may generate a disadvantage is challenging for managers or employees from the home operation because they have internalized the assumptions on which the practices are built and are unlikely to perceive them as problematic. Employees or managers from the host country have to be exposed to the practices before they can point out which ones may clash with deeply held assumptions in the host country and create conflict.

Disadvantage of foreignness. Many EMNCs suffer from the disadvantage of foreignness – when their country of origin is disliked in the host country – especially in advanced economies. This idea, that the country of origin can create problems for a firm, has been widely studied in international marketing. It is generally concluded that foreign products are disliked either because consumers are nationalistic and prefer domestic to foreign products[11] or because consumers feel animosity toward products coming from particular countries for historical reasons and so are unlikely to buy them.[12]

Here we take a much broader view of how the country of origin can create problems and analyze not just how it harms the marketing of products but also how it constrains the investments the firm makes in the host country. Additionally, we go beyond the usual focus on consumers as the individuals judging the country of origin and consider how governments may also have negative perceptions of the country of origin and so create a disadvantage to EMNCs.

Government-based disadvantage of foreignness. A firm encounters a government-based disadvantage of foreignness when the host-country government imposes additional constraints on the firm because it dislikes the firm's origin. For example, in 2006, the US Congress prevented the Emirati port management firm Dubai Port World (DP World) from managing six ports in the United States because US politicians disliked the fact that DP World was headquartered in the United Arab Emirates (UAE).[13] DP World was an offshoot of Dubai Port Authority and specialized in the management of ports internationally. As part of its global expansion, it purchased terminals in Djibouti, India, Saudi Arabia, and Romania, and in 2005 it purchased the international port operations of the US firm CSX World, becoming the seventh largest port operator in the world with operations in Australia, China, Djibouti, Dominican Republic, Germany, India, Romania, Saudi Arabia, United Arab Emirates, South Korea, and Venezuela. In October 2005, DP World expressed interest in acquiring the British firm Peninsular and Oriental Steam Navigation Company (P&O), which was the fourth biggest global player. After a bidding battle with the Singaporean operator PSA, in February 2006, P&O shareholders approved the US$6.8 billion acquisition, and in March 2006, DP World was granted regulatory permission by the British High Court. With this acquisition, DP World became the third largest port operator in the world. Drewy Shipping Consultant's container port analyst Neil Davidson commented that the acquisition resulted in three large operators of similar size (DP World, Singapore's PSA, and Denmark's APM Terminals) after the market leader Hong Kong's Hutchison Ports. He indicated that "overnight, the deal turns DP World into a global operator. [...] It will have a greater geographical scope than any global container terminal operator, including Hutchison, in terms of the number of countries where it will operate."[14]

With the acquisition, DP World also became a port operator on the US East Coast, after receiving approval on January 17 from CFIUS, which DP World had approached in October 2005. However, members of the US Congress and Senate became concerned about the security implications of having an Arab company manage US ports and mounted a campaign to derail the operation. Even though the acquisition of P&O had been widely discussed in the international press and had received approval from CFIUS and that DP world was a well-known and respected company, politicians could not accept that an Arab state-owned firm would be operating US ports. In February, Democratic Senator from New York Charles E. Schumer held a press conference asking for a review of the acquisition, Democratic Senator from New York Hillary Clinton indicated that she would introduce legislation to stop the operation on national security grounds, and Senate Majority Leader Bill First indicated that he would propose legislation to place the deal "on hold" pending an additional review. A US port operator, Eller & Company, which had two joint ventures with P&O, hired a lobbyist to block the deal. Criticisms by politicians were mostly directed at limitations in the effectiveness and capacity of US ports rather than at the ability of DP World or its relationship with Dubai's government. Conservative commentators escalated the rhetoric, accusing Dubai and the UAE of having supported the 9/11 terrorist attacks and helping Iran's nuclear ambitions.

The US administration of President Bush defended the acquisition. Michael Chertoff, Department of Homeland Security secretary, indicated that the deal had been properly investigated and said that "you can be assured that before a deal is approved we put safeguards in place, assurances in place, that make everybody comfortable that we are where we need to be from a national security viewpoint."[15] There were limited concerns about the operation given that DP World was run with little interference from the government and was an efficient and respected operator and that no foreign nationals would have access to the containers when they arrived at US ports because the workers managing containers were US citizens.

On February 23, DP World offered to delay control of the US ports while waiting additional investigation. Despite this, on March 8, the House of Representatives Appropriations Committee voted 62–2 to stop the deal. With this, on March 9, the UAE government told DP World to look for a US buyer of the US port operations, which were sold for US$750 million to the asset management firm AIG Global Investment Group, even though it had little experience managing ports.

Mohammed Sharaf, DP World chief executive, reflected on the imbroglio, indicating that "since Dubai has been a close friend of the United States for three decades, and a staunch ally in the fight against terrorism, and since we at DP World have been serving the US Navy directly since 1990, the misunderstanding came as a real shock,"[16] adding that since the deal happened during a US election year, the timing may have been unfortunate.

The government-based disadvantage of foreignness may arise from multiple causes. In some cases, it arises from concerns about national security, as the case of DP World illustrates. In others, it arises because politicians perceive foreign firms as a threat to national sovereignty, as the ability of multinationals to move production around countries limits the ability of the government to control them.[17] In yet others, it arises because the government has an ideology of economic nationalism and wants to exercise control over economic affairs.[18]

The host-country government may try to impose on foreign firms controls to which domestic firms are not subject, increasing the cost of operating in the host country for the former. In extreme cases, the host-country government may exclude foreign firms from investing in industries it considers strategic for the national security of the country, for example, defense, airlines, or media. In other cases, it may prevent foreign firms from investing in particular industries because lobbying groups campaign against foreign competition. However, in most cases, foreign firms are allowed to invest in the country, but their investments are subject to close scrutiny. Foreign firms may also face other forms of discrimination, such as a limit on the level of investment or the number of expatriates employed or requiring firms to establish joint ventures with local companies.[19]

A foreign firm can identify the government-based disadvantage of foreignness by analyzing whether there are particular constraints, regulations, or legislation against foreign firms. This is relatively simple with the help of local lawyers. However, identifying how such laws and regulations may be applied or whether the government might create new regulations that would discriminate against the firm is more difficult. It is even more challenging to gauge whether the government will discriminate against firms from particular countries, since such regulations are rarely in place. More frequently, politicians may block investments or increase the burden on firms from particular countries, as the case of DP World illustrates. One way to assess the likelihood of this is to observe how other firms from the same home country have previously been treated by the government of the host country.

Customer-based disadvantage of foreignness. EMNCs may also suffer from a customer-based disadvantage of foreignness in which consumers discriminate against foreign firms in general or against firms from particular foreign countries. For example, the Indian firm Titan Watches discovered that it had a country-of-origin image problem in Europe that led to large losses and eventual withdrawal of the firm from the European market.[20] Titan Watches was created in 1987 by the Tata Group, one of India's largest conglomerates. At the time, the market was dominated by the state-owned HMT, and there were high barriers to the importation of foreign watches. By 1993, Titan Watches had 60 percent of the Indian market for quartz movement watches, helped in part by a joint venture with the US firm Timex. As part of the opening of the Indian economy in 1991, the government had scheduled lifting the ban on importing complete watches in 1997. In preparation for this, in the early 1990s, Titan decided to go global. As Titan's managing director Xerxes Desai indicated in 1997, "India is being globalized and the whole world is now turning up in India. So the kind of protection we've enjoyed will go. It's going to get very crowded."[21] At the time, Titan considered becoming a contract manufacturer, but as Bijou Kurien, chief operating officer of watches at Titan Watches, noted, "We strongly felt there was no glory in being a contract manufacturer. You constantly get driven down in terms of price." Instead, Titan focused on building a global brand: "Building your brand abroad and creating value provide the highest return on investment in the long run,"[22] Bijou Kurien stated.

Titan initially concentrated on countries that had a large Indian population. In 1992, it started its globalization in the Middle East, where there was a large nonresident Indian population that already knew the brand. It reached these customers via domestic advertisements in Indian newspapers and television channels that were available in the region. Hence, the firm first entered the UAE, Egypt, Kuwait, Oman, and Saudi Arabia; then focused on nearby countries like Bangladesh, Maldives, Nepal, and Sri Lanka; and eventually extended to countries in the Asia-Pacific region, like Australia, Fiji, Indonesia, Malaysia, Philippines, Thailand, Singapore, and Vietnam.

However, in 1993 it decided to focus on Europe, with the idea that if it could succeed there, it could succeed elsewhere. "If we could crack this market, it would have been an achievement that would have given us the satisfaction that we are as good as the rest of the world,"[23] noted Kurien. As Desai saw it, "We've got to take the bull by the horns at some stage and so we may as well do it from day one. [...] The watches which we retail at the moment are generally in the

US$50 to US$200 range, but we're moving into the US$50 to US$500 range. We see ourselves competing with Longines, Tissot and the upper end of Seiko."[24]

However, the image of India did not support the sale of upscale watches because in the 1990s European consumers perceived Indian products as low quality. The "Made in India" label was a liability, so Titan decided to disguise its origin. As Desai put it, "India's reputation is a bit of a problem, so we're playing it down."[25] In Titan's US$20 million European advertising campaign, created by the British firm Lowe Howard Spink & Associates, in which it aimed to induce European consumers to buy India-made watches priced between US$120 and US$700, it used multicultural female models and the slogan, "No one country could have made faces this beautiful," with the legend "French-Swiss-Indian-Japanese"[26] by the photographs of the watches. The aim was to reduce the association with India and highlight the technological and design collaborations it had used in its product development (French design, Swiss steel, Japanese batteries). The watches were made specifically for Europe with European designers and a separate "Euro" assembly line. The use of skilled and inexpensive Indian labor reduced production costs; for example, the cost of an India-made slim watch movement was one-tenth the cost of a Swiss-made one, as M. S. Shantharam, vice-president of manufacturing, indicated. However, the challenge was not the production of inexpensive watches: it was selling upscale watches to European consumers and after that to US consumers. "The higher the eventual price of the product, the more the marketing muscle needed to sell it at that price,"[27] Shantharam noted. The advertising campaign represented a large investment for the firm, which had spent less than US$9 million on promotion in India. It helped convince consumers to buy the watches and jewelers to stock them. By 1997, Titan had sold 150,000 watches in Europe, amounting to 2 percent of the market, and had exported 600,000 watches, mostly to the Gulf states, making it the sixth largest watch maker in the world, mostly thanks to its dominance of the Indian market. Vikram Rajaram,

Titan's vice-president, noted the reaction of Swiss competitors: "They're afraid of India. We have the technical skills, we can provide the quality, we have a large domestic market, capital, and people who can run complex businesses. Their opposition might stunt our growth, but it will not break our back."[28] Titan was excluded from the Basel Watch Fair for three years in a row. The organizers argued that they excluded firms from countries with high barriers to imports, but A. L. Mudaliar, Titan's chairman, protested that "[t]he [Basel watch] fair authorities are a cartel of Swiss watch makers who are against competition from countries like India where labour is cheap, production costs low, and quality on a par with international standards."[29]

However, by 2002, Titan was unable to sell profitably in Europe, despite its marketing effort. The cumulative losses between 1995 and 2002 were £9 million, and by 2002, its sales were £2.5 million, well below the 1999 sales of £4.5 million. It decided to exit most markets, concentrate on those in which it was relatively well established (Britain, Spain, Greece, and Portugal), reduce costs by moving warehousing from the United Kingdom to Spain, downgrade the European office to a sales office, and coordinate from India.

Reflecting on the setback, Bhaskar Bhat, Titan's managing director, noted, "There is an opportunity for Indian brands. The environment today is better than when we started out. Earlier, the image of India was hampering us. A large part of our losses can, in fact, be attributed to it."[30] In 2006, Titan exited the European market except for a small distribution operation, provisioning the accumulated losses and concentrating in Asia and Africa.

The consumer-based disadvantage of foreignness may arise from consumers' nationalistic sentiments, which lead them to discriminate against all foreign firms, or from animosity toward particular countries, which leads them to discriminate against firms originating there, as was the case of Titan Watches. However, consumers do not necessarily know the firm's true country of origin and respond to the perceived country of origin. Thus, unlike the case of a government-based disadvantage of foreignness in which government officials have the power to know the country of origin of the foreign firm, in the case of a consumer-based disadvantage of foreignness, the EMNC can manage the perception of the country of origin to reduce its negative effect.

Before entering the foreign country, the manager of the EMNC can assess the consumer-based disadvantage of foreignness by running surveys of consumers and their views on products from the home country, assessing whether they dislike the country of origin in general or whether they just dislike the country of origin of particular products, for example, discriminating against high tech but not artisanal crafts coming from emerging markets.

5.4 SOLUTIONS: AVOIDING AND SOLVING DISADVANTAGES ABROAD

To address this disadvantage, the company can focus on actions that avoid it. Table 5.1 summarizes some of the actions that managers can take to prevent the creation of the disadvantages of transfer, government-based disadvantage of foreignness, and consumer-based disadvantage of foreignness.

First, to avoid the creation of disadvantage generated by the transfer of resources to the host country, managers can analyze how each specific management practice fits with local customs or cultural practices. This is relatively straightforward and can be done by asking key local employees for their views of the company's practices. Managers can then assess whether these practices clash with local customs and decide (1) whether they need to educate and train employees in the new practices if they are key to how the company operates, explaining in detail the logic for the practices and how they are crucial for the success of the firm even if they appear to be going against local customs, (2) whether they need to modify or adapt specific practices to fit existing customs and cultural norms if they are not key to how the company operates, or (3) whether to drop specific practices if they risk creating large problems for the operation and the practices are not providing the expected benefits they generate at home.

Table 5.1 *Solutions for addressing establishment challenges*

Issues	Actions
Avoiding transferring disadvantages	Identify how the transferred management practices fit with local customs/cultures, whether they create a problem, and how important this problem is Identify how this problem can be avoided, whether by educating employees, adapting practices, or disusing them
Reducing government-based disadvantages of foreignness	Identify what the regulations against foreign investors are Identify how the political ideology of the government in the host country affects foreign investors or investors from the particular home country Identify how the firm can avoid negative perceptions, whether by educating government officials, using a local partner, or disguising the country of origin
Reducing consumer-based disadvantage of foreignness	Identify the perceptions that citizens in the host country have of foreign firm or firms from the particular home country Identify how can the firm avoid negative perceptions, whether by educating consumers, using a local partner, or disguising the country of origin

Second, to reduce government-based disadvantage of foreignness, the manager can use the help of local lawyers to find out whether there are specific regulations against foreign investors. The manager can then redesign actions to comply with the regulations or work with lobbyists to try to change them. If the opposition the company faces derives from political ideology rather than written regulations, the manager needs to assess whether this negativity is directed against foreign investors in general or investors from the home country in particular. In the first case, the problem is one of economic nationalism, and the company can imitate the strategies used by other foreign companies. It can try to educate politicians about the benefits of having foreign investors in the country; it can lobby the government indirectly by establishing links with a powerful local partner who might influence the government; or it can establish links with the community in which it hopes to invest in order to recruit advocates who will pressure the government. Alternatively, it can hide or change the country of origin by investing from a third country that does not attract such political negativity. For example, it can use offshore financial centers to hide the firm's origin or move the legal registration of the firm to an advanced economy and invest from there.

Third, to solve the consumer-based disadvantage of foreignness, the manager can make an initial assessment of citizens' perceptions of foreign countries to get a sense of the level of nationalism among consumers in the host country. This will help identify their perceptions of products and companies coming from the particular country of origin and foreign countries generally. If the perception is not too negative, the company can educate consumers through advertising campaigns that highlight the quality of the company independently of its country of origin. If consumers have doubts about the products because of the country of origin, the company can establish an alliance with a local partner or purchase a local brand so that the negative image of the country of origin is compensated for by a positive brand image. If consumers will not buy products because they come from a particular country of origin, the company may have to hide the country of origin. This can be done in a variety of ways, for example, by advertising where the product is designed as well as where it is made, by using components from multiple countries that will compensate for the negative image of one particular country, or by modifying the name used to indicate the country of origin (using PRC instead of China or Persia instead of Iran).

5.5 CLOSING CASE: HAVAIANAS – TURNING DISADVANTAGES INTO ADVANTAGES

The Brazilian shoemaker Havaianas provides an example of how managers overcame disadvantages in perceptions of the consumer segment and country of origin. It repositioned inexpensive flip-flops or thongs made in an emerging country as upscale designer shoes and became a successful global brand, even though most apparel global brands were based in Japan, the United States, or Western Europe.[31] The Brazil-based Alpargatas started operations in 1907 as the Brazilian subsidiary of the Argentina shoe maker Alpargatas. It became a Brazilian firm in the 1980s after it was purchased by the one of Brazil's largest conglomerates, the Camargo Correa Group.

In 1958, Alpargatas started manufacturing rubber-made flip-flops. The flip-flops were named Hawaiians, or Havaianas in Portuguese, and trademarked in 1962. The design was derived from the *zori* sandals that Japanese immigrants used. The shoes were very basic, with a white top half of the sole and a bottom half of the sole and straps in five colors (black, blue, brown, pink, and yellow). A proprietary formula of man-made and natural rubber, unlike the competitors' PVC, made the sole soft and durable. They were modestly priced and eventually included in the consumer price index as they were widely used by working classes, becoming known as the "shoes of the poor." As competitors imitated their design, the company came out with an advertisement campaign that highlighted its quality and affordability and promoted them as the genuine Havaianas (*Havaianas legitimas*).

The company repositioned the shoes from lower to upper classes with clever design and advertisement, in part to address a drop in sales. By the 1980s, sales slid, in part affected by the Brazilian economic crisis, dropping from 85 million pairs in 1988 to 66 million in 1992. In the early 1990s, surfers started modifying the shoes by flipping the sole so that straps and the top half of the shoe matched. This inspired the company to launch a new line of shoes called Havaianas Top with matching straps and soles in 13 colors. As manager Carla Schmitzberger noted, "So in 1994 they launched a fully monochromed product. [. . .] By observing consumer behaviour, then selling it back to the consumer, we made the thong more than just a commodity, and it became much more aspirational."[32] The company supported the new design with a premium pricing and advertisement campaign that showed celebrities and upper-class consumers using the shoes. For example, one of the ads targeted stories of people being denied entry into restaurants wearing the flip-flops, with the actor Rodrigo Santoro being turned away and women in the restaurant complaining that "those are not sandals, those are Havaianas" and "if he is leaving, I am also leaving." Schmitzberger noted, "After that campaign, it started to become more acceptable to wear thongs in restaurants."

With the successful repositioning of the brand in Brazil, the company sought to expand abroad. Even though Brazil was a developing country, the company highlighted the positive aspects of the country in its advertisements, building on the positive association with Hawaii in its brand name and being aided by the free publicity gained by their use by celebrities and movie stars. As Carla Schmitzberger, director at Alpargatas, explained, "The first international sales of Havaianas were the result of young Brazilian entrepreneurs wanting to sell the sandal overseas as a business. Hawaii and Australia became the company's first overseas distributors. As more countries heard of the brand's success, more international distributors were signed on. In 2002 the company decided to put more focus on this new opportunity and hired a director specifically dedicated to international sales. The strategy was to position the brand as an aspirational product and involved advertising, proactive product seeding among opinion leaders and celebrities."[33]

The focus on design and building on Brazil's positive attributes was used in the expansion abroad. In 1998, Alpargatas designed flip-flops with the colors of Brazil's national flag and the national flag on the strap as part of the 1998 FIFA World Cup in France. This became a huge sales success in Brazil and abroad. In Australia, a Brazilian entrepreneur, Amelia Maribondo-Aspden, introduced Havainas to the market. Amelia had moved to Australia, and in 1997 she started importing the shoes, initially giving them away at supermarkets and later on selling them. By the early 2000s, the shoes became an accepted fashion item as supermodels like Gisele Bündchen, Naomi Campbell, and Kate Moss wore them by choice. As Amelia explained, "I can say to you without any doubt, I triggered it. Not just me, though, but me and [she names several former executives with Havaianas' Brazilian parent company, Alpargatas SA]. They saw what was happening in Australia with us and our retailers, and they said, 'This is fashionable. This is something we ought to be doing all over the place!'"[34] In a similar way, in 2001, a French-Brazilian entrepreneur became the distributor of Havaianas in France. She used her contacts with leading designers such as John Galliano, Jean-Paul Gaultier, and Lacoste to reposition the shoes upmarket, from fashion to luxury, with exclusive designs and limited editions that sold for over US$200.

Part of the appeal of the shoes was the clever use of the made-in-Brazil branding. In its advertisements, Havainas emphasized the sensuality, vibrancy, and humor of Brazilian culture. Although it made operational sense to move production to other countries, such as China, this idea was quickly dismissed, and production remained in Brazil. A marketing executive in São Paulo emphasized that "consumers love the 'Made in Brazil' factor!" while Brazilian-born fashion consultant Abraao Ferreira indicated "they're cool, colorful, laid-back and chic. They're the quintessence of everything that people find appealing about Brazil."[35]

5.6 CONCLUSIONS

EMNCs can face disadvantages in a host country that will detract from the profitability generated by their sources of advantage. Some of these disadvantages are created by the firm when it imports practices that are incompatible with conditions in the host country. However, and especially in the case of most EMNCs, the country of origin of these firms can become a major source of disadvantage abroad, as governments and consumers discriminate against firms and products from emerging markets.

In some cases, managers are able to turn around the perceptions of consumers and reposition the products and their country of origin in a positive light, as the case of Havaianas illustrates. Havaianas used clever marketing to change two disadvantages it faced: the perception that its products were purchased only by the poor (middle- and upper-class customers would not wear them outside the home) and the association of the products with an emerging country, which meant that consumers in advanced economies would not pay a premium for them. By incorporating ideas from consumers, rethinking the product and its positioning, incorporating design into what was in essence a commodity, and highlighting the positive aspects of Brazil, it was able to move the brand and products into upmarket segments.

Notes

1. Information comes from Fu (2005), Guerrera (2005), Guerrera and Leahy (2005), Guerrera, McNulty, and Kirchgaessner (2005), Kirchgaessner (2005), Kirchgaessner, Alden, and Balls (2005), Leahy, Guerrera, and Politi (2005), and Powell (2005).
2. Guerrera, McNulty, and Kirchgaessner (2005).
3. Kirchgaessner, Alden, and Balls (2005).
4. Kirchgaessner, Alden, and Balls (2005).
5. Guerrera, McNulty, and Kirchgaessner (2005).
6. Fu (2005).
7. Guerrera (2005).
8. Kirchgaessner (2005).
9. Created using information from Iritani (2005), Haier (2014a), NewsWeek (2005), and Prasso (2010).
10. See Schein (2010) for a discussion of corporate culture and how routines and practices are embedded in them.
11. See Shankarmahesh (2006) for a review of consumer nationalism.

12. See Riefler and Diamantopoulos (2007) for a review of consumer animosity.
13. Created using information from Beisecker (2006), King and Hitt (2006), Kirchgaessner (2006), Kirchgaessner and Yuk (2006), Paleit (2006), and Wright (2006a, 2006b).
14. Wright (2006a).
15. Kirchgaessner (2006).
16. Wright (2006b).
17. See Vernon (1977) and Stopford and Strange (1992) for a discussion of the relationships between multinational firms and governments.
18. See Bruton (1998) for a review of import substitution and government control over the economy.
19. See Golub (2003) for a review of the constraints that governments may impose on foreign firms.
20. Created using information from Barone (1996), Nicholson (1997), Rai (2002), Ramswamy (2004), Reuters (1993), Sabharwal (2007), and Sidhva (1997a, 1997b).
21. Nicholson (1997).
22. Ramswamy (2004).
23. Ramswamy (2004).
24. Reuters News (1993).
25. Nicholson (1997).
26. Nicholson (1997).
27. Nicholson (1997).
28. Nicholson (1997).
29. Sidhva (1997).
30. Rai (2002).
31. Information on this case comes from Barchfield (2012), Konishi and Turpin (2009), Robson (2012), and Turpin (2013).
32. Robson (2012).
33. Konishi and Turpin (2009).
34. Robson (2012).
35. Barchfield (2012).

6 Operation

6.1 INTRODUCTION

In the previous chapters we analyzed the challenges that accompany the decisions of EMNCs to establish operations in foreign countries. We now turn our attention to the operational difficulties that occur once an overseas subsidiary has been established. Whereas much attention has been devoted to the initial challenges of expanding abroad, it is less common to give adequate consideration to postinvestment operational issues, which can lead to unexpected problems and ultimately contribute to poor subsidiary performance. This lapse of attention may occur because managers are overfocused on completing a deal quickly and secretly, particularly in the case of cross-border acquisitions. In the case of joint ventures and other strategic alliances, difficulties can also arise in working with partners that seemed like good fits on the basis of their competencies but have incompatible organizational cultures. The lack of experience in operating in different types of environments, which is often the case for managers of EMNCs, undoubtedly contributes to these difficulties as well.

The liability of foreignness, which we discussed in detail in Chapter 4, can create difficulties for firms across multiple aspects of their operations. For EMNCs, these difficulties can be exacerbated due to characteristics associated with their home countries and their collective stage of development within their home markets. Broadly speaking, these difficulties involve identifying the relationship between the EMNC and its customers in the local environment, identifying the advantage of the local operation in comparison to competitors, strengthening sources of competitive advantage, protecting them from mutation and substitution, and identifying new sources of competitive advantage. These issues also involve identifying and meeting institutional and social expectations in the host country.

While these general operational difficulties involve a wide range of activities, based on our examination of actual issues faced by EMNCs, the most common difficulties fall into two main categories: limitations in experience in managing overseas operations and reputational issues. While these difficulties could apply to some degree to any newly internationalizing company, EMNCs are particularly vulnerable due to their lower levels of international experience and sophisticated home-country capabilities when expanding abroad. For example, despite their abundant labor supply, many emerging multinationals find their international growth is limited by the lack of qualified people with the necessary cross-cultural and overseas management skills. These issues, which we analyze in this chapter, are illustrated by the Chinese telecom firm Huawei's foreign expansion.

6.2 OPENING CASE: HUAWEI TECHNOLOGIES

The Chinese telecommunications company Huawei Technologies Company was created in 1987 and by 2012 had become the largest telecommunications equipment maker in the world. The company is a major success story among EMNCs. However, this level of global success has not shielded it from operational difficulties as it has expanded its operations to both developed countries, such as Germany, France, Spain, and the United Kingdom, and emerging countries, including Russia, Brazil, Saudi Arabia, and South Africa, among others. Having developed in the emerging market context of China, the company may have been unprepared for many of the expectations of firms in developed markets or even emerging markets with different types of government. The difficulties Huawei faced in its international operations due to lack of experience, disclosure issues, and reputation are indicative of the multiple operational issues EMNCs face when they invest abroad.

One area of particular difficulty for Huawei has been the issue of intellectual property (IP) concerns and the company's disclosure practices. In 2011, the US government initiated an investigation into Huawei, accusing it of a lack of transparency and disregarding US law related to others' IP rights. In 2012, the US House of Representatives' Permanent Select Committee on Intelligence threatened to forbid Huawei from doing business in the United States.[1] However, Huawei's problems extended beyond the United States and IP issues. As the *Economist* noted, "Westerners fret that the networks the firm is building are used by Chinese spooks to eavesdrop during peace-time and could be shut down suddenly during wartime. They see the firm as a potent weapon in China's burgeoning cyber-arsenal."[2] CFIUS had already prevented Huawei's acquisition of the US tele-com firm 3COM for national security reasons in 2008. Similarly, in 2010, Huawei's bid for the network upgrade of the US telecom carrier Sprint Nextel was stopped by eight Republican senators, and in 2011 the US Department of Commerce blocked Huawei's participation in a national emergency network project tender.[3] Huawei's difficulties are certainly complex, but a contributing factor is that the "company's opaque ownership structure and secretive culture have damaged its reputation."[4] In the United States, the company struggled to establish itself as a legitimate player among the various stakeholder groups with which it interacts.

However, the United States was not the only foreign location where Huawei had experienced operational difficulties associated with political issues. When Huawei invested in India in mid 2000s, the Indian government judged that the company's investment behavior did not match the Indian government's investment policy and constituted a threat to national security.[5] In 2009, India telecom operator Bharat Sanchar Nigam Limited (BSNL) canceled purchase orders for Huawei's equipment, totaling nearly US$2 billion, in response to an Indian government announcement restricting the use of telecommunications equipment from foreign manufacturers, "especially Chinese production facilities."[6] This suggests that

Huawei is fighting not only perceptions of the company but also broader negative perceptions of China itself.

Similar issues occurred in other countries. In 2010, a survey of European Union (EU) members accused Huawei of accepting Chinese government subsidies. In 2012, the Australian government, citing national security reasons, did not allow Huawei to participate in a US$38 billion bid for broadband network infrastructure projects.[7] Facing growing trade and nontrade barriers in advanced economies, Huawei eventually hired former EU Ambassador to China Serge Abou as its telecommunications business consultant[8] and began providing "safe delivery," including its equipment and software security checks, to its customers.[9]

Under pressure, Huawei also pledged to disclose more detailed financial information to shareholders in early 2013, in the hope of clearing obstructions to its global expansion.[10] These difficulties have resulted in Huawei changing its North American focus away from the US market to the smaller but more China-friendly Canadian market.[11] As far as information disclosure is concerned, different expectations in China and Huawei's experience with its initial investments in other emerging countries may have encouraged the company to report on the basis of its home-country expectations rather than those of the host market. Moreover, the security it enjoyed from its strong government ties in China may have contributed to the company's difficulties by making it overconfident in its ability to withstand government and other stakeholder criticisms in other countries.

6.3 LIMITATIONS IN MANAGERIAL EXPERIENCE

Human capital is central to the effective operations of companies. Training employees effectively and retaining developed talent are recognized as crucial to firm success. However, emerging markets lag significantly behind their developed market counterparts in their ability to produce talent, and their "lack of global experience, managerial competence, and professional expertise" is an important challenge for EMNCs.[12] According to the 2014 ManpowerGroup survey of 37,000 employers in 42 countries and territories, talent shortage is a particularly pervasive problem in India, Turkey, and throughout Latin America. As the growth in demand for such talent from EMNCs has consistently outstripped their ability to produce it, firms increasingly face situations where acquiring quality human resources is difficult and costly and where trained talent is often recruited away by competing domestic and foreign firms. Given the relatively limited legal protections offered by noncompete clauses in many of these markets, this can mean that in frequent cases firms actually develop talent for their competitors.

There are four prevailing talent and labor issues for EMNCs: limited home-country talent, inexperienced home-country talent, challenges in using expatriate versus home-country workers, and difficulties with labor unions. We review these now.

Limited home-country talent. A basic issue when considering talent issues in emerging markets is the limited nature of local talent, which may even have received suspect training under earlier government structures. For example, in Russia, the issue is "not so much war for talent as wariness of talent."[13] Much of this wariness results from different expectations and associated training dating from the era of the Soviet Union that have continued into the post-Soviet period. While the Russian case may be an extreme one, it is not unique, and issues around the limited amount of local talent, particularly for managerial positions, are prevalent throughout emerging markets. The lack of local talent in the home market leaves EMNCs at a disadvantage from the start when they invest overseas.

Within Latin America, uneven participation in higher education has created large skill differentials and great variance in job expectations among potential Latin American employees. These differences are further accentuated by a relatively small pool of university graduates and a shortage of skilled workers.

Fortunately, the situation seems to be improving in China relative to other emerging markets, according to the 2014 ManpowerGroup survey, although issues still remain. Yin Tongyao, chief executive officer (CEO) of auto manufacturer Chery International, acknowledged the limitations in talent management: "Talent is a huge bottleneck. On the one hand, we attract domestic and foreign experts and overseas returnees; on the other hand, we groom young professionals. Despite our initial concerns, many of these young people turn out to be fast learners. Given the right opportunities, they can quickly blossom into managerial professionals."[14]

For many firms in China, the problem is also one of succession planning. Most Chinese private enterprises were founded in an unprecedented fast-changing business environment during the past 30 years. Chinese entrepreneurs are not sure if their younger, Western-educated successors have the ability and experience needed to survive in this unique Chinese environment. Moreover, there is a wide cultural gap between generations, reducing trust and cohesion. According to Li Rucheng, founder and CEO of Chinese clothing manufacturer Youngor, "Though I share only 8.5% of the holdings of my company, I still have to choose the next generation carefully to ensure that he or she is able to inherit the Youngor spirit."[15] A recent survey reports that in China "about 70% of the second generation businessmen failed to expand the family enterprise."[16]

Inexperienced employees. Experience generally refers to the act of participating in an activity and the learning that occurs as a result. As such, experience helps companies perform better. It is important because it allows a firm to benefit from its past actions when it pursues future activities. Firms gain expertise and competence by accumulating experience that is incorporated into organizational routines, which have been referred to by various scholars as patterns of action, activity, behavior, and interaction. Given that they represent embedded learning, these organizational routines can become a source of competitive advantage and play a critical role in how organizations make decisions.

Not surprisingly, the limited talent that firms in many emerging markets do possess is generally inexperienced in managing overseas operations. Employment issues are especially problematic for companies pursuing fast global expansion. EMNCs have realized the criticality of international business talent to their overseas success. However, despite the abundant labor supply in many emerging economies, many of them encounter a lack of qualified personnel. Anton Telegin, commercial director for the Commonwealth of Independent States (CIS) countries at VympelCom, a leading Russian telecom group, described human resources as the key organizational issue in expanding abroad.[17] VympelCom has implemented a strategy that gradually replaces Russian expatriates with local talent in management positions, even though local staff often view working in a foreign firm as an opportunity to leave their country.[18] Similarly, when TCL Corporation (TCL) entered US and European markets with large acquisitions, only an estimated 3 to 5 percent of its employees had the requisite international business experience. In response, the company reduced the training period for expatriate managers from three years to one in order to obtain enough personnel.[19]

Another example is provided by Sinochem, one of the four biggest state-owned oil companies in China. While the basic quality of the Sinochem overseas team was good, with rich business experience in general, it lacked people with marketing experience who could handle loss risk – given that its sales in China were virtually guaranteed. When Sinochem explored the South American market, the Chinese employees who were sent to South America took the company's first overseas technical and health, safety, and environment (HSE) roles, pioneering the company's practices.[20]

Many emerging market companies do not have cross-cultural experience, which has hampered their ability to transfer practices abroad. The degree to which management practices and other aspects of firm operations should be uniformly transferred across locations or adapted to local expectations is a fundamental decision for multinationals, with most firms choosing a balance between the two. However, achieving this balance is difficult without significant cross-cultural experience. The shortage of managers with international experience and expertise in global marketing at TCL constitutes a major constraint. Following the company's merger with Thomson Electric, the new company failed to work well with people from different cultures, with different experiences and different routines. Language issues and disagreements about compensation prolonged the period of time it took the new company to develop a common production strategy. In 2007, Beijing-based McKinsey General Manager Wu Hai became the new president of TCL Group subsidiary TCL-Thomson Electronic (TTE). TCL also invited Liang Yaorong, who had abundant international management experience in the electronics industry, to inject new energy into business operation and management. He improved operational efficiency by reorganizing the structure, building key processes, and integrating different kinds of resources.[21]

A common challenge facing MNCs is ideological differences between local managers and home-country managers. For instance, Chinese traditional philosophy emphasizes dedication, which sometimes requires the sacrifice of personal interests in order to protect the collective interest. Consequently, it is quite usual for Chinese employees to give up their personal leisure time and work overtime, which greatly improves the efficiency of Chinese companies. However, in other countries, particularly developed countries from the West, working overtime is much less acceptable. The HQ of Chinese MNCs are often puzzled by the low efficiency of their foreign employees.

Moreover, experience can be misapplied; generalizations of past experience to dissimilar situations do not necessarily lead to positive outcomes. While the benefits of experience are well established, past knowledge can be problematic when applied to situations that have changed or differ. A change in environment or situation can potentially reduce the relevance or value of accumulated experience and, at the extreme, lead to erroneous decisions and actions. For example, acquisitions and joint ventures are two commonly used modes of entry when EMNCs invest in foreign countries. However, the skill sets needed to manage an acquisition differ in sometimes subtle ways from those needed to manage a joint venture. Since firms often gain experience managing both investment types, which is then incorporated into the firm's organizational routines, international managers, who are often responsible for both investment types, may end up applying the same management techniques to both. This could be a contributing factor to the less than optimal operational performance often associated with both acquisitions and joint ventures.

EMNCs typically gain initial international experience by operating in other emerging countries that are similar to their home markets. Emerging markets commonly share the characteristics of "institutional voids," that is, where pro-market institutions and intermediaries that are expected or taken for granted in advanced economies are either missing or underdeveloped in emerging markets or not functioning optimally in them. Operating at home and in other emerging markets means that successful EMNCs gain experience in dealing with uncertain situations and political maneuvering and can apply this experience relatively easily to other emerging markets. For instance, practices created to circumvent an unclear environment based on using connections or favors, such as *guanxi* in China, *jeitinho* in Brazil, and *jugaad* in India, have developed in many emerging markets.[22] These relationship-based practices have facilitated EMNC investments into other emerging markets, such as Chinese investment into Africa and Latin America.

However, while relationship-based capabilities may be advantageous in emerging markets, this may not necessarily be the case in advanced economies. Almost by definition, advanced countries are much more stable and have highly developed, if varied, institutions, which means they supply a high degree of predictability and guidance to firms. Relationship-based practices will still be useful in developed country contexts, as networking is important everywhere, but are much less relevant to ensure successful business transactions. In fact, pursuing these practices can often have unwanted consequences due to the potential legal, political, and reputational ramifications associated with them.

Given this situation, significantly different capabilities are needed for EMNCs to operate in developed countries. However, EMNCs' past experiences in their home markets and other emerging countries may lead these firms to overestimate their abilities, based on successful routines developed from their earlier operations. This may cause these firms to make suboptimal operational decisions that lower their chances of successful performance. Overall, the lack of applicable experience may put these firms at a significant disadvantage when conducting operations in developed world contexts. Quantifying an exact monetary figure for operational losses from misapplied experience is difficult, but in the context of the telecom industry in Brazil, one study found that "firms with institutional experience unrelated to the target country's regulatory environment experience learning penalties and are six times more likely to fail."[23] This evidence suggests that applying inappropriate knowledge represents a huge risk for firms.

There are numerous examples of EMNCs suffering from a lack of experience in developed markets and the legal and other problems this causes them. Like Huawei, Lenovo, the Chinese computer technology firm, has suffered from legal difficulties, stemming partly from its inexperience in international markets. Founded in 1984 as the Beijing-based company Legend, Lenovo sprung into the international spotlight in 2004 when the company acquired International Business Machines' (IBM's) personal computer (PC) business, as we saw in Chapter 4. However, Lenovo's prominence has also made the company a target for multiple lawsuits. In 2014, in response to a class-action lawsuit alleging design defects, Lenovo agreed to refund US$100 or issue a US$250 voucher to an estimated 83,000 owners of its IdeaPad U310 and U410 laptops.[24] As a Chinese firm unaccustomed to facing such consequences, learning to deal with the complexities of the international legal system has been an important operational obstacle for the company.

Some EMNCs have also faced experience-related problems in other emerging markets. Illustrating this point, the Mexican baker Grupo Bimbo entered the Brazilian market wrongly assuming it resembled the Mexican market, given the similarity in development level, size, and location of both countries within the Latin American region. However, the cultural backgrounds of the countries differed greatly: the mass-produced and distributed packaged bread that was so popular in Mexico did not go down well with Brazilian consumers, who preferred artisanal fresh bread.[25] Bimbo learned the hard way that it could not rely on its product-based experience in Mexico when operating in Brazil despite the apparent similarities between the two countries.

Local versus expatriate hiring. A long-standing issue in the management of overseas subsidiaries is achieving the appropriate balance of local versus expatriate employees. The differing advantages of hiring home-country, host-country, and third-country nationals within foreign subsidiaries and the associated benefits and drawbacks of the global mind-set of management have been well established. However, the issues we have noted about limited and inexperienced home-country talent make it all the more crucial to achieve an appropriate balance between these employee types, particularly highly skilled technical labor and managerial talent. For example, many Chinese MNCs opened new production facilities in emerging countries, including Vietnam, Indonesia, and India. While enjoying the advantages of lower labor costs in these countries, the lack of local skilled employees was a big challenge for local production.

This problem can be further exacerbated by restrictions about the employment of expatriates. In order to guarantee the quality of local operations, Chinese MNCs often send expatriates to host countries to set up routines and processes. However, many host-country governments (such as the United States and India) only issue short-term (i.e., three-month) visas for Chinese expatriates. Once the visa expires, they have to leave the host country, which impedes knowledge transfer from Chinese professionals to local employees. Another example is the challenge of dealing with local employment laws and norms. Illustrating this issue, Gianfranco Lanci, former CEO of the Taiwanese PC maker Acer, allegedly breached a noncompete clause in his contract when he left Acer in 2011 and subsequently became a consultant for Lenovo Group.[26]

An additional illustration of the challenges of using expats and difficulties associated with trying to meet government regulations in doing so is the case of the Indian software company Infosys Tech Limited and alleged visa fraud with respect to company expatriates. The company's treatment of the "whistleblower" in a visa fraud case provoked negative reactions as Infosys allegedly violated US policies of nondiscrimination. Furthermore, the allegations triggered investigations by US Homeland Security into company practices in using B-1 visitor visas for work allegedly requiring H-1B work visas. Discrepancies were found in Infosys's short-term business visa paperwork for its Indian employees in the United States, which ultimately resulted in Infosys agreeing to a US$34 million settlement in 2013 with the US Justice Department. The company now faces a retaliation lawsuit from the same plaintiff in the original whistleblower suit.[27]

In some settings, the choice between hiring expatriates and locals can extend beyond the company setting and result in direct confrontation with local populations. Case in point, in 2012, Zijin Mining Group, the biggest gold mining company in China, came into conflict with local residents in Kyrgyzstan who banded together and demanded that Zijin hire more local workers. Zijin responded that the project was at an early stage and pointed out the difficulty in recruiting experienced workers locally. However, the company agreed to increase hiring of local workers in the future.[28]

Labor unions. Inexperience in dealing with labor unions is another employment-related issue common to EMNCs. Given the differences in the power and influence of labor unions across emerging countries, this issue can be particularly problematic when managing subsidiaries overseas. Chinese firms have faced significant difficulties with many of their investments in Africa, often stemming from the application of their home-country practices in the local market. At home, Chinese business practices have been described as a "rough-and-tumble, anything-goes business culture that cares little about rules and regulations." The practice of ignoring local sensitivities in their home market imprints on Chinese firms when they invest abroad, as can been seen in the cases of Chinese oil firms' explorations in a national park in Gabon and creating large oil spills in Sudan. Chinese firms have been accused by Zimbabwe's environment minister of "'operating like *makorokoza* miners,' a scornful term for illegal gold-panners." Further evidence of this systematic trend is found in the case of Chinese-run mines in Zambia's copper belt. In these operations, workers "must work for two years before they get safety helmets. Ventilation below ground is poor and deadly accidents occur almost daily. To avoid censure, Chinese managers bribe union bosses and take them on 'study tours' to massage parlors in China. Obstructionist shop stewards are sacked and workers who assemble in groups are violently dispersed. When cases end up in court, witnesses are intimidated."[29] Because of issues like these, Chinese firms have faced repeated problems with labor unions in several African countries and have been often accused of using union-bashing strategies, often with the support of host governments. "Trade unions see the practices of Chinese companies as a threat to the limited social protections that unions have achieved over the years, through collective bargaining."[30]

The Brazilian steel company Gerdau Ameristeel has experienced difficulties dealing with unions in its various investments in the United States. At one point in 2005, the company was forced to halt operations at its mill in Beaumont, Texas, in response to stalled negotiations with the United Steelworkers of America (USWA) labor union.[31] After the completion of negotiations with Gerdau in Canada, United Steelworkers International President Leo W. Gerard observed that in the United States, "[Gerdau has] hired lawyers who have no experience with steel industry contracts to do their negotiating. Their claim to fame is to fight unions and try to bust them."[32] In 2014, the company came under protest in St. Paul, Minnesota, for hiring an out-of-state nonunion contractor from Georgia for a local expansion project that had received "a package of incentives, grants and forgivable loans" from state and local taxpayers.[33]

6.4 LACK OF REPUTATION AND POOR QUALITY IMAGE

Firm reputation is generally based on the perceptions of a firm in the eyes of its stakeholders. As an intangible asset, reputation can be a source of competitive advantage for firms.[34] As such, managers spend significant energy and resources on building, maintaining, and protecting the reputations of their firms, both in their home markets and when they expand abroad.

Firms face inherent reputational issues when they invest overseas because of a lack of familiarity and legitimacy among host-country audiences. However, while developing reputation is a difficult and long-term process for all firms, EMNCs face an additional hurdle related to the reputations of their home countries. In general, emerging markets are perceived to produce lower-quality products and to have less-developed management systems than their counterparts in developed countries. Additionally, as late movers into global markets, EMNCs have reputational disadvantages. In most overseas markets, well-known MNCs from advanced countries have already established their presence and reputation, while local competitors enjoy familiarity with loyal local customers. Compared to these players, EMNCs are generally seen as inferior in terms of brand recognition and brand quality.

According to one influential review, there are three major reputation conceptualizations: being known, being known for something, and generalized favorability.[35] EMNCs suffer from a lack of "being known." They are generally less established in their host markets than local companies and, given the location of their HQ in emerging markets, are less likely to have received media attention before their arrival. Moreover, when EMNCs are "known for something," it is most likely to be for their home country. This is often linked to an overall country reputation for poor product quality and cheap goods. However, there are notable exceptions. Some specific industries from particular emerging markets have strong reputations, for example, Indian information technology (IT) provision and Brazilian beef. EMNCs also tend to suffer from a lack of "generalized favorability" due to a combination of limited knowledge of the company and a poor home-country reputation. We now go deeper into reputation issues associated with product/brand and country of origin.

Unknown brands. Many EMNCs face reputation issues specifically associated with the lack of awareness of their brands or the brands' association with low quality. This effect is not limited to Chinese firms. Aside from the IT sector, Indian brands commonly lack global appeal and quality. The automobile manufacturer Tata Motors has experienced difficulties with its passenger car products, which are often based on third- and fourth-generation platforms. Despite the global fanfare associated with the Nano as the "people's car," sales both in India and abroad have not been strong.[36] Moreover, being associated with low-end cars has put Tata Motors at a disadvantage when competing against car manufacturers from the United States, Japan, Europe, and most recently South Korea. Although it has achieved success with the Jaguar and Land Rover luxury brands it acquired,[37] the company still faces reputational hurdles.

Many large EMNCs are little known even if they are large and successful competitors. For example, despite being one of the world's largest confectionery providers, ranking seventh in global net sales in the candy industry in 2014,[38] Grupo Arcor of Argentina suffers from a lack of brand recognition.[39] Even in Latin America, where it has massive sales throughout the region, in 2013 it only appeared on two reputation rankings of firms in Latin America (first in Argentina and forty-second in Bolivia), among the eight Latin American countries studied by Merco, which monitors the reputations of firms in Spain and Latin America. By contrast, Swiss competitor Nestlé ranked sixteenth or higher in all eight countries.[40] During earlier stages of the company's development, it was noted that "the ARCOR brand was less well-known than its products."[41] While the company has more recently pursued "a specific institutional communication strategy [that] was carried out to position the main ARCOR brand as an effective umbrella for the rest of the individual brands,"[42] a lack of recognition of the company's core brand still remains a barrier to building a stronger reputation.

These reputational issues are often intertwined and self-reinforcing. In the airline industry, for instance, perceived quality issues are often coupled with a general lack of knowledge. Illustrating this point, Chinese airlines (such as China Eastern Airlines) are generally not well known outside of China, leading to a lower reputation. This may be combined with a general perception that Chinese airlines use older equipment that is less safe, leading customers to prefer other, more established companies even when the prices they charge are higher.

Country of origin. Country-of-origin effects refer to "the impact which generalizations and perceptions about a country have on a person's evaluations of the country's products and/or brands."[43] This impact affects two major areas: (1) how firm actions abroad are impacted by home-country characteristics and (2) how host-country stakeholders make judgments about firms based on the locations of their foreign HQ. We focus on this second category here.

While country-of-origin perceptions can often be positive (e.g., Swiss watches or Japanese cars) with EMNCs, they are more commonly negative, stemming from general perceptions about the quality of a country's products or issues like political instability, which can cast a negative shadow over a country and can make purchasing its products less desirable. The former often applies to manufactured goods, where quality issues can be more quickly judged, whereas the latter may involve a broader range of products and services, in particular, commodities such as oil and natural resources, where variation in quality is less of an issue.

The term "Made in China" is commonly associated with low-quality products and lower technology levels. Compounding this effect, at the beginning of Chinese economic reform, many exported goods from China were fakes that were captured by the media and hurt the image of Chinese products as a whole. This implies a biased attitude toward Chinese companies and their products, which have been the driving force of China's development as an emerging market. Evidence of this effect was seen in the case of Chinese automobile manufacturer Chery and its efforts to enter the Mexican market. Chery hired a local consulting firm to conduct pilot tests. When the marketing firm covered the Chery logo and brand plate on the cars, local respondents evaluated the car relatively well, with a corresponding high price offer; however, after the Chery logo and brand were disclosed, respondent evaluations and the associated car price dropped steeply.[44] Additionally, in spite of its size, the China National Cereals, Oils and Foodstuffs Corporation (COFCO), the largest agricultural and food products company in China, needed to contend with a general perception that food products from China were unsafe. Some, like COFCO's chairman, questioned this perception: "I don't think China's food safety problem is that serious, because ... over the past three decades, China has seen improvement in its [food] quality and nutrition level."[45] However, perceptions often trail reality, and reputations are slow to change, limiting COFCO's ability to overcome this issue. Nonetheless, recent company marketing campaigns to educate the public about its healthy foods and lifestyle promotion aimed to combat this perception, although this remained a serious issue for food companies from China.

It is not only the lower level of development but also the existence of political instability in the home country that may cast a negative perception on EMNCs. For example, despite Venezuela's vast oil wealth, the national oil company Petróleos de Venezuela S.A. (PDVSA) has faced a number of challenges abroad stemming from the political climate within Venezuela. In the United States, the association of Citgo Petroleum Corporation (CITGO) with PDVSA, and until recently with the socialist regime in Venezuela, has turned public opinion against the company. To help counter this effect, in 2005 CITGO began a program that provided subsidized heating oil to poor Americans. Between 2005 and 2014, this program provided 235 million gallons of heating oil to over 1.8 million people in 25 US states, aiding an average of 145,000 single-family households per year since its inception.[46] Another example is the problem of perception of the Russian oil firm Gazprom. While the position of Russia's oil and gas company Gazprom remains strong in former Soviet republics, Russia's disputes with neighboring countries have caused the company's reputation to suffer in Western Europe, particularly when those disputes have resulted in cuts to the gas and oil supplies of these countries. Political considerations have frequently constrained the acquisition attempts of Russian firms in Western Europe.

6.5 SOLUTIONS: DEVELOPING TALENT AND BUILDING REPUTATION

Successful EMNCs have developed multiple tactics for addressing the issues highlighted here. Table 6.1 summarizes some of the solutions that can be used to address these problems. We start with solutions for the limitation of managerial experience and conclude with solutions for the lack of reputation.

Solving the limitations in international experience. A set of solutions deals with the lack of managerial talent that limits both local and foreign operations. First, one of the primary ways of addressing the

Table 6.1 *Solutions for addressing operations challenges*

Issues	Actions
Limited managerial experience	Work with home-country national and regional governments to develop the home-country workforce
	Send managers and select talent to establish training facilities within the host country
	Home-country training for host-country workers
	Cross-cultural training
	Emphasize win–win with unions
Limited reputation	Promote home country
	Become locally embedded
	Participate in industry associations and events
	Demonstrate quality
	Target an unfilled product niche to gain a foothold in the market
	Leverage local partners and acquisitions

issue of limited talent in the home country is for a firm to work with its national or regional government to develop trained personnel. The lack of a trained workforce is a societal-level issue common across the majority of emerging markets. While some emerging markets have been able to advance their economies by taking advantage of a large, cheap, unskilled labor force (e.g., China) or abundant natural resources (e.g., Brazil), it requires some degree of skilled labor to move to higher development levels, as countries such as South Korea or Japan have done. Given the limitations of education in emerging markets, focused national policies could work effectively to develop the human talent needed. While these are obviously not under the direct control of EMNCs, given that they often possess strong ties with local governments, EMNCs can be a force in influencing the government to adopt such policies. EMNCs could also take more care to nurture sufficient people capabilities before going abroad. An example is Monterrey Tec, a private Mexican University with 31 campuses in 25 cities in Mexico that was created in 1943 by a group of local businessmen in Monterrey interested in developing the skilled employees they needed for their companies and that the state-owned universities were unable to train.

Second, host-country training also helps address this issue. A large portion of EMNC investment occurs in emerging markets, which, as we noted earlier, generally have less-developed educational institutions. This often creates a need for firms to develop their own talent when entering these markets. For example, Chinese telecom equipment manufacturers Huawei Technologies and ZTE Corporation (ZTE) operate together in 50 countries in Africa.[47] A lack of trained telecommunications workers in Africa initially restricted both companies' entry to the market. To combat this issue, both companies established extensive training efforts throughout the continent. Huawei established six regional training centers in South Africa, Nigeria, Kenya, Egypt, Tunisia, and Angola, which can provide technical training for up to 2,000 people annually.[48] Similarly, ZTE developed remote learning infrastructure as well as local training centers. Both companies worked with local educational institutions as part of their efforts. In 2007, ZTE cofounded the North Africa Training Academy at Algeria's national school for post and telecommunications (Entreprise Nationale de Travaux aux Puits, ENPT).[49] Another example is Sinochem Group and its cultivation of local employees, including the internationalization, diversification, and localization of its employees. The company's community policies provided that 100 percent of unskilled workers would be employed from local areas, while local skilled workers were given priority in local market recruitment. At the same time, the company offered training for employees at all levels in order to create better employment opportunities and broader development space for them. In its annual appraisal of excellent employees, the company established the "Foreign Model Worker" award. Winners were invited to

China with their families to attend the awards ceremony and the spring party held at the company's HQ, enabling them to experience the enthusiasm and warmth of the "Sinochem family."[50] Sinochem's local employment policy played a significant role in raising the income level of local residents and improving the quality of life for the communities where it operates. For example, its rubber business created more than 18,000 jobs in Africa and will create more employment opportunities with sustained development of its overseas business.[51]

Third, home-country training of host-country workers also addresses the challenge. EMNCs often bring local employees to their HQ for training. This is expensive, but for a limited number of high-level employees it can be a very viable option for developing key talent. Illustrating this point, every year, a significant number of foreign employees were brought to ZTE HQ for training.[52] Similarly, the Sinopec subsidiary in Saudi Arabia worked hard to develop local talent. According to Yang Guangwei, the company's head of administration there, "We have created our own training center based in Abqaiq to help the young Saudi nationals train and gain employment within the services and also send the best trainees to China to gain further knowledge and experience."[53]

A fourth solution to the limitations in international experience is cross-cultural training. To help ease difficulties in merging with SsangYong, Shanghai Automotive Industry Corporation (SAIC) hired an international management consultancy firm to help develop a "Hundred Days" integration plan. During the acquisition period, SAIC employed specialists to organize training on Korean customs, culture, and tradition. Everyone stationed in South Korea received a booklet titled, "Comic Korea," which was edited by a Korean and outlined Korean culture and national traditions and characteristics. Chinese officials gradually became accustomed to drinking as an opportunity to communicate with Koreans and set up a special fund to finance the cultural gifts widely expected in Korea. Meanwhile, South Korean executives and employees started to learn Chinese.

Similarly, after acquiring MG Motor UK Ltd. in 2007, SAIC spent a lot of time and effort in settling down the engineers and integrating them into the SAIC family. Both Western and Chinese food were provided in the SAIC UK Technology Center cafeteria. Young Chinese workers and older British engineers sat together in the same large space to discuss issues, and all computers and telephones were connected to the Shanghai System so that any transoceanic communication problems could be resolved as quickly as possible.

Fifth, the EMNC can foster efforts to develop its relationships with unions to get a win–win relationship. When dealing with unions and issues related to employee relations, successful EMNCs have emphasized policies and practices that provide benefits to both the company and its employees. For example, the Mexican baker Grupo Bimbo had gained little experience dealing with unions in Mexico, its home country. However, when the company expanded to the United States, it quickly realized that unions could significantly influence its operations, particularly in the case of Teamster-affiliated unionized truckers.[54] Moreover, variation in labor rights between US states meant that a one-size-fits-all approach was not possible in the US market. One approach that brought the company success in multiple locations was to attempt to convert unionized truck drivers to independent operators. This allowed drivers to gain benefits from being a small entrepreneurial business while simultaneously reducing company costs and adding flexibility to union-negotiated driving schedules. While this move had been resisted in locations where the unions are strong[55] and had even led to some lawsuits against the company,[56] the result was often a win–win for both drivers and the company. In a broader sense, Grupo Bimbo is also recognized for its many employee-centered policies, such as avoiding layoffs during economic downturns which has led to the company being rated one of the best places to work in Mexico[57]. Although these policies represent a significant expense to the company, over time in return Bimbo has gained the loyalty of its employees, something company executives consider an important factor in the company's sustained success.[58]

Finally, the EMNC can build local support. A common postacquisition difficulty of EMNCs involves the loss of executives and skilled personnel from the acquired firm. This is particularly prevalent in international acquisitions when a foreign parent is perceived to be less integrated into the local environment. After the Chinese oil company Sinopec set up its subsidiary in Argentina, the entire local management team walked out. They were used to a relaxed management style, which had resulted in high costs and low-quality raw materials. The first difficulty the Chinese management team faced was how to assume responsibility for the company and its employees. They reacted fast and adopted an icebreaker approach. Their first step was to reorganize the subsidiary's expense authorization system to strictly control nonproduction costs. The management team adjusted the authorization of purchases and made it clear that it was acting in the mutual interest of the company and its employees, which helped gain the employees' understanding, support, and recognition. The second step was to react proactively to the management strike. The company set up a Labor Union Relationship Department within the overall Human Resource Department. The new department was in charge of communications with local government and the labor union. The company also worked to influence local residents through public relations and social responsibility actions. The third step was to lead from the front, establishing a base in the oilfield production site. The managers of the Argentine HQ operated from the site and ate and lived together with local workers, using their relations to influence them.

Solutions for overcoming reputation difficulties. Efforts to overcome EMNC reputation issues involve two levels. First, firms need to address issues related to knowledge and perceptions about their firm, their specific products, and other characteristics. Second, they need to address the overall perception of their home country and/or specific industry effects associated with their country. Tactics could include promoting the home country, becoming more locally embedded, participating in industry associations and events, demonstrating quality, targeting an unfilled niche, using local partners, and making local acquisitions. Let us look more closely at these.

A first solution is to promote the home country. A home country's reputation can cast a shadow over the reputations of EMNCs when they invest abroad, particularly when the company is not well known in the host market, which is often the case. Given this inherent difficulty, EMNCs must work with their governments to help improve the reputations of their home countries. Perceptions of a country's products and its economy are recognized as important components of country reputations. The fates of companies are to a certain degree intertwined with those of their home country, and it can serve companies well to consider country issues in their policies and actions. For example, emerging Chinese MNCs are trying their best to change foreigners' negative perceptions and biased attitudes toward China and Chinese products. First of all, they try to influence foreign customers to make a more objective evaluation of today's China. For instance, every year, the telecommunications equipment producer Huawei invites experts and commercial leaders in the industry to visit China and participate in the "New Silk Road."[59] They also print and distribute illustrated booklets that reflect China's economic development. By targeting these influential stakeholders, they hope to create a ripple effect that will help improve country, and ultimately firm, reputation in the broader communities in which they operate.

A second solution is to become locally embedded. Local stakeholders are much more likely to be positively inclined toward a company when they perceive it as part of the local environment. It is critical for EMNCs to pursue actions that allow them to be perceived as more "local" that can help them gain legitimacy among local stakeholders and that ultimately improve their reputations. For instance, when Huawei entered Russia in 1996, the Huawei brand had no influence in the local market, and product quality was mistrusted. To help overcome this lack of trust, Huawei staff stayed in Russia, in continual communication with clients, for four years, remaining throughout Russia's economic crisis in 1997.[60] Sticking with a market even in difficult times can help demonstrate a commitment that will resonate with local stakeholders. A common method for achieving brand recognition in a local economy is to sponsor sports events or teams – such as Haier's sponsorship of the US National Basketball Association (NBA). These sponsorships provide instant brand awareness and recall while also conveying some benefits of association through image transfer. Successfully competing to win international sponsorship contracts can also be a reputation-enhancing signal that a firm is competent, has resources, and holds market power. Within Ecuador, Sinopec continued the tradition of hosting entertainment and sports events during local festivals to motivate local employees in its subsidiary. The celebratory dinner for the foundation of the subsidiary coincided with the Ecuador national football team qualifying for the World Cup. At the event, Chinese managers wore national football team uniforms and sang and danced with local workers. This shortened the cultural distance with local workers and established a solid foundation for cultural integration.

A third solution is participation in industry associations and events. In addition to becoming locally embedded in host markets, EMNCs can also benefit from greater participation in industry associations. Many successful EMNCs are active participants in global industry exhibitions. Each year, Huawei Group spends more than US$10 million participating in more than 20 major global telecommunications equipment exhibitions.[61] This helps build Huawei's brand name and establish relational networks.

A fourth solution is to demonstrate quality. While reputation is a perceptual measure, perceptions are often rooted in a company's earlier performance. For EMNCs trying to overcome the negative effects of their home-country reputations, demonstrating quality results can have an important signaling effect that influences a company's reputation. According to Yin Tongyaio, CEO of Chery International, "We are aware that people have concerns regarding product lines made in China. To respond to these concerns, we must overdesign, overtest, and overservice. We think concerns about the quality of goods in China will quickly disappear if consumers cannot find problems, even with very picky eyes."[62]

Along with efforts to improve the knowledge and perceptions of their products, many firms are pursuing initiatives to improve the quality of those products. In order to follow international customs and rules and meet the standards of host countries, many EMNCs apply for various types of standard certifications, such as International Organization for Standardization (ISO) 9000 and Six Sigma. These quality guaranties provide a premise for EMNC products to compete globally. In terms of firm reputation assessment, even more important than their influence on actual quality, these certifications serve as important signals to the marketplace that firms are producing quality goods. Social constructionists view reputation as a composite of different types of stakeholder perceptions of a firm. By achieving an externally recognized certification, firms provide a signal to important stakeholders that can help overcome previous conceptions of poor quality. Haier is another good example of a firm improving its brand recognition. Its globalization strategy started in the United States, which imposed much higher quality requirements for Haier's products than would have been expected from developing markets. Haier's CEO, Zhang Ruimin, believed that if the American market accepted Haier, the company could then compete anywhere in the world in terms of product quality.[63]

A fifth solution is to target an unfilled niche. In addition to demonstrating quality in general, EMNCs can also pursue a differentiation strategy by targeting an unfilled niche in the host market. For example, a major strategy of Haier was to target market niches, such as small-scale refrigerators in the United States. This allowed them to compete less directly with the major competition and gradually build a brand name. In France and Italy, it followed a similar strategy, focusing on air conditioning, which was a relatively new market without well-established brands. In each case, it introduced additional product lines after becoming established.[64]

A sixth solution for overcoming reputation difficulties is to use local partners and acquisitions. Few emerging market firms have the luxury of appointing a dedicated reputation manager, especially when it comes to entering a foreign market. A local partner can help a firm navigate the host environment more easily. Illustrating this point, the Brazil Hotels Group, which is a relatively new multinational, has overcome this challenge by partnering with global brands that give Brazil Hotels brand recognition and know-how in global hotel management. In order to improve brand recognition, some Chinese MNCs collaborate with world-famous companies to enhance legitimacy. For example, in December 2007, Chrysler reported that it would sell a Dodge-badged Chery A1 in Mexico. The A1 was built at Chery's Wuhu plant and exported to Mexico. This news signaled that Chery is a high-quality Chinese auto producer. In 2007, Chery also announced that it would enter a joint venture with Israel Corp. – an Israeli holding company – to create a new automaker. This joint venture would develop a new brand that targeted high-end consumers. Professionals from McKinsey would help Chery to develop and promote the new brand. In order to get rid of the low-quality image associated with Chinese brands, some Chinese MNCs have purchased established, well-known brands. The Chinese computer firm Lenovo is the best example: in 2004, Lenovo bought the PC division from IBM and was authorized to use the ThinkPad brand. While Chinese firms may play a leading role among EMNCs in terms of their abilities to purchase foreign firms, this is by no means an exclusively Chinese-firm strategy. The Brazilian food producer Brasil Foods (BRF) is known to target well-established companies with strong brands as a central component of its acquisition strategy. In doing this, BRF further strengthens its own reputation and brand.

6.6 CLOSING CASE: EMBRAER

The Brazilian aircraft manufacturer Embraer has emerged as one of a handful of global players in the passenger aircraft industry, competing with the Canadian firm Bombardier, the US maker Boeing, and the

European consortium Airbus. Despite coming from an emerging market and operating in a high-tech industry, it has "built a reputation for excellent performance and low operational costs"[65] and achieved world-class success. However, given the technical sophistication of its product line, it is also highly dependent on a well-trained workforce. While the company used other short-term strategies to build its technical employee base at different points during its development, its long-term advancement was contingent upon a reliable supply of engineers. Given the limited number of qualified technical workers being trained in Brazil, in order to ensure a qualified workforce for its products, Embraer worked with the Brazilian government to establish an Aeronautical Technology Institute, which supplied Embraer with a large percentage of its engineers.[66] While the establishment of a training institute has certainly had societal benefits beyond simply supplying Embraer with employees, it is unlikely that this effort would have been pursued if the Brazilian government's goal to have a reliable supply of short-range aircraft had not aligned so well with Embraer's needs.

Besides addressing labor issues, Embraer also successfully addressed reputation issues at both company and country levels. At the company level, Embraer targeted a niche market of short-range passenger jets that was relatively unattended by its major industry competitors (Boeing and McDonnell Douglas, and later Airbus), which focused on larger, more profitable long-range aircraft. Embraer specifically developed designs based on the flying conditions of these smaller aircraft rather than just scaled-down versions of larger aircraft. As a result, the company achieved significant results. One source notes that "the biggest difference is that Embraer has designed what I call a 'vertical oval' shape into its cabin, which gives much more room than a traditional cylinder shape."[67] The company also focused on low fuel consumption, reduced operating costs, ease of maintenance, and outstanding reliability.[68] These efforts helped Embraer to be ranked among the top companies in Brazil in 2014.[69] By establishing its capabilities as an airplane manufacturer and competing successfully with developed world competitors over a sustained period of time, Embraer has overcome issues associated with its home country's reputation to establish its own unique identity.

6.7 CONCLUSIONS

Establishing operations in a foreign market requires specific capabilities that differ in significant ways from those that may be necessary in a firm's home market. EMNCs often lack these capabilities, particularly when making initial investments in markets that differ in the level of institutional development and other ways from their home market.

Unfortunately, managers commonly make inadequate plans for managing postinvestment operations after their foreign subsidiaries have been established, which can lead to unexpected operational problems and ultimately contribute to poor firm performance. We have suggested that the most common operational difficulties faced by EMNCs in their initial postinvestment period fall into two broad categories: limitations in experience to be able to manage overseas operations and lack of reputation.

With respect to the lack of managerial talent and other qualified labor, we suggest a multipronged approach to developing the talent needed to compete in the firm's new environment. This includes working with a firm's home-country government to develop a home-country workforce with international skills to help manage foreign operations, sending managers and select talent to the host country for training, and providing home-country training for host-country workers. Embraer, Sinochem, and ZTE are all examples of firms that have made effective strides in addressing training concerns. Regarding lack of experience in the host market and associated legal issues, as many of these issues deal with local employee organizations, firms must establish win–win relationships with unions and employees. Participating in industry associations can help the firm to be seen as part of the broader community. Moreover, making efforts to become more locally embedded and not seen as a foreign entity is crucial.

Grupo Bimbo is a good example of a firm that has overcome these types of difficulties in its local markets.

Regarding a firm's reputation with potential customers and a broad range of local stakeholders, firms need to demonstrate the quality of their products and how the company's offering fulfills an unmet need in the local environment. Leveraging local partners or making acquisitions can also help the firm seem less of an outsider and provide legitimacy. Additionally, in cases where the firm suffers from a strong bias against its home country, it may need to work with other home-country forces to improve the country's image while simultaneously endeavoring to be seen as more of a local player. Haier, Embraer, and Chery are among the EMNCs that have succeeded in overcoming reputation issues.

Our focus in this chapter has been primarily on operations in the host country, as we examine issues that are particularly troublesome in the postinvestment startup period for EMNCs. In the next chapter we overview factors related to the integration of foreign subsidiaries with the HQ and other firms in an EMNC's international network.

Notes

1. Hille (2013).
2. Economist (2012b).
3. Ao, Liang, and Gao (2012).
4. Economist (2012b).
5. Anon (2006).
6. Wang (2010).
7. Ojo (2012)
8. Chen (2013).
9. Ojo (2012).
10. Hille (2013).
11. Einhorn, Mayeda, and Argitis (2014).
12. Luo and Tung (2007).
13. Holden and Vaiman (2013).
14. Gao (2008).

15. Anon (2011b).
16. Anon (2011b).
17. Skolkovo (2009).
18. Skolkovo (2009).
19. Skolkovo (2009).
20. Sinochem (2013).
21. Zhang (2007) and Wang (2008).
22. See Smith et al. (2012).
23. Perkins (2014).
24. Shaw (2014).
25. Siegel (2009).
26. Kwong (2012).
27. Wides-Munoz (2014).
28. Li, Liu, and Bi (2012)
29. Anon (2011d).
30. Jauch (2014).
31. Economist (2005).
32. United Steelworkers (2006).
33. Union Advocate (2014).
34. See Fombrun (1996), Rindova & Martins (2012) and Fombrun, Ponzi & Newburry (2015) for discussions of reputations and stakeholder perceptions.
35. Lange, Lee, and Dai (2011).
36. McLain (2013).
37. Bajaj (2012).
38. Scully (2014).
39. Webber (2012).
40. Merco (2015) (see individual country rankings within the website).
41. Kosacoff et al. (2014), p. 46.
42. Kosacoff et al. (2014), p. 190.
43. Lampert and Jaffe (1996).
44. Skolkovo (2009).
45. Huang (2013).
46. CITGO (2015).
47. Anon (2011c).
48. Anon (2011c).
49. Economist (2007).
50. Economist (2012a); Sinochem (2012).
51. Economist (2012a); Sinochem (2012).

52. Economist (2007).
53. Arab News (2014).
54. See Anon (2009) for an example of the Teamster influence on Bimbo's operations in the U.S.
55. See, e.g., Kosman (2014).
56. See, e.g., Tabakman (2010).
57. Great Place to Work (2014).
58. Siegel (2009).
59. Wildau (2014); Gupta, Pande, and Wang (2014).
60. Yan (2005).
61. Li and Cui (2009).
62. Gao (2008).
63. Palepu, Khanna, and Vargas (2006).
64. Duysters et al. (2009).
65. Grundig (2013).
66. Ghemawat, Herrero, and Monteiro (2009).
67. McMclellan (2006).
68. Ghemawat, Herrero, and Monteiro (2009).
69. Merco (2014).

7 Integration

7.1 INTRODUCTION

After overcoming the initial tasks of establishing a subsidiary within a foreign country, and often simultaneously, managers of EMNCs must address governance issues to ensure the integration of the new operation with the rest of operations in the multinational. Managing the relationships between HQ and their overseas subsidiaries, along with the optimal management and integration of MNC networks, is a major concern for MNCs. The integration of foreign subsidiaries is also a major area of importance for developed country MNCs, but some specific characteristics make this a particularly problematic area for EMNCs. Inefficiencies caused by organizational structures developed to compensate for the deficiencies in institutions and market intermediaries in the home country, the so-called institutional voids, along with limited capabilities in corporate governance, make integration issues within EMNCs troublesome. These compound the relationship between the foreign subsidiary and the parent corporation. Effective integration includes identifying the mandate of the local operation and its relationship with HQ and other subsidiaries – in other words, how the subsidiary fits within the overall MNC network.

There are additional governance challenges that EMNCs tend to face because of their state and family ownership. For example, some large EMNCs have inherited the bureaucratic structures of their original state-owned enterprises (SOEs), which may complicate the management of overseas subsidiaries. Issues of current government ownership and legacies of recent government ownership are much more prevalent in emerging markets than in developed countries, where they tend to be associated with only a few select industries. Additionally, family-run enterprises, another major component of the emerging market landscape, can also have organizational structures that stifle overseas managers.

Hence, in this chapter, we examine the integration of the new subsidiary within the network of subsidiaries of the EMNC. Specifically, we analyze integration between the subsidiary and HQ and throughout the firm's broader intersubsidiary network, as well as coordination with alliance partners and acquisitions. We also discuss governance issues relating to organizational ownership by the state or family-owned business groups.

7.2 OPENING CASE: HAIER'S ACQUISITION OF SANYO

The acquisition of the Japanese Sanyo's white goods operations by the Chinese white goods manufacture Haier illustrates the difficulties EMNCs face in establishing subsidiary roles and controlling overseas operations effectively. The Haier group operated a global network of subsidiaries producing home appliances and consumer electronics. By a significant and growing margin, Haier was the largest home appliance or white goods manufacturer in the world in terms of net sales.[1]

Company chairman and chief executive officer (CEO) Zhang Ruimin has been famous for his efforts to transform this formerly state-run company into a globally respected home appliance brand since he was appointed managing director in 1984. Nonetheless, the company's growth over the past three decades has created a need to develop new capabilities to address the challenges of managing and integrating the components of its multinational network.

In March 2012, Haier completed its acquisition of Sanyo's white goods operations in Japan, Indonesia, Malaysia, the Philippines, and Vietnam. This acquisition was projected "to enhance Haier's R&D, manufacturing and marketing capabilities in Japan and Southeast Asia to better serve the needs of local consumers."[2] As part of the agreement, Japan was to serve as Haier's Asian HQ. According to Jingguo Du, vice-president of the Haier Group, "The key success factor of any acquisition is neither the amount of capital investment nor is it merely an acquisition of resources; it is dependent on the integration of cultures and management philosophies."[3] This integration of cultures and management styles created several difficulties for Haier. First, when Du came to Japan, Sanyo employees had difficulty communicating with a Chinese. To overcome this, Du eventually adopted a version of the Japanese drinking culture. He divided the 170 employees into 17 groups, and over the period of a year drank tea with each of these groups twice. By adopting this local custom, he was able to develop trust with the employees and communicate that he was working hard on behalf of the merged company.[4]

Other challenges facing Haier related to the positions of individual subsidiaries within the overall corporation. For example, before the acquisition by Haier, Sanyo employees served only the Japanese market. However, after the acquisition, they had to serve the Chinese market as well, although they were not acquainted with Chinese consumer habits and markets. To overcome this, Du proposed setting up a professional market research company in China to investigate Chinese consumer behavior. His proposal was opposed, on the grounds that the Chinese market should be the responsibility of the Chinese parent company. In response, Du emphasized that the new joint company was there to serve its customers and ensure a future in the market and not to serve either Haier or Sanyo. As a result of these efforts, the company finally set up a research and planning company in Shanghai.[5]

7.3 INTEGRATION CHALLENGES IN THE NETWORK OF SUBSIDIARIES

In an MNC context, control is generally defined in terms of the influence that HQ has over its subsidiaries. A challenge for EMNCs is integration of the network of subsidiaries to ensure control. An example is Kaspersky Labs, a fast-growing Russian provider of security software. For years, it has tried to penetrate foreign markets through trade representatives, without fundamentally changing its flat, startup-like corporate structure. "The old structure wasn't scalable, that was its main shortcoming," explained founder Evgeni Kaspersky at the end of 2007, when the company finally decided to restructure radically. Five regional HQ were created, each providing support and oversight to local offices. Overall, with respect to the foreign investments of Russian firms in general, "Russian multinationals need to introduce more transparency, improve reporting procedures, and protect minority shareholders' rights. It is increasingly acknowledged that long-term competitiveness of Russian companies depends on best practices in corporate governance."[6]

Integration challenges in acquisitions. There are numerous examples of difficulties EMNCs encounter in the area of integration, and these are particularly acute in international acquisitions because many EMNCs use foreign acquisitions in order to gain know-how and other assets. A prime case was the Chinese electronics firm TCL Corporation's acquisition of the French electronics firm Thomson, which we discussed in Chapter 4. Another example is the expansion of the UAE-based airline Emirates. Sir Maurice Flanagan, executive vice chairman of Emirates, commented that, as a growth strategy, taking stakes in smaller airlines was "just not worth it. … It eats up an enormous amount of senior management time. … They want you to develop that airline to be like Emirates."[7] Flanagan's position may stem from Emirates' earlier experience with SriLankan Airlines. Emirates had previously acquired a 43.6 percent stake in the company, which also gave it management control. However, the Sri Lankan government continuously sought greater control over the airline's day-to-day business decisions, leaving Emirates in the undesirable position of losing control of corporate governance. This led to Emirates not renewing its management control contract and eventually selling its stake in the airline.[8] Similarly, the Indian car company Tata Motors also experienced governance challenges. Due to Tata Motors' rapid expansion, the company experienced problems with internal control and corporate governance, which had at least partially been driven by the company's high rate of acquisitions, joint ventures, and product diversification. In 2012, Tata hired Carl Slym, former head of General Motors India, as managing director. Slym brought with him a new team to address some of these issues and bring quality to the forefront: "The new team has identified three problem areas – poor quality, a lack of model upgrades and a perception that the company's cars are only good enough to be used as taxis."[9]

Finally, China's first and the world's fastest-growing construction machinery company Zoomlion Heavy Industry's acquisition of Italian construction equipment manufacturer Compagnia Italiana Forme Acciaio (CIFA) in 2008 provides another example of difficulties in establishing effective corporate governance and control. Zoomlion established a special international management company with no capital ties to the parent out of consideration for promoting integrated management and to ensure no interference at the operational level. Chen Xiaofei, who was the general manager of the Concrete Division, was made chief of the company, and Davide Cipolla from CIFA was put in charge of R&D. Cipolla was also responsible for assigning tasks and setting up project teams. Italian team members regularly attended meetings in China, and Zoomlion technicians would occasionally go to Italy to work. Integration developed slowly and extended to living and working habits. However, despite these efforts, integration difficulties nonetheless emerged. The Italians did not like working overtime and maintained that the Chinese operated without effective planning. The Chinese thought the Italians were lazy and rigid, as they were unwilling to depart from written plans. Chen Peiliang noted that on the factory manager's occasional visits to his office, his most frequent complaint was that internal processes were too complicated and that approvals needed too many signatures.

Chen would respond by explaining each time that Zoomlion had 30,000 people and CIFA 700. On that scale, Zoomlion had to sacrifice some efficiency to strengthen management and control.[10] The Zoomlion–CIFA relationship emphasizes the potential tradeoffs between control and local operational efficiency in EMNCs.

Integration challenges in alliances. Integration challenges are even more pronounced when having to coordinate with partners in other countries. While the alignment of partner goals is a critical issue in all international joint ventures and alliances, it is a particularly difficult issue when the foreign partner is a developing country firm. The potential for differing expectations from the joint venture, particularly when the foreign partner is stateowned or influenced, is greatly increased. Differing goals can lead to differences in operation strategies and ultimately poor performance and accusations of mismanagement by the joint venture partners.

For example, in 2013, US home-comfort product manufacturer Soleus International, which partnered with Gree USA, a subsidiary of China's Gree Electrical Appliances, accused the Chinese company of asking Soleus to hide facts relating to defects found in their air dehumidifiers sold in the United States and then threatening retaliation after the fault was reported to the US government. According to Soleus, Gree USA signed a contract worth US$150 million with Sears Holdings Corp., a top US retailer, in December 2011, but the agreement was sabotaged because of "unreasonably high price quotes" for Gree USA products from the Chinese side. Furthermore, Gree Electronic Appliances was also said to have allegedly tried to do business directly with Sears, without participation from Gree USA.[11]

Soleus then asked for more than US$150 million in compensation for violations under the terms of their contract agreement and fair trade practices. Soleus said it hired product-testing experts to investigate the faulty products and confirmed that there was a design problem with the dehumidifiers produced for Gree USA and that the products made between 2010 and 2012 were all made with disqualified material. As a result, Soleus removed the products from the market. Soleus claimed that Gree Electronic Appliances pressured them to hide customer complaints and then tried to ruin Soleus by ignoring contracts, regardless of their relationship as business partners, as well as luring customers to engage in under-the-table dealings. Gree Electronic Appliances admitted that there were some disputes between the two companies but claimed that accusations made in the court in California were "fabricated and groundless" and completely inconsistent with the facts.[12]

Gree USA had received some complaints from customers that the dehumidifiers were prone to catch fire. The company reported them to the US Consumer Product Safety Commission and hired a third-party organization to assess the problem. Gree Electronic Appliances stated, "The number of fire-prone dehumidifiers is only 0.005 percent of all the similar products on sales in the US. Meanwhile, Gree Electronic Appliances has not received any legal documents from the California federal court so far." As for their partnership with Soleus, Gree Electronic Appliances said it never ever threatened or pressured them, and it would take legal action to assert its rights and protect Chinese companies abroad.[13]

7.4 CORPORATE GOVERNANCE CHALLENGES

In addition to coordination challenges, EMNCs face particular corporate governance challenges – "the ways in which suppliers of finance to corporations assure themselves of getting a return on their investment"[14] – which are paramount to address in order to succeed in foreign markets. Although a major focus of corporate governance has been the protection of shareholder rights, it can be extended to include not only capital but also labor and management. Suppliers of capital vary from country to country; labor quality and rights vary transnationally; and cultural preferences and management capabilities also vary across countries, thus affecting how EMNCs coordinate across countries.

Emerging markets are noted for their deficiencies in capital, labor, and management capabilities, which translate into poor corporate governance when these firms invest abroad. "Owing to underdeveloped stock markets at home, poor accountability, and lack of transparency stemming from their ties with their host government, corporate governance of [EMNCs] is generally weak."[15] Compounding these issues, corporate governance in emerging markets is often relationship based, which may be poorly perceived by foreign stakeholders as lacking accountability, transparency, and trustworthiness. These issues are further complicated by EMNCs' general lack of familiarity, experience, and managerial capability, as companies cannot rely on established routines.

Sharing control can also be a critical issue in managing EMNCs. VimpelCom, a leading telecommunications service provider in Russia, has been affected by a major dispute between its two principal shareholders: Altimo (Russia's Alfa Group Consortium's telecommunications unit) and Telenor (a Norwegian multinational telecommunications provider). Russian shareholders do not believe Telenor should have equal shares, and this has raised legal issues between the two parties.[16] Illustrating the complexities of overcoming difficulties between partners, disputes between these shareholders have occurred for many years. For example, when Alfa Group wanted to purchase WellCOM in Ukraine in 2005, Telenor complained because Alfa Group and Telenor already shared ownership of Kievstar in Ukraine. This dispute occurred despite the fact that WellCOM had an estimated 50,000 users at the time compared to 6.25 million for Kievstar.[17] Shareholder disputes have proved to be an ongoing challenge that impacts some aspects of the company's managerial capabilities because they reflect inconsistencies in the companies' objectives in international expansions.

In addition to these general corporate governance challenges, EMNCs face the additional challenges of dealing with two ownership structures that are common in emerging markets: state ownership and family ownership.

Corporate governance in state-owned enterprises (SOEs). A major organizational integration issue for many EMNCs is the influence of state ownership, either current or a legacy in recently privatized firms that maintain government contacts and/or minority ownership. The privatization wave of the 1980s and 1990s created various types of SOEs. Regardless of the level of ownership, state-owned firms often have broader and sometimes conflicting goals compared to private firms.[18] However, these firms have also gone through a transition in recent years, from being primarily focused on the domestic market to being encouraged by their state owners to internationalize in order to compete in the global economy, often with the incentive of government capital for these investments. Indeed, investment funding can be a strong motivator for firms in economies where there are still institutional voids regarding access to capital. However, even more important to the management of these relatively new foreign subsidiaries is that SOEs are notorious for their bureaucratic management processes, which can hinder operational decision making and the integration of a firm's global network.

This issue is particularly prevalent in large companies in China, which have inherited the bureaucratic structures of their original SOEs and which may in turn become obstacles to overseas expansion. Even for private Chinese multinationals, "the long shadow of the state" has been noted.[19] This challenge is especially obvious in the oil, electricity, metal, telecommunications, airlines, and financial service sectors – all industries of continuing strategic interest to the government.[20]

Jin Zhiguo, CEO of the previously state-owned Chinese brewer Tsingtao Brewery, recorded his experience of taking control of the company in 2001, where he needed to deal with an employee population used to working based on the practices of an SOE, where job competition and performance review were not expected: "In my first six months as president I replaced seven of the eight general managers who were running big departments at Tsingtao and more than 20 general managers at our breweries. Many of these people had been supervisors or colleagues of mine. To be honest, I found the firing process extremely difficult. When you're at a company for a long time, you know everyone. But I believed that the market should rule, and that only those who performed well should be able to stay. I stuck to that belief. I needed to create a team of wolves who wanted to compete."[21]

Corporate governance in family-run firms and business groups. A large percentage of foreign subsidiaries of many EMNCs are family owned. One particular issue related to family firms is scalability. When firms aim to maintain family control over operations, they can face difficulties attracting talent. This problem can intensify when the family internationalizes. Moreover, these firms often have relatively flat organizational structures, which limit the ability to manage foreign expansion effectively, suggesting a need to redesign the structure. Jollibee, the Filipino fast-food company, is one example of a family-owned firm that did phenomenal business in its home market, even outcompeting major foreign competitors such as McDonald's, but struggled in its early efforts to internationalize. Even after bringing in foreign managerial talent with international fast-food experience to run its international division, the company still had difficulty managing its rapid international expansion into multiple countries, largely due to having insufficient trained personnel at HQ to manage a foreign franchise network.[22]

These issues are compounded in the case of business groups, or multi-company organizations bound together under joint control and operating in different industries.[23] In the Indian context, research has found that belonging to a business group increases the odds of subsidiary survival in emerging countries but not necessarily in developed countries.[24] This is consistent with the notion that the benefits of business group affiliation in emerging markets may not transfer to developed country contexts.

Corporate governance in politically challenging countries. Political uncertainties certainly play a key role in the abilities of EMNCs to maintain and expand their foreign operations. Emerging markets tend to be less politically stable than markets in developed countries; EMNCs seem disproportionately prone to difficulties arising from home- and host-country political dynamics. In many instances, political uncertainties may even result in the retraction of investment. Illustrating this point, a few years ago, Leonid Fedun, vice-president of the Russian oil giant Lukoil, informed the *Financial Times* that some "Russian investors have started to withdraw from countries such as Poland and Lithuania because of political antagonism."[25]

Political relations issues seem particularly problematic in Russia. This may result from a combination of the long-term political hegemony of Russia, stemming from its former position within the Soviet Union, and the large concentration of the country's foreign investments in oil and other politically sensitive industries. The Russian government is perceived as more likely to interfere in the activities of its companies than most other emerging markets. Indeed, "there is a growing consensus in the literature that Russia's economy today resembles some form of state capitalism."[26] Russian firms have also been criticized for a lack of transparency in their investments, reinforcing political concerns.

Nowhere is the impact of political issues on the actions of Russian companies more apparent than in Ukraine. Because of its geographic position, Ukraine plays a critical role in the transport and trade of Russian gas. In 2013, for example, about half of Russian gas exports to Europe went through Ukraine, which accounted for about 15 percent of European consumption and 49 percent of Russia's total gas exports.[27] However, Ukraine has arguably been the greatest source of challenge for Gazprom, the Russian gas conglomerate that provided about 30 percent of Europe's gas needs in 2013.[28] In 2012, European Union (EU) regulators launched an investigation into Gazprom that resulted two years later in the European Commission threatening to make several antitrust allegations against the company relating to abusive gas pricing and other anticompetitive practices.[29] Ultimately, these threats resulted in sanctions against Gazprom and other companies starting in July 2014.

Political issues with Gazprom's pipelines in Ukraine date back to at least the 1990s, causing the company to expend significant efforts developing additional pipelines through other countries, as well as expanding other means of gas transport (e.g., shipping). However, events demonstrated that the impact of Russia's relationship with Ukraine extended well beyond the oil and gas industry. European and US sanctions have had much broader impacts on European company profitability.[30] Meanwhile, Russia developed support funding for companies targeted by sanctions.[31] Nonetheless, the effect of sanctions extended well beyond the limited range of companies targeted (oil and gas, banks), with "officials and industry executives say[ing] they've had a much broader indirect effect, dragging on a Russian economy that was already stalling before the Ukraine crisis exploded."[32]

While the Russian example is noteworthy, political dynamics played prominent roles in the expansion of companies from other countries as well. Much of the income of the Venezuelan state-owned oil and gas company Petróleos de Venezuela S.A. (PDVSA) was used by President Hugo Chávez for political motives rather than development of the company. PDVSA was a cash cow for the country[33] and "PDVSA's chairman, Rafael Ramírez ... made it an explicit company policy to employ only supporters of the president."[34] Before his death, Chávez railed against Citgo Petroleum Corporation, PDVSA's wholly owned subsidiary in the United States, insisting that it was a bad investment and that he wanted to sell it.[35] Whether true or not, given the contentious relationship between Venezuela and the United States, it was hard to disentangle political and economic motives in the case of PDVSA's Citgo operations.

Political issues are also often intertwined with corruption charges against EMNCs. For example, in 2013, ZTE Corporation (ZTE) faced a corruption probe in Mongolia, adding to the Chinese company's difficulties as it tried to fend off Western suspicions about its government connections. The management of ZTE was being investigated following the arrest of the Mongolian tax official who handled ZTE's tax affairs. The probe into ZTE was triggered by the authorities' investigation into the assets of the tax official and his family. The authorities were also looking at tenders and purchases made by the Mongolian Ministry of Education, Science, and Culture.[36] Similarly, in January 2013, top executives from Cencosud, the largest retail company in Chile, were put on probation in relation to a smuggling and tax fraud lawsuit.[37] The lawsuit, filed in 2011, accused Cencosud of smuggling products from Argentina into Chile, evading taxes (US$2.8 million) under the guise that the goods were for a humanitarian cause. The lawsuit stated that 183 Cencosud trucks crossed the border between March 3 and March 30, 2010, without paying any taxes or fees. Cencosud denied the allegations, maintaining that the goods were sent as aid for earthquake victims in Chile in 2010.[38]

7.5 SOLUTIONS: HOW EMNCS CAN OVERCOME INTEGRATION AND CORPORATE GOVERNANCE ISSUES

Successful EMNCs have developed multiple tactics for addressing the integration and corporate governance issues highlighted within this chapter. Table 7.1 summarizes some of the solutions that can be used to address these problems. We start with solutions for achieving better integration, followed by ways to achieve better corporate governance.

Solving integration difficulties. Successful EMNCs have developed multiple approaches to addressing the integration issues highlighted here. We highlight several in the following sections.

First, clearly defining subsidiary missions and associated HQs' roles is crucial. As the case of Haier's acquisition of Sanyo's white

Table 7.1 *Solutions for addressing integration challenges*

Issues	Actions
Lack of effective integration	Clearly define subsidiary mission and associated HQ's roles Establish scalable organizational structures Structure integration Adopt international standards and best practices
Corporate governance challenges	Establish clear control guidelines with partner organizations Learn to balance broader expectations of state ownership with market-based demands For family-owned firms, develop global capabilities of family members and bring in outside talent with international experience Develop contingencies for operating in politically unstable regions

goods operations in Japan shows, clearly defining the roles of subsidiaries is imperative for their effective functioning. This may be particularly true for acquired subsidiaries, whose roles will change after integration into an EMNC's overall network. While acquisitions cause stress during the transition process, employees in target firms will face less uncertainty and manage it better when EMNCs present clear strategic directions and roles for their acquired subsidiaries.

Second, EMNCs need to establish scalable organizational structures. One overarching concern of the bureaucratic state- and family-owned structures common in many EMNCs is the lack of capability to incorporate overseas subsidiaries effectively. The ability of an organization's structure to incorporate rapid increases in capacity is crucial to the growth of EMNCs. Without this, the addition of new subsidiaries and substantial growth in existing ones can mean loss of control, lower their efficiency, and reduce their ability to compete. Scalability of a company's organizational structure is an important issue. Russia's largest mobile operator Mobile TeleSystems (MTS) restructured into a four-level geographic structure to create this capability. At the top level were three geographic businesses combined with a corporate center. Former MTS CEO Leonid Melamed remarked, "As the business grows, this managerial functionality is easily scalable."[39] The structure also made it possible for the company "to separate strategic functions from operational ones, and to create a simple and transparent structure, increasing the business unit managers' motivation to achieve goals" while also making sure overall company goals remained embedded throughout the company.[40]

Traditional examinations of international business structure usually note that MNCs new to internationalization adopt an international division structure, which allows flexibility in international expansion and avoids giving core domestic operations the additional burden of learning new routines for an international environment. Indeed, Filipino firm Jollibee provides a high-profile example of an EMNC using this organizational form.[41] However, EMNCs have largely shied away from this form, adopting a range of structures according to the nature of their business, suggesting a more global outlook from the start of their internationalization. This indicates that EMNCs need to consider a structure that accommodates their international goals and leaves room for expanding international operations.

Third, integration efforts need to be well structured. While integration is certainly difficult, there are success stories that can serve as examples for other emerging market firms. One prominent example is Chinese computer company Lenovo, which is well known for its acquisition of IBM's PC business. A major driver in successfully integrating the two companies involved a purposeful integration plan that helped overcome differences in business models and cultures across 12 time zones and capture the best practices and knowledge from both parties in the acquisition.[42] According to Lenovo executives, "What Lenovo brings to the table is the best from East and West. From the original Lenovo we have the understanding of emerging markets, excellent efficiency and a focus on long-term strategy. From IBM we have deep insights into worldwide markets and best practices from western companies."[43] By projecting an air of excitement about the prospects for the integrated company, Lenovo was able to generate positive attitudes among its new US employees about being part of the global team.[44] In the end, Lenovo acquired not only notebook computer technology but also a former IBM R&D team, who felt more valued by Lenovo than they did by IBM, which at the time was less focused on computer hardware.

Companies available for purchase by EMNCs are often small, and their size may allow tacit knowledge to flow relatively easily within company borders. However, they are unlikely to have a knowledge management program, which can create difficulties for integration with an acquiring company, particularly one located in a foreign country. The acquiring company may need to develop capabilities within its acquisition before being able to fully capitalize on its venture. This was the situation faced by Russian equipment manufacturer Concern Tractor Plants (CTP) when it acquired the Danish company Silvatec. CTP pursued the acquisition to increase production and market Silvatec's harvesters and forwarders in the Russian market. However, it soon found out that engineering at Silvatec was done on such an ad hoc basis that "you could just as well consider every one of those Danish harvesters as unique."[45] CTP needed to expend significant effort standardizing processes and then ensuring that they were adequately documented before it could realize the goal of its acquisition.

Fourth, one particularly effective method for EMNCs to demonstrate competency is through the adoption of international standards and best practices. For example, among software firms, resources like capability maturity model integration (CMMI) accreditation signal the firm's capabilities to external markets. Firms that adopt this standard are more likely to attract developed country partners, increasing their ability to internationalize at a faster rate.[46] This has been a prevalent practice among Indian software firms working to gain global legitimacy. Similarly, as we noted in

Chapter 6, many EMNCs apply for various types of standard certification, such as ISO 9000 and Six Sigma. As well as being quality guarantees, these standards also have a control function in helping to manage differing employee expectations.

Solutions for corporate governance challenges. In addition to methods of addressing integration difficulties highlighted earlier, we also suggest the following approaches to overcoming corporate governance challenges.

First, when EMNC foreign investments involve partner organizations, clear control guidelines with these partners must be established in order for EMNCs to adequately make decisions regarding their overseas investments without partner interference. These must include which organization is in charge of what types of decisions or when decisions will be made jointly. As the case of VimpelCom and its two principal shareholders, Alfa Group and Telenor, noted earlier illustrates, the impact of partnerships can extend beyond the scope of the actual partnership to include related investments.

Second, EMNCs must learn to effectively balance the demands and wider expectations of being a SOE versus those of competing in markets where meeting market expectations is key to success. The case of Chinese brewer Tsingtao Brewery's CEO Jin Zhiguo and his efforts to transform the management of the company to operate according to market principals noted earlier in this chapter illustrates the severity that such changes may entail. Even after a state-owned company has been privatized, the influence of the state may remain through informal channels. EMNC managers must recognize that despite such pressures, the importance of responding to market forces must be addressed in foreign markets if the firm is to succeed financially in its investments.

Third, family firms must realize that the effective governance of their corporations in international environments requires specific skills and a mind-set that may not have been developed in the process of operating in their home-country environment. These skills need to be honed at the top levels of the corporation to ensure that strategic decisions are aligned with the company's global operating conditions and not just those of the home market. If the management of the company is to remain within family control, family members must be groomed from an early age not just regarding the basic workings of the company but also regarding the management of foreign subsidiaries, with significant overseas experience being a must. Additionally, family firms are also advised to complement talent developed within the family by bringing in trustworthy outsiders. As an EMNC grows, it will become increasingly difficult to fill all important positions with family members, particularly when the company is also a business group involving multiple business lines that may require different skill sets to effectively manage. Bringing in outside talent may be a must to succeed in this setting.

Fourth, as EMNCs are more prone to have operations located in politically unstable markets, corporate governance policies must address contingencies associated with contentious political settings. This may include the development of talent with specific expertise in handling crises such as those plaguing Russian firms in Ukraine. While such unexpected issues may be difficult to avoid completely when firms operate in such markets, putting steps in place to minimize problems when they occur will aid a firm in overcoming such obstacles. Luckily, many EMNCs have significant experience they can apply in politically unstable markets stemming from recent institutional changes in their own markets.[47] A governance structure that enables the firm to harness this experience when needed is crucial.

7.6 CLOSING CASE: ZTE

In its vision statement, ZTE, China's leading manufacturer of telecommunications equipment, aimed to be "a global communications leader, which provides the clients worldwide with satisfying and customized products and services, to become a world-class excellent enterprise."[48] In accordance with this, and depending on local circumstances, subsidiaries played different roles: some emphasized sales, some took advantage of local resources to build factories, and some concentrated on innovation and R&D. Some of ZTE's overseas projects were doomed to experience financial loss but nevertheless had huge strategic value. In these cases, the subsidiaries did not want to be penalized for supporting an overall company strategic goal that had negative performance implications at the individual subsidiary level. In the end, the company president made the decision to bear the costs of such strategic investment.[49] This illustrates the importance of establishing clear relationships between HQ and subsidiaries and understanding the role of each subsidiary not only as a standalone unit but also as part of broader corporate strategy.

A more specific example of the multiple roles of subsidiaries in ZTE occurred in the African market. In order to serve local customers better and reduce market costs and risks, the company built several overseas offices and maintenance departments that employed local technicians and marketing personnel.[50] However, in addition to these offices, in 2007, ZTE, together with the Algerian Ministry of Posts and Telecommunications, also cofounded the North Africa Training Academy at Algeria Entreprise Nationale de Travaux aux Puits (ENPT) University. Associated with the training academy were a number of English–French teachers who taught employees how to build win–win models with key clients.[51] By developing different types of units in the local environment, each fulfilling a complementary role, the company was able to serve the market better.

7.7 CONCLUSIONS

Following expansion overseas, there are inherent issues about the relationship of a subsidiary with its parent company. These should be borne in mind throughout the process leading up to investment; however, they become paramount once the subsidiary becomes operational. In this chapter, we examined these issues as they relate to identifying the mandate or mission of the local operation, structuring the relationship of the local operation with HQ to allow effective governance and control, establishing mechanisms to effectively integrate between the HQ and subsidiary and among the firm's broader subsidiary network, and working to overcome issues related to corporate governance problems.

This chapter provided examples of these issues while advocating some potential solutions. We note the importance of clearly defining a subsidiary's mission while also clearly stating the role HQ will play in the operation of the subsidiary. Regarding the lack of effective governance and control, we advocate the establishment of scalable organizational structures and adopting international standards and best practices. Lenovo and Jollibee provide examples of firms that have overcome issues related to subsidiary mandates and governance.

Regarding difficulties in knowledge transfer, firms need to pursue efforts to make the tacit knowledge of the firm explicit and also structure the integration of the subsidiary to allow knowledge flow. Firms must also develop communication and organizational learning capabilities. Russian company CTP is an example of an EMNC that has made effective strides in this area.

Overall, this chapter reviews some of the difficulties EMNCs face in integrating their overseas subsidiaries into the HQ organization. In the next chapter, we move on to discuss operation-related difficulties associated with firm expansion once operations have been established in a market and integrated into the firm.

Notes

1. Statista (2014).
2. Anon (2012a).
3. Haier (2011).
4. Li, Y. F. (2010).
5. Li, Y. F. (2010).
6. Filippov (2010).
7. McGinley (2012).
8. Saleem (2010).
9. Raj (2013).
10. Hu, W. and Li, Y. (2013).
11. Ziyan (2013).
12. Ziyan (2013).

13. Ziyan (2013).
14. Shleifer and Vishny (1997).
15. Luo and Tung (2007), p. 494.
16. Wembridge, Milne, and Belton (2012).
17. Anon (2004).
18. Cuervo-Cazurra et al. (2014).
19. Nölke (2014).
20. Ciravegna, Fitzgerald, and Kundu (2014).
21. Zhiguo (2012).
22. Bartlett (2001).
23. Khanna and Yafeh (2007).
24. Garg and Delios (2007).
25. Panibratov and Kalotay (2009).
26. Grätz (2014).
27. CIEP (2014).
28. CIEP (2014).
29. Chazan (2014).
30. Reuters (2014).
31. Kolyandr and Ostroukh (2014).
32. Kolyandr and Ostroukh (2014).
33. Anon (2011a).
34. Anon (2012c).
35. Coronel (2011).
36. ZTE (2013).
37. Siekierska (2013).
38. Siekierska (2013).
39. Skolkovo (2009).
40. Skolkovo (2009).
41. Bartlett (2001).
42. Stahl and Koster (2013).
43. Quelch and Knoop (2007).
44. Stahl and Koster (2013).
45. Skolkovo (2009).
46. Jain, Kundu, and Newburry (2015).
47. del Sol and Kogan (2007).
48. ZTE (2014).
49. Sun, J. X. (2012).
50. Cai, Q. (2004).
51. Du, J. (2007)

8 Expansion

8.1 INTRODUCTION

In this chapter, we examine the final process issue of our operational difficulties framework related to EMNC expansion. After managers of EMNCs overcome the hurdles associated with establishing operations in foreign countries and integrating these operations into the overall corporation, they must attempt to build upon the initial investments by identifying new business opportunities in the local country and the competitive advantages they can use to pursue them. They may also attempt to build upon MNC networks to identify new business opportunities outside the country that can be served from the local operation and identify advantages that can be used to set up new business operations outside the country in coordination with other subsidiaries. By pursuing these activities, EMNCs may be able to consolidate and supplement their initial investments within a country to develop synergies and a stronger overall presence.

As we have seen in previous chapters, there are differences in institutionalized expectations about organizational practices between developing country home markets and developed country host markets, and EMNCs have relatively little experience operating in these markets to guide them in incorporating local practices into their subsidiary operations. While these issues may be present in any MNC, for EMNCs with operations in developed countries, the possibilities for differences in such role expectations and the need to develop abilities to reconcile them are exponentially higher. In this chapter, we review operational difficulties associated with EMNC expansion, focusing particularly on issues related to learning and innovation and expanding EMNC competencies. We begin our exploration with the case of Tata Motors and its efforts to expand geographically as well as into higher-level automobile categories.

8.2 OPENING CASE: TATA MOTORS

Tata Motors is an Indian car company with manufacturing subsidiaries in Argentina, South Africa, Thailand, and the United Kingdom and research and development (R&D) operations in South Korea, Spain, and the United Kingdom. The company had revenues of US$38.6 billion and 66,000 employees in 2014. While Tata had initial success in investing overseas, these investments did not significantly improve the company's reputation, and Tata was primarily seen as a manufacturer of low-cost automobiles, the most notable being the Tata Nano launched in 2009. Partly as a way to combat this, Tata Motors acquired the British brands Jaguar and Land Rover from the US automaker Ford Motor Company in 2008.[1] This highly reported acquisition emphatically announced Tata's entry into a luxury level of automobiles based on the status of the long-standing Jaguar and Land Rover automobile brands.[2] The aim of the acquisition was to expand the scope of the company and its subsidiary network to include a broader range of car brand levels.

While the acquisition certainly made headlines, it was not without its difficulties, which were compounded by the global financial crisis that occurred shortly afterward. The acquisition was made possible by the fact that Jaguar Land Rover had been performing poorly under Ford ownership, although analysts suggested that Tata overpaid for the company.[3] However, Tata did not have significant prior experience in luxury cars, and the firm's ability to manage and improve the performance of such an acquisition was questioned. Relatively few emerging market firms had been able to turn around a struggling acquisition from a developed market, particularly an acquisition that required a significant leap in capabilities. This also applied to another firm in the Tata Group, Tata Steel, which struggled with its purchase of the United Kingdom's Corus Steel in 2007.[4] By

November 2008, the firm had reportedly laid off 850 Jaguar/Land Rover employees, with more layoffs predicted.[5] For Tata Motors, expanding its brand scope and capabilities was proving a difficult task.

Fast forward a few years, and Jaguar/Land Rover's situation had changed significantly. As Tim Urquhart, a senior analyst at IHS Automotive in London, noted in the *New York Times*, "I think people were a bit skeptical and snobbish and maybe had some old colonial hangover. . . . If you look at Land Rover and Jaguar now, they probably have the strongest product line in their recent history if not ever."[6] However, the factors behind Tata Motors' ability to successfully upgrade and expand its capabilities, when few EMNCs had been able to do so, remained unclear. One source attributed this partially to the company's allocation of managerial autonomy to local executives in the United Kingdom.[7] However, this answer left open the question of whether Tata would be able to integrate these capabilities into other facets of its global operations. Moreover, aside from its operational issues, will Tata be able to improve the global reputation of the Tata brand from this successful acquisition? These and other expansion-related issues will be important to the company as it strives to expand and build upon its global competitive advantage in terms of geographic and product scope.

8.3 LEARNING AND INNOVATION IN MNC NETWORKS

As EMNCs continue to develop, they encounter greater opportunities to benefit from their international networks. Taking advantage of networks to build organizational capabilities is particularly important for emerging market firms, which are less likely to possess other advantages common among developed country multinationals. Integration and organizational difficulties are particularly important for EMNCs, which "can range from building effective working relationships with host country stakeholders, reconciling disparate national- and corporate-level cultures, organizing globally dispersed complex activities, to integrating home and host country operations."[8] However, most EMNCs must work to develop the ability to take advantage of international networks. EMNCs need to learn to optimize their investments, which creates the potential for role differentiation, when individual subsidiaries or units within a corporation play different roles within a country. With role differentiation also comes the potential for role conflict and ambiguity. Role conflict refers to "a situation in which the priorities of one system conflict with the priorities of other systems."[9] Role ambiguity is created when a person's role in the corporation is uncertain or vague. "[T]he process of organizational role-taking is simplest when a role consists of only one activity, is located in a single subsystem of the organization, and relates to a role-set all of whose members are in the same organizational subsystem."[10] This is not the case with roles within EMNC subsidiaries, where the risk of role conflict and role ambiguity may be particularly high, potentially hindering EMNC expansion. Here we overview several network-based challenges that EMNC subsidiaries may face in their expansion efforts.

Integrating location-based network knowledge. A primary challenge in learning from EMNC networks to facilitate expansion is leveraging location-based knowledge. Before proceeding to develop new expansion-based knowledge, it makes sense for EMNCs to harness the knowledge of their network partners, both within and external to the EMNC. In the process of their initial expansions, EMNCs commonly develop ties beyond the HQ-subsidiary relationship that can prove valuable to their future expansion efforts. These may include internal ties within the broader EMNC or external ties in their local operating environment. For example, scholars have found that Indian firms "draw on the international experience of their parental and foreign networks to build such capabilities."[11] Given that many EMNCs are relatively smaller and less globally dispersed than their advanced economy competitors, the scope of a firm's network may be particularly important because small- and medium-sized firms may not be able to benefit from size advantages. Also, firms without market power in the home country may benefit more from foreign partnerships when internationalizing, again potentially overcoming a size-based limitation.

While it is beneficial to take advantage of knowledge from an EMNC's network, it requires specific capabilities to analyze that knowledge and ascertain its applicability in other locations in which the EMNC operates. A good example of the difficulties of reconciling location-based expectations across multinational networks can be found with Chinese firm Gree Electric Appliances. Gree faces differing expectations across its operations in the Americas. The North American market expects high-quality, high-end products and high energy efficiency, while the South American market demands low-end, low-cost products. These two extremes make market development difficult for the company. The products sold in the North American market need strict certification and sampling tests, while the company requires strict cost control to meet the needs of the Latin American market, which requires very low prices. This in turn increases the risk of failed product-sampling tests. In terms of pursuit of quality, it is difficult for Gree to balance the principles of high quality and low cost.[12]

The direction of knowledge flow often begins from the HQ to the subsidiary but can later evolve to include flow from subsidiary to HQ and even between subsidiaries, as they assume increasingly important roles in the larger corporation. This may be particularly the case in EMNCs that have invested with the explicit purpose of obtaining advanced knowledge and technology that would be more difficult, costly, and time-consuming – even impossible – to develop on their own. This can be viewed as reverse diffusion, where best practices of the subsidiary are used to inform domestic operations in the home country. This trend has partially resulted in EMNCs' dissatisfaction with international joint ventures that were entered into with the goal of obtaining technical knowledge but were often unsuccessful due to the foreign company's reluctance to share core technologies. For example, while Shanghai Automotive Industry Corporation (SAIC) has international joint ventures with developed world companies GM and Volkswagen, most of the critical parts used in their joint production operations are imported. Because of this, SAIC acquired the Korean firm SsangYong in order to upgrade their technologies to include new components such as hybrid engines.[13] However, the anticipated benefits of such acquisitions can still be difficult to obtain due to the numerous obstacles created by cultural differences and the complexity of knowledge transfer. One example is seen in Russian automotive conglomerate Gorkovsky Avtomobilny Zavod (GAZ) Group's acquisition of the British LDV Group (LDV) in 2006.[14] GAZ hoped to use its acquisition of the van company to make a technological gain, enabling it to compete with higher-level competitors, but by 2009 it had abandoned the plan, citing the "specific and not very modern" design of LDV's Maxus.[15] After receiving rescue aid from the United Kingdom,[16] LDV has since been acquired by SAIC.[17]

Learning from industry clusters. Aside from learning from their network partners, EMNCs may learn from industry competitors operating in their geographic location. Network learning might also originate in informal networks as a result of locating within a cluster of firms to take advantage of others within the industry. Firm clusters and associated agglomeration effects, commonly noted in developed countries, are also present in emerging markets, such as India's Bollywood cluster for movies and the Bangalore cluster for information technology (IT).[18] However, when firms from these industries invest abroad, they will need to locate purposefully to maintain cluster advantages in other markets. Moreover, while industry clusters may benefit local players in a number of ways, they also mean much higher competition in a geographic area than an EMNC would normally experience. EMNCs locating in an industry cluster may need to develop specific skills in navigating the competitive environment.

8.4 COMPETENCY EXPANSION AND UPGRADE

While we have addressed the need for EMNCs to develop competencies to compete in foreign markets in several chapters in this book, in the context of EMNC expansion, it is worth noting that the quest for competency development does not end with the establishment of an initial foreign investment. Expanding their initial foreign investment, in terms of either geographic or product scope, requires EMNCs to expand their competency base to address the needs of their new target market(s). This may also require them to develop higher-order competencies and the ability to address their international operations with a global mind-set.

People who have the capabilities to operate in cross-national settings are often said to have a global mind-set, which has been defined as "possessing positive attitudes towards a company's global capabilities."[19] There are multiple frameworks for assessing cross-cultural competence and global mind-sets, all of which incorporate multiple dimensions, suggesting that it is difficult to attain an advanced level of intercultural competence. One framework, for example, distinguishes between psychological, social, and intellectual capital,[20] suggesting that all three are needed to operate successfully in a global environment. Another distinguishes between integration, responsiveness, and coordination expectations,[21] focusing on the types of activities common in managing global operations.

Network service. An additional element associated with the management of EMNC networks is service. Despite the efforts of many EMNCs in exploring overseas markets, they are still short of extensive service networks and capabilities to serve local customers, which may limit their expansion efforts. First, most EMNCs have not established widespread service networks in host countries. Consequently, they have difficulty in providing responsive and high-quality services to local customers. This constrains the abilities of these firms to expand, since developed country customers expect a high level of service for their purchases. Second, growing EMNCs have to serve customers from different countries, whose demands vary in line with cultural differences. This is a big challenge for most EMNCs, which have not accumulated sufficient experience to deal with varying demands.

Network overextension. While integrating networks can provide significant benefits to EMNCs, they also pose risks if the network expands too quickly without adequate support. The case of the Filipino fast-food company Jollibee illustrates this issue. One of the main company strategies in its early internationalization efforts was to "plant the flag," that is, to be the first fast-food retailer in any market it entered. In this way, it hoped to replicate the first-mover advantage that had worked extremely well in its home market of the Philippines. But the company soon learned that planting too many flags without an adequate support structure behind them resulted in a network of international franchises and subsidiaries without efficient HQ control.[22] EMNCs are noted for their rapid expansion efforts. However, expanding too quickly can create problems of failing to meet customer expectations, which ultimately hurts both a firm's profits and its long-term reputation.

Stakeholder demands. As EMNCs grow from small to midsized organizations to large multinationals, demands from their stakeholders increase, as these firms are better known and expectations of them as leaders in their industries make them symbolic targets for groups advocating for broader societal changes.[23] Additional media attention to these firms also increases awareness of these firms and their actions as they seek to expand their networks of foreign operations. Brasil Foods (BRF) provides a prototypical example of how stakeholders can influence the operations of a firm. The company faced problems from importing countries that had increased measures and trade barriers in order to protect their local producers. Case in point, the United States had very restrictive rules regarding the chicken industry, in which BRF was a global leader, and allowed only a few select countries that met its auditing standards to export to the United States. These did not include Brazil. The European Union (EU) similarly limited chicken imports to 11 countries, one of which was Brazil. It has been speculated that a "huge surplus in the US and EU chicken-production and their position in the top five global chicken-producing and the top three chicken-exporting countries may be the underlying factors behind the highly restrictive US and EU chicken markets."[24] Given the nature of animal-borne diseases such as avian and swine flu, BRF also recognized its vulnerability to future restrictive measures, even when there was no evidence of disease in its animals.[25] Overall, the BRF case illustrates how institutional differences in the regulation of an industry could adversely impact the competitiveness of emerging market firms, whose home governments are less likely to meet the generally stricter and better-enforced standards of developed countries.

The impact of stakeholder demands can also extend to a firm's suppliers. In 2011, China's textiles and clothing company Youngor was the subject of a report by the environmental group Greenpeace, which accused Youngor of working with suppliers in China that were contributing to the pollution of the Yangtze and Pearl rivers. According to the Greenpeace report, "Dirty Laundry," samples were collected from a facility belonging to the Youngor Group on the Yangtze River Delta and from the Well Dyeing Factory near the Pearl River Delta. The results showed the presence of hazardous and persistent hormone disruptor chemicals.[26] In the report, Greenpeace stated that the Youngor Group had the power to improve the environment through better control of its suppliers. Fabric and clothing manufacturing industries rely heavily on businesses with brands and suppliers. The report cited China's relative lack of national regulation or directives on restricted chemicals as one of the major causes of pollution in the industry.[27] Large companies face a big challenge when outsourcing operations, not the least of which is that the level of compliance with environmental regulations is not assured in high-risk countries.

8.5 SOLUTIONS: OVERCOMING EXPANSION-RELATED DIFFICULTIES

Some examples of EMNCs that have successfully expanded their operations can provide guidance for future EMNC efforts. We start

Table 8.1 *Solutions for addressing expansion challenges*

Issues	Actions
Learning and innovation	Develop communication and organizational learning capabilities Build environmental scanning capabilities at the HQ and subsidiary levels
	Capitalize on adaptability
	Develop network management protocols
Competency expansion	Organic and competence-based growth
	Competence upgrade and expansion
	Management of postsales service
	Stakeholder responsiveness building

with some recommendations related to innovation and learning and then discuss suggestions for harnessing and further developing EMNC networks. Table 8.1 summarizes the solutions.

Solving innovation and learning. The first set of recommendations aims to solve the problems with learning and innovation. There are several actions that managers of EMNCs can take.

First, develop communication and organizational learning capabilities. Integrating knowledge from their foreign subsidiaries into the main company also requires EMNCs to develop capabilities to incorporate acquired knowledge. Not all knowledge can be explicitly written and transmitted, and the "tacit" portion is often the most sustainable, and therefore the most valuable, element of a company's competitive advantage once obtained. However, the more tacit the knowledge, the more sophisticated these acquisitive capabilities must be, since knowledge lies in the workers themselves. Because of this, transferring tacit knowledge generally requires intensive personal interaction, like site visits and meetings, often involving lengthy stays. According to Erik Eberhardson of GAZ, two of his primary lessons from the company's integration of acquired firm LDV were the importance of "'mix[ing]' people more actively" and "pay[ing] more attention to internal communication."[28]

Transferring knowledge effectively requires firms to develop capabilities in both the home country and its subsidiaries to communicate information on the one hand and to absorb it in a way that informs company practices on the other. While knowledge transfer routines can be complex and require advanced global mind-sets and competencies, at a basic level, core issues like speaking the same language fluently or working on the basis of the same operational standards are essential capabilities for communication and eventual knowledge transfer. In certain industries, this may involve obtaining particular industry accreditations. Mikhail Bolotin, president of the Russian agricultural machinery manufacturer Concern Tractor Plants (CTP), noted, "Our engineers have solid knowledge, but they are not used to designing equipment using a modern computer-based environment – which is a basic skill for European engineers."[29]

Second, build environmental scanning capabilities at the HQ and subsidiary levels. In addition to developing management protocols, EMNCs must simultaneously develop the capability to scan their different environments for growth opportunities in order to facilitate expansion in new markets. This requires cooperation from both the local subsidiary and the HQ. The local subsidiary must develop capabilities to identify opportunities for growth in the host country or neighboring countries in the host region. The HQ must be open to receiving scanned input from the subsidiary and develop the capability to integrate these inputs with the overall company strategy. This requires the EMNC to have a global strategic mind-set.

Third, capitalize on adaptability. While EMNCs may suffer from their limited scope and experience, these characteristics can also provide benefits. If they are not constrained by a well-established network, EMNCs may find it much easier to adapt to the requirements of globalization than their more traditional MNC counterparts. As the global economy does appear to be reaching what has been referred to as a "turning point" in the twenty-first century, where numerous game-changing trends are occurring, such as the dominance of emerging markets,[30] the ability to adapt may become increasingly crucial.

EMNCs may also have a higher level of ambidexterity, which has been defined as "to be aligned and efficient in the management of today's business demands while simultaneously adaptive to changes in the environment."[31] Ambidexterity has been described as a multi-dimensional concept, based on the dimensions of co-orientation, co-competence, co-opetition, and co-evolution. The Chinese firms Sinohydro, Huawei, Hong Kong Prosperous Clean Energy Company (HPEC), and China National Petroleum Corporation (CNPC) illustrate how these four firms demonstrate the four types of ambidexterity in their international operations.[32] For example, Huawei has demonstrated co-opetition by actively collaborating with some of its global competitors, despite its reputation for aggressive competition. The company's CEO Ren Zhengfei, has gone so far as to call on employees to use the term "friendly partner" (*you ban*) to refer to competitors instead of the more competitive term "rival" (*dui shou*).[33]

More broadly, adaptability and ambidexterity capabilities can help EMNCs to gain competitive advantages. The flexibility they imply can make EMNCs more able than established firms to meet market demands.

Fourth, develop network management protocols. One important strategy for EMNCs expanding their subsidiary networks is the development of best practices and protocols for integrating new subsidiaries into the overall corporate structure. The Chinese construction equipment manufacturer Zoomlion Heavy Industries has merged with and acquired dozens of domestic and foreign enterprises since 2001. Integrating overseas resources represents a new practice in the Chinese construction machinery industry. For example, Zoomlion acquired Compagnia Italiana Forme Acciaio (CIFA), an enterprise based in Italy, in 2008. This acquisition was an important step for Zoomlion as it brought the most advanced technology into the company, making Zoomlion a pioneer in the internationalization of the industry and allowing it to maintain a leading industry position. Zoomlion's corporate culture was certainly beneficial in integrating the acquired enterprises into the company. In addition, the company employed talent with extensive acquisition experience to help solve postmerger and acquisition management problems.[34] Its continuous M&As made Zoomlion a real M&A master, enabling it to identify five basic principles for Chinese cross-border M&As: inclusiveness, sharing, responsibility, rules, and cooperation. Zhan Chunxin, chairman of Zoomlion, said, "Chinese enterprises need to not only go global but get globally involved as well. 'Going global' is more than selling products abroad, sending people abroad, and setting up plants abroad. We still need to get involved in the global industrial ecology as a world-class enterprise jointly supported by different nations, different countries, and different cultures."[35]

Another example of a company successfully managing network dynamics is Haier, China's leading consumer electronics company. On March 28, 2014, the Haier Asia International (HAI) team gathered in Osaka, Japan, where the company's senior management team announced a series of new initiatives to drive growth across the Asian region. Recently appointed CEO Yoshiaki Ito announced a range of strategic changes aiming to position HAI as one of Asia's leading enterprises. To achieve that goal, HAI has established unified marketing, sales, finance, R&D, and strategy and administration divisions, uniting resources from around Asia, and has reduced the number of job bands from more than ten to five, to ensure maximum efficiency and cooperation.[36]

HAI outlined plans to follow the "three-in-one" approach to localization (localizing R&D, manufacturing, and sales) in order to drive growth while furthering Haier Group's strategic objective of becoming a "platform-based" company adapted to the needs of the Internet age. The objective is to achieve "zero distance" between the company, its staff, suppliers, and customers and move toward building itself as a self-managed company and the market leader in its industry in the coming years.[37]

Managing competence expansion. A second set of solutions addresses the challenges of managing the expansion of competences. We propose several solutions.

First, pursue organic and competence-based growth. As we noted earlier, while the growth of many EMNCs is tremendous, it is not necessarily profitable. Recent evidence relating to more than 100,000 firms operating in the BRIC (Brazil, Russia, India, and China) countries has found that sustaining profitable growth requires "qualified sales growth (i.e., organic growth), competence-based and competence-enhancing growth, and continuous product diversification."[38] In other words, firms that want to sustain profitability over time cannot just blindly pursue increased sales but need to pursue growth opportunities that either stem from their specific firm competencies or allow the firm to improve upon its competencies in order to compete better in the future. As we have remarked in several places in this book, capable talent is in short supply for most emerging market firms, and growing beyond a firm's capabilities only deters the firm from being able to control its overseas operations.

Jollibee faced difficulties arising from the overextension of its international operations to a point where the company could not effectively manage its international franchise network. However, the company has since developed capabilities to manage these efforts better. Following its initial internationalization difficulties, Jollibee changed its strategy to focus on markets where it can achieve a minimum efficient scale in the number of franchises that can be supported by the local economy. The result is that the Jollibee chain now operates in fewer countries but generally has a deeper presence: in early 2015, the US market was leading with a total of 32 of the company's 71 Jollibee stores outside the Philippines.[39] Adding to the Jollibee brand, through acquisitions of other chains, the company managed over 541 overseas outlets, which accounted for 20 percent of the company's revenue.[40] A core component of Jollibee's strategy has been to invest in locations with a significant Filipino population, a market segment in which it could better leverage its core competencies.

However, the company's strategy expanded to include looking more to other markets with was a smaller Filipino presence, like Europe, while recognizing that it needed adequate personnel to manage them. CEO Tony Tan recently noted, "Filipinos are asking for it. And interested parties [in Europe] are asking for a joint venture or franchise. So it's a matter of internal capability and whether we have the people and support team. Right now we have not focused there yet."[41]

Second, upgrade and expand competencies. EMNC expansion often necessitates obtaining new capabilities and integrating them into the organization. These capabilities may be needed to reach new customer niches in developed markets that are already being served or to meet the needs of new geographic markets. The Tata Motors example in the introduction to this chapter illustrates how a company can acquire higher-level capabilities through the acquisition of an ongoing developed country operation in order to service a higher-level customer niche and new geographic markets that demand a higher-level product. We discussed acquisitions in detail in Chapter 4 in the context of choice of entry mode. However, acquisitions are also important as a method of upgrading capabilities for the future expansion of existing operations. It is common for EMNCs to make a series of acquisitions to continually upgrade their capabilities while expanding their geographic scope.

Third, manage postsales service. An important component of expanding a company's presence in both a single market and a broader region is building a solid reputation. In many industries, postsales service is a crucial element of this. In addition to demonstrating quality, providing strong postsales service signals that a company is committed to a market, which in turn inspires confidence among potential investors, customers, and employees that a company's expansion efforts are worthy of their support. EMNCs have developed a number of measures to serve local customers in a more responsive, effective, and satisfactory way. First, some EMNCs try to establish an extensive independent service network in host countries and promote the so-called service follows markets policy – wherever the products enter, their service will follow. For example, the Chinese heavy machinery manufacturer Sany Heavy Industry's 15 overseas parts centers, together with its overseas parts dealers, have formed a worldwide parts provision network. The company promises response within five hours for delivery of parts globally, relying on a logistics system that integrates sea, land, and air transportation. Functions of Sany's Global Customer Portal (GCP) system include online inquiry, purchase, and dynamic management of parts.[42] Second, some EMNCs form strategic alliances with local companies that have already established high-quality service networks. Illustrating this point, Chinese firm Ningbo Bird Co. Ltd. (Bird) entered into an agreement with German firm Siemens Mobile to develop after-sale service networks together. These would integrate 180 Siemens Mobile Service Centers and 450 Bird Service Centers in China while simultaneously giving Bird access to Siemens' global sales network. In addition, the partnership allowed for Bird to sell Siemens Mobile's phones throughout China, while Bird also gained access to Siemens Mobile's phone platforms in order to develop its own phones for the Chinese market.[43] Third, in order to deal with varying demands and cultural differences among global customers, some EMNCs develop multiple-nationality service teams. For instance, the cabin crew teams of many emerging market airlines include members with different nationalities. Air China, for instance, employs flight attendants from Japan, Korea, and Germany. This helps the company communicate better with global customers.

Fourth, pursue efforts to improve stakeholder responsiveness. In order to expand within host-country environments, it is generally desirable to be integrated into local networks. While a company may be able to establish an initial investment on its own in specific industries, expansion in a host market requires a greater level of embeddedness if it is to gain local support for its expansion efforts. China's chemicals and oil giant Sinochem has integrated corporate social responsibility (CSR) into its "Go Global" process. As a member of the United Nations Global Compact (UNGC), the company has made significant efforts to promote local social and economic development, build a harmonious overseas community, protect the environment, and build an image as "Responsible Sinochem, Responsible Chinese Corporate." The company's philosophy is "being friendly with and being partner of the neighbors" and "achieving win-win development," and it has explored a distinctive model to develop together with the local communities in which its projects are located. Through cultural exchange, local recruitment, local sourcing, engaging in local social welfare activities, and protecting the local environment, it strongly promotes local economic and social progress.[44]

For example, in Colombia, Sinochem Group entered into an annual contract with the nonprofit healthcare organization Healing the Children. The company also worked with the Colombian Ministry of National Social Security to purchase medical emergency vehicles for 22 communities in the Gigante oilfield area. The company has cooperated with various social organizations in constructing, reconstructing, and expanding school cafeterias and dormitories, education centers, medical stations, kindergartens, and other infrastructure projects.[45] By pursuing these efforts in Colombia and other countries where it conducts business, the company has built local support that aids its expansion efforts.

For the Chinese firm Gree's operations in Brazil, language was a natural barrier, coupled with differing social and cultural attitudes toward work, resulting in ineffective management and operations. Also, the level of protection given by Brazilian labor law was close to European levels, but the quality of labor did not match that of the United States and Europe; some employees used the law to shield slack work and troublemaking. To solve these problems, Gree adopted a localized development strategy. In addition to production workers, many middle managers were hired locally, and the Chinese in charge of supervision and management worked behind the scenes. Gree's localization strategy involved a large number of employees and structural adjustments; however, it reflected the management's philosophy of gradually moving factory and market operations closer to those of Brazilian companies.[46] In Brazil, Gree employed local economists, accountants, lawyers, and consultants, who helped develop policies and regulations to assist in the practical operation of the company, minimize mistakes, and avoid economic losses when possible.[47]

8.6 CLOSING CASE: FALABELLA AND CONSUMER CREDIT

Given strong institutional voids in the credit market in many emerging countries, consumer purchasing is often limited by a general lack of access to credit. Microfinance efforts in many emerging countries have helped a multitude of small entrepreneurs to start and maintain their businesses. However, these programs are not necessarily geared toward general consumer purchases. Company expansion in these markets is often stymied by issues related to consumer purchasing power.

S.A.C.I. Falabella is a Chilean multinational company that owns department stores, supermarkets, home improvement stores, and Banco Falabella. The company operates in Argentina, Brazil, Colombia, and Peru as well as Chile, making it one of the largest retail companies in Latin America. The company is best known for its Falabella department stores, the first of which was founded in 1889 by Salvatore Falabella, an Italian immigrant to Chile. However, Falabella really took off when it established Banco Falabella a century later and expanded into the banking industry. Banco Falabella built on an earlier initiative in the 1980s, when the company began issuing credit cards to its store customers. As Maria Soledad Martinez Peria noted, "The high penetration of the retail sector in Chile is related to the introduction of in-house credit cards. These credit cards issued by department stores became popular in Chile because they offered consumer credit, especially to the middle-income segment of the population, when the bank credit market serving this segment was still in its early stages."[48] As a result of efforts such as those of Falabella, private retailers provided 17 percent of consumer credit in Chile.[49] In 2014, the value of Falabella's financial services throughout Latin America exceeded any of its other three principal business areas (department stores, home improvement, and supermarkets).[50]

The extension of Falabella's main retail segment to include credit is a major component of the expansion of its investments throughout Latin America, where access to credit was still an issue in many economies. Falabella alone accounted for approximately 6 percent of all consumer loans in Peru.[51]

8.7 CONCLUSIONS

In this chapter, we examined issues related to EMNC expansion after local operations are established. This type of expansion requires higher-level skills and more conscious consideration of the individual roles that subsidiaries play in the overall EMNC than initial foreign investments, building on the capabilities discussed in earlier chapters.

After establishing operations in foreign countries and integrating these operations into the overall corporation, EMNCs face operational challenges related to their expansion. At this stage of their development, EMNCs attempt to build upon their initial investments by managing learning and innovation. Additionally, EMNC managers need to identify new business opportunities in the host country and leverage their networks to identify new business opportunities outside the country that can be served by the host-country subsidiary. This implies a more sophisticated strategy within a country and/or region beyond an initial investment and, as such, presents new challenges.

In this chapter, we discussed how expansion creates the potential for role differentiation of operations within a country, which in turn creates difficulties related to role ambiguity and conflict. We examined innovation and learning and then competency expansion as crucial factors that impact firm expansion efforts. With respect to innovation and learning, we recommend developing communication and organizational learning capabilities, building environmental scanning capabilities at the HQ and subsidiary levels, capitalizing on adaptability, and developing network management protocols. Firms such as Zoomlion Heavy Industries and Haier have excelled in these types of activities. Regarding competency expansion, we advocate practices such as pursuing organic and competence-based growth. Jollibee provides an example of a firm that has successfully overcome difficulties in these areas. We also identified management of postsales service networks and stakeholder responsiveness as important factors in EMNC expansion. Here Sany Heavy Industry's GCP System illustrates a firm that has overcome this obstacle.

Notes

1. Ford Motor Company (2008).
2. Chandran (2008).
3. Singh (2009).
4. Bajaj (2012).
5. Singh (2009).
6. Bajaj (2012).
7. Bajaj (2012).
8. Luo and Tung (2007), p. 494.
9. Shenkar and Zeira (1992).
10. Katz and Kahn (1978).
11. Elango and Pattnaik (2007).
12. Xiaoyan (2013).
13. Skolkovo (2009).
14. Milner (2006).
15. Skolkovo (2009).
16. Figel (2009).
17. Anon (2010).
18. See Lorenzen & Mudambi (2013).
19. Newburry, Belkin, and Ansari (2008), p. 816. See also Murtha, Lenway, and Bagozzi (1998).
20. Thunderbird (2014).
21. Murtha, Lenway, and Bagozzi (1998).
22. Bartlett (2001).
23. See, e.g., Gardberg & Newburry (2012).
24. Kingkaew (2014), p. 177.
25. Brazil Foods (2010).
26. Greenpeace (2011).
27. Greenpeace (2011).
28. Skolkovo (2009).

29. Skolkovo (2009).
30. Guillén and Ontiveros (2012).
31. Luo and Rui (2009).
32. Luo and Rui (2009).
33. Luo and Rui (2009).
34. Zoomlion (2013a), p. 18.
35. Zoomlion (2013b).
36. Haier (2014b).
37. Haier (2014b).
38. Zhou, Park, and Ungson (2013).
39. Jollibee (2015).
40. Anon (2013).
41. Anon (2013).
42. Sany (2012).
43. Lisheng (2004).
44. Sinochem (2012), p. 48.
45. Anon (2012b); Sinochem (2012).
46. Lijuan (2012).
47. Xie Chunfang, and Meng lin (2008).
48. Martinez Peria (2014).
49. Martinez Peria (2014).
50. Falabella (2014).
51. Martinez Peria (2014).

9 Conclusions

Along with the fast growth of emerging markets over the last couple of decades, there has been a surge in a new breed of global players from these countries. Their entry into the global market has disrupted the competitive landscape and presented a threat to traditional global leaders from developed countries. The sources of competitive advantage and unique capabilities of these newly emerging global challengers and leaders have been well documented in academic research and consulting reports. So far, most research on EMNCs has focused on how they differ from incumbent advanced-economy global players, especially in terms of their direction of global growth and modes of entry into selected countries. However, scant attention has been paid to the operational issues these new players face at all stages of their global expansion, from country selection to managing local growth.

Based on in-depth case studies of a large pool of EMNCs from various emerging markets, we have examined factors relating to the operational difficulties EMNCs face when they invest overseas. While there are differences specific to certain sectors and countries, we have been able to identify common elements of these operational challenges. In Chapter 2, we presented our findings in a process-oriented framework that provided the structure for our discussion of issues related to the operational challenges occurring at different stages of EMNC development. We divided these challenges into two broad sets – challenges EMNCs face as they seek to enter and start operating in a foreign country and challenges managers face once the firm has established operations overseas. In Chapters 3 to 8, we systematically reviewed these issues with the aim of producing more operationally successful EMNCs. In this concluding chapter, we summarize some key lessons and our final thoughts on managing successful EMNC operations. Each of the companies we have discussed experienced particular challenges in moving abroad, some of which detracted from their ability to benefit from the perceived advantages and opportunities of internationalization, due to resource, capability, and environmental issues. Nevertheless, we can distill some lessons from the analysis of these firms that will be useful to managers of emerging market firms that are considering taking their companies abroad.

First, it is important to consider the country of origin. Operating in emerging markets provides many comparative advantages, including lower labor costs, underdeveloped natural resources, and new, young consumers, which provide a base for continuous growth. However, these countries can also constrain the ability of firms to expand abroad because they have comparative disadvantages in the form of higher costs of capital, less sophisticated consumers, or weaker protection of intellectual property (IP), which limit their ability to create sophisticated resources and capabilities. This double-edged sword results in particular patterns of international expansion. On the one hand, the comparative advantages provide firms with the ability to grow and hone their abilities to serve customers in other countries. On the other, the comparative disadvantages may not only limit their international competitiveness but in some cases also may even induce firms to escape the underdeveloped conditions of the home country and expand abroad in search of more nurturing environments.

Second, as firms consider going abroad, they need to identify not only their sources of competitive advantage but also their sources of competitive disadvantage and the resources they lack. Most of the current analyses of EMNCs focus on identifying their sources of competitive advantage but neglect to examine possible sources of disadvantage. The result is a bias in the recommendations provided. Managers are well informed about how to hone the advantages of their firms but in many cases may not be able to compensate for sources of disadvantage or the lack of complementary resources. The latter are relatively easy to solve and address; by dealing with them, the manager can ensure a higher likelihood of success abroad at relatively lower costs.

Third, in this book we provide the process view of internationalization (see Figure 2.1). Most analyses of internationalization discuss different options as discrete choices. Here we have taken a process approach in which we present a series of interconnected decisions that can help facilitate not only the analysis but also the solution of the challenges that EMNCs may face abroad. Although many of the steps proposed here are implicitly taken by managers of EMNCs when considering the expansion of their firms abroad, we provide a logical sequence that can help improve analysis and decision making. While the book provides detailed discussions of challenges and solutions in each stage, it should be pointed out that the nature of issues and responses in each stage is not necessarily independent of decisions in prior stages of the process. How EMNCs enter and establish an initial operation in foreign markets will affect the nature and extent of the challenges they face in subsequent stages of local operation and growth.

Fourth, there should also be caution about firm-specific issues. This book provides discussions of managerial decisions in which we not only identify the challenges that companies have faced but also provide specific recommendations for dealing with them. It is a given that the particular characteristics of a firm will affect the problems it faces and its corresponding responses. However, this does not mean that managers cannot learn from the experiences and lessons of other companies. A detailed analysis of the experiences of other firms can provide inspiration and guidance for making better decisions that improve the likelihood of success in managing EMNC growth.

Fifth, industries differ systematically across emerging markets and affect the internationalization of firms. The examples we give suggest that there are also patterns across industries, with natural resource-based industries differing from manufacturing industries. For example, in China, EMNCs are more likely to have grown through manufacturing; in India, growth has often been seen in the information technology (IT) and pharmaceuticals industries; and in Brazil and Russia, natural resources have often been the main catalyst for EMNC growth. These factors may in turn influence the types of capabilities developed by EMNCs and, ultimately, the degree to which they face operational difficulties in foreign host countries due to the lack of appropriate capabilities to manage operations in their chosen markets.

Sixth, building on these points, our discussion illustrates that operational difficulties faced by EMNCs at different stages in the process of EMNC internationalization have interconnected multilevel influences. While it is common to think of operational issues as being associated with the firm, we illustrate through the examples in this book how home- and host-country-level factors and industry-level factors contribute to the operational difficulties of firms. With respect to operational difficulties, we explain that EMNCs are not monolithic and that these issues need to be examined as a collection of influences that interact at multiple levels. This requires managers to develop the ability to consider influences as part of a system.

Figure 9.1 illustrates the multilevel nature of influences on EMNC operational difficulties. While the figure generally shows a downward flow of influences from country to industry to firm, it should be noted that this might not always be the case. For example, firms that experience operational difficulties in one market might learn from these efforts, prompting the firms to develop additional capabilities for use in future international growth. Thus, a company like Haier has learned from its early investment difficulties to develop capabilities that can be used in other markets. Similarly, a country that observes multiple firms experiencing difficulties overseas might pursue country-level actions to assist them. A noticeable trend in this area is the increasing number of countries working to develop their country brands, which ultimately helps change the reputations of firms from these countries as they operate overseas.

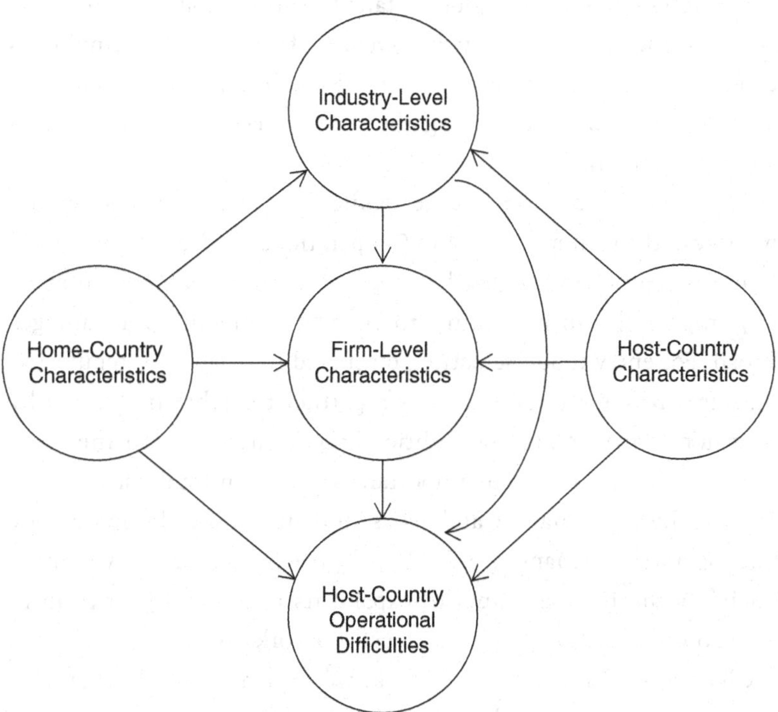

FIGURE 9.1 Multilevel influences on host-country operational difficulties

The multilevel sources of operational challenges are also reinforced by the country-specific issues in EMNCs' home and host countries. There are general patterns of variance across emerging markets that might largely be traced to country differences in patterns of resources, government policies, culture, and institutions that either promote or hinder certain industries and formulate specific types of firm capabilities. For example, Chinese culture and current government policies have long supported educational efforts, which may help EMNCs in China to overcome the operational issues associated with training and international management skills that we note in several chapters in this book.

ManpowerGroup's 2014 global talent survey found China (at 24 percent) well below the global average of 36 percent of employers reporting difficulties filling jobs, whereas both India (64 percent) and Brazil (63 percent) were among the top five countries where firms report this difficulty.[1]

Finally, reputation and recognition in the host market are important throughout the EMNC operational process. This starts from the selection of country discussed in Chapter 3, where reputation may impact the firm's ability to transfer competitive advantages abroad. For entry mode selection, discussed in Chapter 4, reputation impacts a firm's attractiveness as a partner for other firms, and by extension, entry mode possibilities become available to the firm. Reputation continues to be important as the firm establishes operations in the local market and seeks to demonstrate the legitimacy of its operations (Chapters 5–7). This legitimacy becomes even more crucial as the firm attempts to expand its operations in a country or region and needs to rely on local networks to do so, as shown in Chapter 8. Throughout this book, we present multiple examples of firm activities geared toward increasing their reputation and legitimacy.

9.1 MOVING FORWARD

While the EMNCs highlighted in this book have all gone through a process of internationalization, it is important to remain aware that these companies will continue to evolve to address even more complex operational issues, while other companies from the same markets will address issues at earlier stages of the EMNC process as their economies become even more global.

Additionally, while firms continue their path of internationalization, so do countries, so the home countries of the major EMNCs highlighted in the book may evolve past the point of being considered emerging and become advanced economies, as has happened to countries like South Korea and Singapore. In their place, new countries will continue to enter the emerging market category.

Multiple classifications of these countries have developed, such as the CIVETS (Colombia, Indonesia, Vietnam, Egypt, Turkey, and South Africa) or MINT (Mexico, Indonesia, Nigeria, and Turkey) countries. These countries may benefit from the lessons learned by earlier EMNCs.

EMNC foreign investment decisions are complex endeavors. While operational difficulties are only one component of the overall EMNC picture, it is nonetheless a critical one, which has been largely ignored in previous studies. EMNCs must continually build upon their existing capabilities. Initial operational capabilities transferred from their home-country operations will not be enough to succeed in new host countries. Additional capabilities need to be constantly added as EMNCs proceed through the growth phases overseas to enable them to prosper and sustain profitable growth in the host market and region. In this book, we demonstrate a hierarchy of skill sets that EMNCs need to develop and provide guidance for the future planning of operations. By focusing attention on this important EMNC component and illustrating its manifestation throughout the EMNC investment and operational process, we hope to have provided useful guidance for managers and academics alike.

Note

1. ManpowerGroup (2014).

References

Ahrens, N., and Zhou, Y. 2013. *China's Competitiveness: Myth, Reality, and Lessons for the United States and Japan. Case Study: Lenovo*. Washington, DC: Center for Strategic and International Studies.

Aguilera, R. V., & Jackson, G. 2003. The cross-national diversity of corporate governance: Dimensions and determinants. *Academy of Management Review*, 28(3): 447–465.

Agtmael, A. V. 2007. *The Emerging Markets Century: How a New Breed of World-Class Companies Is Overtaking the World*. New York: Free Press.

AJE. 2014. About AJE. www.ajegroup.com/about-aje/ (accessed December 3, 2014).

Allam, A. 2003. Making near beer acceptable in Near East. *New York Times*, January 4. www.nytimes.com/2003/01/04/business/international-business-making-near-beer-acceptable-in-near-east.html (accessed November 27, 2014).

Amado, G., & Brasil, H. V. 1991. Organizational behaviors and cultural context: The Brazilian "jeitinho." *International Studies of Management and Organization*, 21(3): 38–e.

Anholt, S. 2003. *Brand New Justice: How Branding Places and Products Can Help the Developing World*. Oxford: Butterworth Heinemann.

Anon. 2004. Telenor and Alpha face off in the Vimpelcom boardroom. TeleGeography.com. www.telegeography.com/products/commsupdate/articles/2005/04/14/telenor-and-alfa-face-off-in-the-vimpelcom-boardroom/ (accessed May 22, 2015).

Anon. 2006. The Huawei Way. Newsweek. January 15. http://www.newsweek.com/huawei-way-108201 (accessed January 2, 2016).

Anon. 2009. Bimbo Bakeries workers vote overwhelmingly to join Teamsters. PR Newswire. April 21. http://www.prnewswire.com/news-releases/bimbo-bakeries-workers-vote-overwhelmingly-to-join-teamsters-61898537.html (accessed January 1, 2016).

Anon. 2010. SAIC to resurrect LDV Maxus. ChinaAutoWeb, August 15. http://chinaautoweb.com/2010/08/saic-to-resurrect-ldv-maxus/ (accessed February 25, 2015).

Anon. 2011a. Brazil's oil boom: Filling up the future. *The Economist*, November 5. www.economist.com/node/21536570 (accessed December 30, 2014).

Anon. 2011b. China Inc's succession problem: Entrepreneurs unsure if children can cope with business model demands. *The Economic Times*. http://articles.economictimes.indiatimes.com/2011–04-24/news/29466852_1_youngor-entrepreneurs-enterprises (accessed July 29, 2014).

Anon. 2011c. China's mighty telecom footprint in Africa. www.newsecuritylearning.com/index.php/archive/75-chinas-mighty-telecom-footprint-in-africa (accessed November 11, 2014).

Anon. 2011d. The Chinese in Africa: Trying to pull together. *The Economist*, April 20. www.economist.com/node/18586448 (accessed March 14, 2015).

Anon. 2012a. Haier completes SANYO acquisition in Southeast Asia. *PR Newswire*, March 31. www.prnewswire.com/news-releases/haier-completes-sanyo-acquisition-in-southeast-asia-145305625.html (accessed December 7, 2014).

Anon. 2012b. Sinochem Group: Actively fulfilling social responsibilities and promoting local development in "going global" process. December 12. http://english.sinochem.com/g1007/s1771/t7798.aspx (accessed February 20, 2015).

Anon. 2012c. Venezuela's oil industry: Up in smoke. *The Economist*, August 27. www.economist.com/blogs/americasview/2012/08/venezuelas-oil-industry (accessed December 30, 2014).

Anon. 2013. Billionaire Tony Tan Caktiong takes Jollibee Foods global. Forbes Asia. January 30. http://www.forbes.com/sites/forbesasia/2013/01/30/billionaire-tony-tan-caktiong-takes-jollibee-foods-global/#4cb29bf717d5 (accessed March 4, 2015).

Antonioli, S. 2014. UPDATE 2: Rio Tinto sues Vale, Steinmetz, BSGR over Guinea iron deposit rights. *Reuters*, April 30. www.reuters.com/article/2014/04/30/rio-tinto-guinea-idUSL6N0NM66Q20140430 (accessed November 27, 2014).

Ao, X. F., Liang, L., & Gao, L. 2012. Huawei and ZTE face barriers in their expansion to the States, *Chongqing Economic Times*, October 10. http://business.sohu.com/20121010/n354540799.shtml (accessed October 19, 2015).

Arab News. 2014. Sinopec remains strong because of strong values. www.arabnews.com/news/637991 October 1. (accessed February 20, 2015).

Aulakh, P. S. 2007. Emerging multinationals from developing economies: Motivations, paths, and performance. *Journal of International Management*, 13: 338–355.

Backaler, H. 2010. Haier: A Chinese company that innovates. *Forbes*, June 17. www.forbes.com/sites/china/2010/06/17/haier-a-chinese-company-that-innovates/ (accessed May 17, 2015).

Bajaj, V. 2012. Tata Motors finds success in Jaguar Land Rover. *New York Times*, August 30. www.nytimes.com/2012/08/31/business/global/tata-motors-finds-success-in-jaguar-land-rover.html?pagewanted=all&_r=0 (accessed December 13, 2014).

Ballon, M. 2002. Jollibee struggling to expand in U.S. *Los Angeles Times*, September 16. http://articles.latimes.com/2002/sep/16/business/fi-jollibee16. (accessed February 20, 2014).

Barchfield, J. 2012. At 50, Havaianas flip-flops are symbol of Brazil. *Seattle Times*, July 24. http://seattletimes.com/html/nationworld/2018758962_apltbrazilhalf centuryofhavaianas.html. (accessed September 13, 2015).

Barkema, H. G., & Schijven, M. 2008. How do firms learn to make acquisitions? A review of past research and an agenda for the future. *Journal of Management*, 34: 594–634.

Barney, J. B. 1991. Firm resources and sustained competitive advantage. *Journal of Management*, 17: 99–120.

Barney, J. B. 1999. How a firm's capabilities affect boundary decisions. *Sloan Management Review*, 40(3): 137–145.

Barone, A. 1996. Lowe helps Titan stand out in crowded watch market. *Advertising Age*, October 14, A3.

Barros de Castro, A. 2011. Entrevista com Siegfried Kreutzfeld, director Superintendente da WEG Motores (Interview with Siegfried Kreutzfeld, CEO of WEG Motores). Conselho Empresarial Brasil-China, Carta Brasil-China, Edição 2, Agosto www.cebc.org.br/sites/default/files/entrevista_siegfried_0.pdf. (accessed September 13, 2015).

Bartlett, C. A. 2001. *Jollibee Foods Corporation (A): International Expansion*. Harvard Business School Case 9-399-007 (revised December 17).

Bartlett, C. A., & Ghoshal, S. 1989. *Managing Across Borders: The Transnational Solution*. Boston, MA: Harvard Business School Press.

Basdeo, D. K., Smith, K. G., Grimm, C. M., Rindova, V. P., & Derfus, P. J. 2006. The impact of market actions on firm reputation. *Strategic Management Journal*, 27: 1205–1219;

BBCNews. 2001. Britons face lash in Saudi Arabia. BBCNews, May 31. http://news.bbc.co.uk/2/hi/uk_news/1363200.stm (accessed November 27, 2014).

BBCNews. 2004. Has TV changed Bhutan? BBCNews, June 17. http://news.bbc.co.uk/2/hi/entertainment/3812275.stm (accessed May 17, 2015).

BCG. 2014. Redefining global competitive dynamics. *2014 BCG Global Challengers*. Boston, MA: Boston Consulting Group.

Becker, M. C. 2004. Organizational routines: A review of the literature. *Industrial and Corporate Change*, 13(4): 643–677.

Beisecker, R. 2006. DP World and U.S. port security. *NTI*, March 1. www.nti.org/analysis/articles/dp-world-and-us-port-security/ (accessed September 13, 2014).

Bilkey, W. J., & Tesar, G. 1977. The export behavior of smaller Wisconsin manufacturing firms. *Journal of International Business Studies*, 9: 93–98.

Birkinshaw, J., Hood, N., & Jonsson, S. 1998. Building firm-specific advantages in multinational corporations: The role of subsidiary initiative. *Strategic Management Journal*, 19: 221–241.

Bland, B. 2014. Drinks groups lose some fizz in Indonesia. *Financial Times*, November 5. www.ft.com/intl/cms/s/0/b2eafa70-601a-11e4-98e6-00144feabdc0.html#axzz3Klf8RLRU.

Bland, B., & Schipani, A. 2014. Peruvian upstart AJE takes on Coke and Pepsi in Asia. *Financial Times*, July 21. www.ft.com/intl/cms/s/0/dd0e0c00-0cf2-11e4-bf1e-00144feabdc0.html#axzz3Gi4SxEAK.

Brazil Foods. 2010. U.S. Securities and Exchange Commission Form 20-F for BRF – Brazil Foods S.A., fiscal year ending December 31, 2010.

Bruton, H. 1998. A reconsideration of import-substitution, *Journal of Economic Literature*, 37 (2).

Burgis, T. 2014. Timeline: The battle for Simandou. *Financial Times*, November 26. http://ig.ft.com/sites/2014/guinea-timeline/ (accessed November 27, 2014).

Cai, Q. 2004. ZTE's oversea expansion strategy shows effects in Africa. *Communications Weekly*, May 17, 2004.

Capron, L., & Mitchell, L. 2012. *Build, Borrow, or Buy: Solving the Growth Dilemma*. Boston, MA: Harvard Business School Press.

Casanova, L. 2009. *Global Latinas: Latin America's Emerging Multinationals*. France: Insead Business Press.

Cavusgil, T. S. 1980. On the internationalization process of firms. *European Research*, 8: 273–281.

Chandran, R. 2008. Tata Motors completes acquisition of Jag, Land Rover. *Reuters*, June 2. www.reuters.com/article/2008/06/02/us-tata-jaguar-idUSBMA00084220080602 (accessed December 13, 2014).

Chattopadhyay, A., Batra, R., & Ozsomer, A. 2012. *The New Emerging Market Multinationals: Four Strategies for Disrupting Markets and Building Brands*. New York: McGraw-Hill.

Chazan, G. 2014. Gazprom faces EU antitrust charge threat. *Financial Times*, February 7. www.ft.com/intl/cms/s/0/e42946bc-8fed-11e3-aee9-00144feab7de.html#axzz3NDAG7w7T (accessed December 28, 2014).

Chen, D., Newburry, W., & Park, S. H. 2010. Operational challenges facing emerging multinationals: a study of multinationals from China, Russia and Brazil. Paper presented at the Strategic Management Society Annual Meeting, Rome.

Chen, D., Park, S. H., & Newburry, W. 2009. Parent contribution and organizational control in international joint ventures. *Strategic Management Journal*, 30(11): 1133–1156.

Chen, X. 2013. Huawei's "diplomatic card." *Tencent Technology*, October 12. http://tech.qq.com/a/20131013/001392.htm (accessed October 19, 2015).

Chen, Z., Hu, R., Yu, D., Chenzhong, X., & Liang, D. 2009. Cultural collision sends carmakers reeling. *Caijing Magazine*, February 25. http://english.caijing.com.cn/2009–02-25/110073536.html. (accessed November 27, 2014).

Chosun Nilbo. 2009. SAIC's takeover of SsangYong was simple theft. *Chosun Nilbo*, November 12. http://english.chosun.com/site/data/html_dir/2009/11/12/2009111200904.html (accessed November 27, 2014).

CIEP. 2014. Russian Gas Imports to Europe and Security of Supply – Factsheet. Clingendael International Energy Programme (CIEP). www.clingendaelenergy.com/files.cfm?event=files.download&ui=9C1DEEC1-5254-00CF-FD03186604989704 (accessed December 28, 2014).

Ciravegna, L., Fitzgerald, R., & Kundu, S. K. 2014. *Operating in Emerging Markets*. Upper Saddle River, NJ: FT Press.

CITGO. 2015. CITGO-Venezuela Heading Oil Program. www.citgoheatingoil.com/about-programoverview.html (accessed February 20, 2014).

Coronel, G. 2011. A crime of passion – Chavez destroys Venezuela's Citgo. *Latin American Herald Tribune*, November 28. www.cato.org/publications/commentary/crime-passion-chavez-destroys-venezuelas-citgo (accessed March 14, 2015).

Cuervo-Cazurra, A. 2012. How the analysis of developing country multinational companies helps advance theory: Solving the Goldilocks debate. *Global Strategy Journal*, 2: 153–167.

Cuervo-Cazurra, A., & Genc, M., 2008. Transforming disadvantages into advantages: Developing – country MNEs in the least developed countries. *Journal of International Business Studies*, 39: 957–979.

Cuervo-Cazurra, A., Maloney, M., & Manrakhan, S. 2007. Causes of the difficulties in internationalization. *Journal of International Business Studies*, 38(6): 709–725.

Cuervo-Cazurra, A., & Montoya, M. A. 2014. Building Chinese cars in Mexico: The Grupo Salinas–FAW alliance. *Innovar*, 24(54), 219–230.

Cuervo-Cazurra, A., Inkpen, A., Musacchio, A., & Ramaswamy, K. 2014. Governments as owners: State-owned multinational companies. *Journal of International Business Studies*, 45: 919–942.

Cuervo-Cazurra, A., Narula, R., & Un, C. A. 2015. Internationalization motives: Sell more, buy better, upgrade and escape. *Multinational Business Review*, 23: 25–35.

Cuervo-Cazurra, A., & Ramamurti, R. (Eds). 2014. *Understanding Multinationals from Emerging Markets*. Cambridge University Press.

Cuervo-Cazurra, A., & Un, A. 2007. Types of difficulties in internationalization and their consequences. In: Tallman, S. (Ed.), *A New Generation in International Strategic Management*. Northampton, MA: Edward Elgar, pp. 63–83.

Czinkota, M. R. 1982. *Export Development Strategies: US Promotion Policies.* New York: Praeger.

Donaldson, T. 1996. Values in tension: Ethics away from home. *Harvard Business Review,* 74(5), 48–56.

Downie, A. 2010. South American neighbours living worlds apart. *Financial Times,* November 22. www.ft.com/intl/cms/s/2/62a2bdec-f655-11df-846a-00144feab49a.html#axzz3Klf8RLRU (accessed September 13, 2015).

Doz, Y. L., Santos, J., & Williamson, P. J. 2001. *From Global to Metanational: How Companies Win in the Knowledge Economy.* Boston, MA: Harvard Business School Press.

Du, J. 2007. ZTE searches for "win-win" models in oversea markets. *Communications World Weekly,* January 31. www.c114.net/news/127/a107101.html (accessed October 19, 2015).

Dunning, J. H. 1993. *Multinational Enterprises and the Global Economy.* New York: Addison-Wesley.

Duysters, G., Jacob, J., Lemmens, C., & Yu, J. 2009. Internationalization and technological catching up of emerging multinationals: A comparative case study of China's Haier group. *Industrial and Corporate Change,* 18(2): 325–349.

Ebenkamp, B. 2007. Jollibee is on fast (food) track in virgin markets. *Brandweek,* 48(41): 14.

Economist. 2001. The Cemex way. *Economist,* June 14. www.economist.com/node/655858 (accessed November 27, 2014).

Economist. 2005. Gerdau Ameristeel halts operations at Beaumont steel mill pending labor agreement. PR Newswire, May 26. www.prnewswire.com/news-releases/gerdau-ameristeel-halts-operations-at-beaumont-steel-mill-pending-labor-agreement-54533567.html (accessed February 20, 2015).

Economist. 2006a. Heading for the exit. *The Economist,* August 3. www.economist.com/node/7253227 (accessed November 27, 2014).

Economist. 2006b. Crashing prices make TV-set manufacture a horrible business to be in. *Economist,* November 2. www.economist.com/node/8119231.

Economist. 2007. ZTE opens training academy at Algerian university. Telcompaper, January 31. www.telecompaper.com/news/zte-opens-training-academy-at-algerian-university–544180 (accessed 29 July 2014).

Economist. 2008. Emerging-market multinationals: The challengers. *The Economist,* January 10. www.economist.com/node/10496684 (accessed September 13, 2014).

Economist. 2012b. Who's afraid of Huawei? *The Economist,* April 4. Accessed from online edition at: www.economist.com/node/21559922 (accessed September 13, 2015).

Economist. 2013a. Ready-mixed fortunes. *Economist*, June 22. www.economist.com/news/business/21579844-worlds-cement-giants-look-set-recoverybut-will-it-be-durable-ready-mixed-fortunes (accessed November 27, 2014).

Economist. 2013b. Why are sales of non-alcoholic beer booming? *Economist*, August 11. www.economist.com/blogs/economist-explains/2013/08/economist-explains-3 (accessed November 27, 2014).

Economist. 2015. Missing the target. *The Economist*, January 16. www.economist.com/news/business-and-finance/21639887-exit-discount-store-offers-cautionary-tale-foreigners-trying-enter-canadian (accessed May 16, 2015).

Eden, L., & Miller, S. R. 2004. Distance matters: Liability of foreignness, institutional distance and ownership. *Advances in International Management*, 16: 187–221.

Einhorn, B., Mayeda, A., & Argitis, T. 2014. China's Huawei, unwelcome in the U.S., finds favor in Canada. BloombergBusinessweek, August 7. www.businessweek.com/articles/2014–08-07/chinas-huawei-finds-favor-in-canada-amid-u-dot-s-dot-rejection (accessed February 20, 2015).

Elango, B., & Pattnaik, C. 2007. Building capabilities for international operations through networks: A study of Indian firms. *Journal of International Business Studies*, 38: 541–555.

Elvira, M. M., & Davila, A., 2005. Emergent directions – HRM in Latin America. In: Elvira, M. M., & Davila, A. (Eds.), *Managing Human Resources in Latin America* London: Routledge, pp. 235–252.

Falabella. 2014. Fact Sheet SACI. www.falabella.com/static/staticContent/content/minisitios/Inversionistas/images/contenidoDescargable/presentaciones/2014/Fact_Sheet_Falabella_2Q2014.pdf (accessed December 14, 2014).

Figel, J. 2009. State aid NN 41/2009 (ex N 313 / 2009) – United Kingdom Rescue Aid for LDV Group Limited. Correspondence dated August 7. http://ec.europa .eu/competition/state_aid/cases/232269/232269_983777_18_2.pdf (accessed February 25, 2015).

Filippov, S. 2010. Russian companies: The rise of new multinationals. *International Journal of Emerging Markets*, 5(3/4): 307–332.

Fleury, A., & Fleury, M. T. L. 2011. *Brazilian Multinationals: Competences for Internationalization*. Cambridge University Press.

Fombrun, C. J. 1996. *Reputation: Realizing Value from the Corporate Image*. Boston: Harvard Business School Press.

Fombrun, C. J., Ponzi, L. J., & Newburry, W. 2015. Stakeholder tracking and analysis: The RepTrak® system for measuring corporate reputation. *Corporate Reputation Review*, 18(1): 3–24.

Fontanella-Khan, J., & Song, J. A. 2010. Mahindra close to deal with Ssangyong. *Financial Times*, August 10. www.ft.com/intl/cms/s/0/f6a9139a-a5b7-11df-a5b7-00144feabdc0.html#axzz3KUiNWsIy (accessed November 27, 2014).

Forbes. 2015. The world biggest public companies. www.forbes.com/global2000/list/#page:1_sort:0_direction:asc_search:_filter:All%20industries_filter:All%20countries_filter:All%20states (accessed October 09, 2015).

Ford Motor Company. 2008. Ford Motor Company announces agreement to sell Jaguar Land Rover to Tata Motors. Press release. http://web.archive.org/web/20080612192629/http://media.ford.com/newsroom/release_display.cfm?release=27953 (accessed December 13, 2014).

Fu, C. 2005. Letter from CNOOC to the US Congress. *Financial Times*, June 27. www.ft.com/intl/cms/s/0/7624beca-e755-11d9-a721-00000e2511c8.html#axzz33CvB3BWr. (accessed September 13, 2014).

Gammeltoft, P., Barnard, H., & Madhok, A. 2010. Emerging multinationals, emerging theory: Macro- and micro-level perspectives. *Journal of International Management*, 16: 95–101.

Gao, P. 2008. Selling China's cars to the world: An interview with Chery's CEO. *McKinsey Quarterly*, May. www.mckinsey.it/storage/first/uploadfile/attach/140151/file/seca08.pdf (p. 5) (accessed September 13, 2015).

Garg, M., & Delios, A. 2007. Survival of the foreign subsidiaries of TMNCs: The influence of business group affiliation. *Journal of International Management*, 13: 278–295

Gardberg, N. A., & Newburry, W. 2013. Who boycotts whom? Marginalization, company knowledge and strategic issues. *Business & Society*, 52(2): 318–357.

Ghemawat, P. 2001. Distance still matters. *Harvard Business Review*, 79(8): 137–145.

Ghemawat, P. 2007. Redefining global strategy: Crossing borders in a world where differences still matter. Boston, MA: Harvard Business School Press.

Ghemawat, P., Herrero, G. A., & Monteiro, L. F. 2009. *Embraer: The Global Leader in Regional Jets*. Harvard Business School Case 9–701-006.

Ghoshal, S., & Bartlett, C. A. 1990. The multinational corporation as an interorganizational network. *Academy of Management Review*, 15: 603–625.

Gianatasio, D. 2009. People wash their clothing in Barf every day. *Adweek*, June 17. www.adweek.com/adfreak/people-wash-their-clothing-barf-every-day-14028 (accessed September 13, 2015).

Goldstein, A. 2007. *Multinational Companies from Emerging Economies: Composition, Conceptualization and Direction in the Global Economy*. London: Palgrave Macmillan.

Golub, S. S. 2003. Measures of Restrictions on Inward Foreign Direct Investment for OECD Countries. Paris: OECD. www1.oecd.org/eco/growth/33638671.pdf (accessed September 13, 2014).

Grant, J., & Pearson, S. 2014. Vale inaugurates $1.4bn Malaysia port. *Financial Times*, November 7. www.ft.com/intl/cms/s/0/84073b2e-6623-11e4-898f-00144feabdc0.html?siteedition=intl#axzz3KUiNWsIy (accessed November 27, 2014).

Grätz, J. 2014. Russia's multinationals: Network state capitalism goes global. In: Nölke, A. (Ed.), *Multinational Corporations from Emerging Markets: State Capitalism 3.0*. London: Palgrave Macmillan (p. 91).

Greenpeace. 2011. Dirty laundry: Unravelling the corporate connections to toxic water pollution in China.

Great Place to Work. 2014. Best workplaces in Mexico: More than 5,000 employees 2014. http://www.greatplacetowork.net/bestworkplaces/a2480000005kC5x (accessed January 1, 2016).

Grundig, J. 2013. The costs of buying and operating an Embraer Phenom 300. July 2. www.sherpareport.com/aircraft/aircraft-overview/costs-embraer-phenom-300.html (accessed December 14, 2014).

Guerrera, F. 2005. CNOOC at odds with Congress over Unocal deal. *Financial Times*, July 26. www.ft.com/intl/cms/s/0/07ca91da-fdfc-11d9-a289-00000e2511c8.html#axzz33CvB3BWr. (accessed September 13, 2014).

Guerrera, F. and Leahy, J. 2005. CNOOC considers $13bn bid for Unocal. *Financial Times*, January 7. www.ft.com/intl/cms/s/0/4c32b332-5fed-11d9-bd2f-00000e2511c8.html?siteedition=uk#axzz3o5BNA1kM. (accessed September 13, 2014).

Guerrera, F., McNulty, S., & Kirchgaessner, S. 2005. Unocal to hold talks with CNOOC over $20bn bid. *Financial Times*, June 24. www.ft.com/intl/cms/s/0/ebef88fc-e3ee-11d9-a754-00000e2511c8.html#axzz33CvB3BWr (accessed September 13, 2014).

Guillen, M., & Carcia-Canal. 2012. *Emerging Markets Rule: Growth Strategies of the New Global Giants*. New York: McGraw-Hill.

Guillén, M. F., & García-Canal, E. 2009. The American model of the multinational firm and the "new" multinationals from emerging markets. *Academy of Management Perspectives*, 23(2): 23–35.

Guillen, M., & Garcia-Canal, E. 2012. *Emerging Markets Rule: Growth Strategies of the New Global Giants*. New York: McGraw-Hill.

Guillén, M. F., & Ontiveros, E. 2012. *Global Turning Points: Understanding the Challenges for Business in the Twenty-First Century*. Cambridge University Press.

Gupta, A. K., Pande, G., & Wang, H. 2014. *The Silk Road Rediscovered: How Indian and Chinese Companies Are Becoming Globally Stronger by Winning in Each Other's Markets*. San Francisco: Jossey-Bass.

Gupta, A. K., Wakayama, T., & Rangan, U. S. 2012. *Global Strategies for Emerging Asia*. San Francisco: Jossey-Bass.

Haier. 2011. Haier and Sanyo sign final agreement. October 18, 2011. www.haier.net/en/about_haier/news/201110/t20111028_83307.html (accessed September 13, 2014).

Haier. 2014a. About Haier. www.haier.net/en/about_haier/ (accessed December 5, 2014).

Haier. 2014b. Haier Asia International unveils new strategy. www.haier.net/en/about_haier/news/201403/t20140329_212372.shtml (accessed September 13, 2014)

Harvard Business Review. 2011. *Harvard Business Review on Thriving in Emerging Markets*. Boston, MA: Harvard Business School Press.

Hawwari, A. 2001. Getting a drink in Saudi Arabia. BBCNews, February 8. http://news .bbc.co.uk/2/hi/middle_east/1160846.stm (accessed November 27, 2014).

Hille, K. 2013. Huawei in pledge to disclose more information. Retrieved from www.ft.com/cms/s/0/4b0ab5ce-6398-11e2-84d8-00144feab49a.html#axzz2QNpOiKEs (accessed January 21, 2013).

Holden, N., & Vaiman, V. 2013. Talent management in Russia: Not so much war for talent as wariness of talent. *Critical Perspectives on International Business*, 9(1/2): 129–146 (p. 129).

Hook, L. 2013. China permits giant Valemax to dock. *Financial Times*, April 18. www.ft.com/intl/cms/s/0/ab14aba8-a7fb-11e2-b031-00144feabdc0.html#axzz3KUiNWsIy (accessed November 27, 2014).

Hook, L., & Wright, R. 2012. China blocks Vale's large iron ore carriers. *Financial Times*, January 13. www.ft.com/intl/cms/s/0/b0fa84e6-4bf6-11e1-b1b5-00144feabdc0.html#axzz2QUkjKtQ6 (accessed November 27, 2014).

Hornby, L. 2014. Vale in deal with China Merchants Group to expand large ore fleet. *Financial Times*, September 26. www.ft.com/intl/cms/s/0/dfef5f92-4590-11e4-ab10-00144feabdc0.html#axzz3KUiNWsIy (accessed November 27, 2014).

Hu, W., & Li, Y. 2013. M&A under crises. *Caijing Magazine*, December 16, 2013. http://finance.sina.com.cn/chanjing/gsnews/20131216/143217647933.shtml (accessed October 19, 2015).

Huang, Y. 2013. Fatal misperception: How unsafe is Chinese food? Asia unbound. Council on Foreign Relations, July 10. http://blogs.cfr.org/asia/2013/07/10/fatal-misperception-how-unsafe-is-chinese-food/ (accessed July 29, 2014).

Hymer, S. H. 1976/1960. *The International Operations of National Firms: A Study of Direct Foreign Investment*. Cambridge: MIT Press.

ICMR. 2006. TCL-Thomson Electronics Corporation, TCL Multimedia Technology Holdings Limited and Thomson SA. ICMR case BSTR198. www.icmrindia.org/casestudies/catalogue/Business%20Strategy/BSTR198.htm (accessed September 13, 2015).

IMF. 2011. Offshore financial centers (OFCs): IMF staff assessments. www.imf.org/external/NP/ofca/OFCA.aspx (accessed September 13, 2014).

IMF. 2013. Washington, DC: IMF. www.imf.org/external/pubs/ft/weo/2014/01/weodata/groups.htm (accessed September 13, 2013).

Iritani, E. 2005. Fostering goodwill with jobs. *Los Angeles Times*, July 31. http://articles.latimes.com/2005/jul/31/business/fi-uschina31 (accessed December 6, 2014).

Jain, N. K., Kundu, S. K., & Newburry, W. 2015. Efficiency-seeking emerging market firms: Resources and location choices. *Thunderbird International Business Review*, 57(1): 33–50.

Jamasmie, C. 2014. Valemax finally allowed at Chinese port. *Mining*, October 10. www.mining.com/valemax-finally-allowed-at-chinese-port-51195/ (accessed November 27, 2014).

Jauch, H. 2014. Chinese investments in Africa: Twenty-first century colonialism? *New Labor Forum*, May 17. http://newlaborforum.cuny.edu/2014/05/17/chinese-investments-in-africa-twenty-first-century-colonialism/ (accessed March 14, 2015).

Johanson, J., & Mattsson, L. G. 1988. Internationalization in industrial systems: A network approach. In: Hood, N., & Vahlne, J. E. (Eds.), *Strategies in Global Competition*. Croom Helm: New York.

Johanson, J., & Vahlne, J. E. 1977. The internationalization process of the firm: A model of knowledge development and increasing foreign market commitments. *Journal of International Business Studies*, 8: 23–32.

Johanson, J., & Vahlne, J. E. 2003. Business relationship learning and commitment in the internationalization process. *Journal of International Entrepreneurship*, 1: 83–101.

Johanson, J., & Vahlne, J. E. 2009. The Uppsala internationalization process model revisited: From liability of foreignness to liability of outsidership. *Journal of International Business Studies*, 40: 1411–1431.

Johanson, J., & Wiedersheim-Paul, F. 1975. The internationalization of the firm: Four Swedish case studies. *Journal of Management Studies*, 12: 305–322.

Jollibee. 2015. International. www.jollibee.com.ph/international/ (accessed February 6, 2015).

Katz, D., & Kahn, R. L. 1978. *The Social Psychology of Organizations* (2nd ed.). New York: Wiley, p. 178.

Khanna, T., & Palepu, K. G. 1997. Why focused strategies may be wrong for emerging markets. *Harvard Business Review*, 75(4): 41–51.

Khanna, T., & Palepu, K. 2010. *Winning in Emerging Markets: A Road Map for Strategy and Execution*. Boston, MA: Harvard Business School Press.

Khanna, T., & Yafeh, Y. 2007. Business Groups in Emerging Markets: Paragons or Parasites? *Journal of Economic Literature*, 45(2): 331–372.

Khanna, T., Palepu, K. G., & Sinha, J. 2005. Strategies that fit emerging markets. *Harvard Business Review*, 83(6): 63–74.

King, N., & Hitt, G. 2006. Dubai Ports World sells U.S. assets. *Wall Street Journal*, December 12. http://online.wsj.com/articles/SB116584567567746444. (accessed September 13, 2014).

Kingkaew, S. 2014. The action-reaction in the global grade: Comparing the cases of the Brazilian check and the Thai tuna industries. In: Nölke, A. (Ed.), *Multinational Corporations from Emerging Markets: State Capitalism 3.0*. London: Palgrave macmillan.

Kirchgaessner, S. 2005. "Congressional angst" scuppers Chinese bid. *Financial Times*, August 2. www.ft.com/intl/cms/s/0/838c1610-0390-11da-b54a-00000e2511c8.html#ixzz38p814Zjo (accessed September 13, 2014).

Kirchgaessner, S. 2006. White House defends ports takeover stance. *Financial Times*, Februray 19. www.ft.com/intl/cms/s/0/0b682dc4-a177-11da-9ca4-0000779e2340.html#axzz3pf1Tpavl (accessed October 26, 2015)

Kirchgaessner, S. Alden, E. and Balls, A. 2005. Washington could be obstacle to CNOOC. *Financial Times*, June 24. www.ft.com/intl/cms/s/0/51eeb3d0-e44e-11d9-a754-00000e2511c8.html#axzz33CvB3BWr (accessed September 13, 2014).

Kirchgaessner, S., & Yuk, P. 2006. Opposition mounts over P&O ports takeover. *Financial Times*, Februray 22. www.ft.com/intl/cms/s/0/138b9850-a349-11da-ba72-0000779e2340.html#axzz3pf1Tpavl (accessed October 26, 2015)

Knickerbocker, F. T. 1973. *Oligopolistic Reaction and Multinational Enterprise*. Boston, MA: Division of Research, Graduate School of Business Administration, Harvard University.

Knight, G. A., & Cavusgil, S. T. 2004. Innovation organizational capabilities and the born-global firm. *Journal of International Business Studies*, 35: 124–141.

Kogut, B. 1985a. Designing global strategies: Comparative and competitive value-added chains. *Sloan Management Review*, 26(4): 15–28.

Kogut, B. 1985b. Designing global strategies: Profiting from operational flexibility. *Sloan Management Review*, 27(1): 27–38.

Kolyandr, A., & Ostroukh, A. 2014. Russia plans emerging fund for companies hurt by Ukraine sanctions. *Wall Street Journal*. Updated September 15. www.wsj.com/articles/russia-plans-emergency-fund-for-companies-hurt-by-ukraine-sanctions-1410802572 (accessed December 28, 2014).

Konishi, T. N., & Turpin, D. 2009. *Havaianas: A Brazilian Brand Goes Global*. IMD case study IMD-5–0748.

Kosacoff, B., Forteza, J., Barbero, M. I., Porta, F., & Stengel, E. A. 2014. *Going Global from Latin America: The Arcor Case* (3rd ed.). New York: McGraw-Hill Education, pp. 46 & 190.

Kwong, R. 2012. Acer sues former chief exec Lanci. *Financial Times* Tech Blog. February 7. http://blogs.ft.com/tech-blog/2012/02/acer-sues-former-ceo-lanci/? (accessed September 13, 2015).

Kosman, J. 2014. Entenmann's drivers brace for contract talks. New York Post. March 21. http://nypost.com/2014/03/21/entenmanns-drivers-brace-for-contract-talks/ (accessed January 1, 2016).

Laçon, J. P. 2009. *Chinese Multinationals*. Singapore: World Scientific.

Lampert, S., & Jaffe, E. 1996. Country of origin effects on international market entry, *Journal of Global Marketing*, 10(2): 27–52 (quote on p. 29).

Lange, D., Lee, P. M., & Dai, Y. 2011. Organizational reputation: A review. *Journal of Management*, 37: 153–184.

Lau, J. 2006. TCL to close most European operations. *Financial Times*, November 1. www.ft.com/intl/cms/s/0/4424358c-690d-11db-b4c2-0000779e2340.html#axzz33CvB3BWr (accessed September 13, 2014).

Leahy, J., Guerrera, F., & Politi, J. 2005. CNOOC's bid attempt hits a snag. *Financial Times*, April 4. www.ft.com/intl/cms/s/0/2b1d373c-a4a6-11d9-9778-00000e2511c8.html#axzz33CvB3BWr (accessed September 13, 2014).

Lessard, D. R., & Lucea, R. 2009. Embracing risk as a core competence: The case of CEMEX. *Journal of International Management*, 15(3): 296–305.

Lessard, D. R., & Reavis, C. 2009. *CEMEX: Globalization "The CEMEX Way."* MIT Case 09–039. https://mitsloan.mit.edu/LearningEdge/CaseDocs/09%20039%20CEMEX%20%20Lessard.pdf (accessed November 27, 2014).

Levinson, R. 2014. The Jollibee burger comes to Canada. *Canadian Business*, 87(1): 13–14.

Li, C., & Cui, H. Y. 2009. Huawei's internationalization, *IT Time Weekly*, October 15. www.c114.net/news/126/a450100.html (accessed October 19, 2015).

Li, J., Liu, Y. P., & Bi, F. Y. 2012. Zijin's workers got into conflicts with local people in Kyrgyzstan. *Global Times*, October 25. http://finance.ifeng.com/stock/ssgs/20121025/7200352.shtml (accessed October 19, 2015).

Li, Y. F. 2010. The integration story between Haier and Sanyo, June 29, 2010. http://blog.sina.com.cn/s/blog_6097fc250100jm1h.html (accessed October 19, 2015).

Lira, A. 2013. Franquia Nosso Bar pretende chegar a 800 unidades até o fim do ano. *Revista Pequenas Empresas Grandes Negocios*. http://revistapegn.globo.com/Revista/Common/0,EMI305841-17183,00-FRANQUIA+NOSSO+BAR+PRETENDE+CHEGAR+A+UNIDADES+ATE+O+FIM+DO+ANO.html. (accessed September 13, 2014).

Lisheng, Z. 2004. Siemens, Bird initiate strategic partnership. China Daily.com.cn, June 21. www.chinadaily.com.cn/english/doc/2004–06/21/content_341165.htm (accessed December 31, 2014).

Liu, B. 2007. TCL declares European unit insolvent. *China Daily*, May 26. www.chinadaily.com.cn/cndy/2007–05/26/content_880825.htm. (accessed September 13, 2014).

Liu, L. 2012. Gree, revelation armed with Brazil. *China Forex*, 07.

Lorenzen, M., & Mudambi, R. 2013. Clusters, connectivity and catch-up: Bollywood and Bangalore in the global economy. *Journal of Economic Geography*, 13: 501–534.

Lucas, L. 2012. AmBev to launch bars across Brazil. *Financial Times*, November 25. www.ft.com/intl/cms/s/0/b7970730-3597-11e2-bd77-00144feabdc0.html?siteedition=intl#axzz38UdoUPoP. (accessed September 13, 2014).

Luo, Y. 2002. *Multinational Enterprises in Emerging Markets*. Copenhagen Business School Press.

Luo, Y., & Rui, H. 2009. An ambidexterity perspective toward multinational enterprises from emerging economies. *Academy of Management Perspectives*, November: 49–70.

Luo, Y., & Tung, R. L. 2007. International expansion of emerging market enterprises: A springboard perspective. *Journal of International Business Studies*, 38: 481–498.

ManpowerGroup. 2014. The talent shortage continues: How the ever changing role of HR can bridge the gap. www.manpowergroup.com/wps/wcm/connect/0b882c15-38bf-41f3-8882-44c33d0e2952/2014_Talent_Shortage_WP_US2.pdf?MOD=AJPERES&ContentCache=NONE (accessed July 29, 2014).

ManpowerGroup. 2014. ManpowerGroup's Ninth Annual 2014 Talent Shortage Survey: Interactive Talent Shortage Explorer Tool. www.manpowergroup.com/talent-shortage-explorer/#.VQ2sztF0yUk (accessed March 21, 2015).

Marsh, P. 2007a. Weg powers up from an unlikely site. *Financial Times*, January 25. www.ft.com/intl/cms/s/0/4902a02a-ac1a-11db-b011-0000779e2340.html#axzz3Klf8RLRU. (accessed September 13, 2014).

Marsh, P. 2007b. Weg's way of operating. *Financial Times*, January 25. www.ft.com/intl/cms/s/0/497a4526-ac1a-11db-b011-0000779e2340.html#axzz3Klf8RLRU.

Martinez Peria, M. S. 2014. Financial inclusion in Latin America and the Caribbean. In: Didier, T., & Schmukler, S. L. (Eds.), *Emerging Issues in Financial Development: Lessons from Latin America*. Washington, DC: World Bank, pp. 25–90.

Mathews, J. A. 2006. Dragon multinationals: New players in 21st century globalization. *Asia Pacific Journal of Management*, 23: 5–27.

McGinley, S. 2012. Airline acquisitions "not worth it" says Emirates boss. Arabian Supply Chain.com, May 8. www.arabiansupplychain.com/article-7493-airline-acquisitions-not-worth-it-says-emirates-boss/ (accessed February 25, 2015).

McLain, S. 2013. Why the world's cheapest car flopped. *Wall Street Journal*, October 14. www.wsj.com/articles/SB10001424052702304520704579125312679104596 (accessed February 25, 2015).

McMclellan, J. M. 2006. Left seat: Big company makes little jet. *Flying Magazine*, February: 13–17 (quote on p. 14).

Merco. 2014. Merco Empresas. www.merco.info/br/ranking-merco-empresas (accessed December 14, 2014).

Merco. 2015. Qué es Merco. http://merco.info/es/que-es-merco (accessed September 13, 2015).

Milner, M. 2006. Russians take the wheel at LDV. *The Guardian*, August 1. www.theguardian.com/business/2006/aug/01/russia.motoring (accessed February 25, 2015).

Murphy, C. 2012. Beijing wields big stick against megaships. *Wall Street Journal*, November 13. http://online.wsj.com/news/articles/SB10001424127887324595904578116702590372508?cb=logged0.4119602390564978 (accessed November 27, 2014).

Murtha, T. P., Lenway, S. A., & Bagozzi, R. P. 1998. Global mind-sets and cognitive shift in a complex multinational corporation. *Strategic Management Journal*, 19(2): 97–114.

Narula, R., & Santangelo, G. D. 2012. Location and collocation advantages in international innovation. *Multinational Business Review*, 20(1), 6–25.

Newburry, W. 2012. Waving the flag: The influence of country of origin on corporate reputation. In: Barnett, M. and Pollock, T. (Eds.), *Oxford Handbook of Corporate Reputation*. Oxford University Press, pp. 240–259.

Newburry, W., Belkin, L., & Ansari, P. 2008. Perceived career opportunities from globalization: Influences of globalization capabilities and attitudes towards women in Iran and the U.S. *Journal of International Business Studies*, 39(5): 814–832.

Newburry, N., Gardberg, N. A., & Sanchez, J. I. 2014. Employer attractiveness in Latin America: The association among foreignness, internationalization and talent recruitment. *Journal of International Management*, 20(3): 327–344.

Newburry, W., & Zeira, Y. 1997. Generic differences between equity international joint ventures (EIJVs), international acquisitions (IAs) and international greenfield investments (IGIs): Implications for parent companies. *Journal of World Business*, 32(2), 87–102.

Newsweek. 2005. Business: A Jack Welch of Communists. *Newsweek*, May 8. www.newsweek.com/business-jack-welch-communists-118987 (accessed December 5, 2014).

Nicholson, M. 1997. Titan hindered by India's reputation. *Financial Post*, September 16.

Nölke, A. 2014. Private Chinese multinationals and the long shadow of the state. In: Nölke, A. (Ed.), *Multinational Corporations from Emerging Markets: State Capitalism 3.0*. London: Palgrave Macmillan.

Nueno, J. L., Bazan, M., & Rodriguez, S. 2011. AJE – Taking on bigger rivals. *Financial Times*, November 7. www.ft.com/intl/cms/s/0/462d0582-0577-11e1-8eaa-00144feabdc0.html?siteedition=intl#axzz3Klf8RLRUCASE STUDIES. (accessed September 13, 2014).

Ojo, B. 2012. Huawei faces barriers in Australia again. *Electronics Supply and Manufacturing China*, March 28, 2012. www.esmchina.com/ART_8800120171_1400_2300_0_4300_7305094c.HTM?jumpto=view_welcomead_1382928926571 (accessed October 19, 2015).

O'Neill, J. 2011. *The Growth Map: Economic Opportunity in the BRICs and Beyond*. New York: Penguin.

Oviatt, B. M., & McDougall, P. P. 1994. Toward a theory of international new ventures. *Journal of International Business Studies*, 25: 45–64.

Pacek, N., & Thorniley, D. 2004. *Emerging Markets: Lessons for Business Success and the Outlook for Different Markets*. London, GBR: Profile Books.

Paleit, A. 2006. How the DP World deal unraveled. *Financial Times*, March 11. www.ft.com/cms/s/0/f7587b96-b0a2-11da-a142-0000779e2340.html#ixzz3pfBxHUjn. (accessed October 26, 2015).

Palepu, K., Khanna, T., & Vargas, I. 2006. *Haier: Taking a Chinese Company Global*. Harvard Business School Case 9–706-401, revised August 5.

Panibratov, A., & Kalotay, K. 2009. Russian outward FDI and its policy context. FDI Profile, Vale Columbia Center on Sustainable International Investment, New York, October 13, p. 4.

Panibratov, A. 2012. *Russian Multinationals: From Regional Supremacy to Global Lead*. London: Routledge.

Park, S. H., Zhou, N., & Ungson, G. 2013. *Rough Diamonds: The Four Traits of Successful Breakout Enterprises in BRIC Countries*. San Francisco, CA: Jossey Bass/Wiley.

Park, S. S. 2009. Chinese carmaker SAIC accused of tech theft. *Korea Times*. www.koreatimes.co.kr/www/news/nation/2009/11/113_55305.html (accessed November 27, 2014).

Peng, M. W. 1997. Firm growth in transitional economies: Three longitudinal cases from China, 1989–96. *Organization Studies*, 18: 385–413.

Perkins, S. E. 2014. When does prior experience pay? Institutional experience and the multinational corporation. *Administrative Science Quarterly*, 59(1): 145–181 (p. 145)

Perlmutter, H. 1969. The tortuous evolution of the multinational corporation. *Columbia Journal of World Business*, 1(January/February): 9–18.

Porter, M. E. 1980. *Competitive Strategy*. New York: Free Press.

Porter, M. E. 1985. *Competitive Advantage*. New York: Free Press.

Powell, B. 2005. Sunset for a deal. *Time*, August 5. http://content.time.com/time/magazine/article/0,9171,1090826,00.html (accessed December 5, 2014).

Prahalad, C. K., & Doz, Y. L. 1987. *The Multinational Mission*. New York: Free Press.

Prasso, S. 2010. American made ... Chinese owned. *Fortune*, May 7. http://archive.fortune.com/2010/05/06/news/international/china_america_full.fortune/index.htm (accessed December 6, 2014).

Quelch, J. A., & Knoop, C. I. 2006. *Lenovo: Building a Global Brand*. Harvard Business School Case 507–014.

Quelch J., & Knoop C. I. 2007. *Lenovo – Building a Global Brand*. Harvard Business School Case Study 9-508-703. Boston, MA: HBS Publishing.

Rai, A. 2002. Titan's European foray wasn't worth the time. *Economic Times*, September 7. http://articles.economictimes.indiatimes.com/2002–09-07/news/27362717_1_indian-brand-titan-brand-bhaskar-bhat (accessed December 7, 2014).

Raj, A. 2013. Tata Motors' market share shrinks to single digits. Livemint and the *Wall Street Journal*, August 19. www.livemint.com/Industry/5boWEXwyJoCZa2xMasQHNK/Tata-Motors-market-share-shrinks-to-single-digits.html?utm_source=copy.

Ramamurti, R. 2012. What is really different about emerging market multinationals? *Global Strategy Journal*, 2(1): 41–47.

Ramamurti, R., & Singh, J. V. (Eds). 2009. *Emerging Multinationals from Emerging Markets*. Cambridge University Press.

Ramstad, E. 2003. Venture with Thomson gives TCL global role. *Wall Street Journal*, November 4. http://online.wsj.com/articles/SB106789214823565200. (accessed September 13, 2014).

Ramswamy, S. 2004. Living in interesting times. *Tata*. www.tata.com/article/inside/8xXL3Vvjg!$$$!4=/TLYVr3YPkMU= (accessed December 7, 2014).

Reid, S. D. 1981. The decision-maker and export entry and expansion. *Journal of International Business Studies*, 12: 101–112.

Reputation Institute. 2009. *CountryRep ™ 2009*. www.reputationinstititute.com.

Reuters. 1993. Indian watch firm Titan plans to go global. *Reuter News*, September 10.

Reuters. 2014. Factbox: The effect of Russia sanctions on European companies, August 7. www.reuters.com/article/2014/08/07/us-ukraine-crisis-companies-idUSKBN0G70OR20140807 (accessed December 28, 2014).

Riefler, P., & Diamantopoulos, A. 2007. Consumer animosity: a literature review and a reconsideration of its measurement. *International Marketing Review*, 24 (1), pp. 87–119.

Rindova, V. P., & Martins, L. L. 2012. Show me the money: A multidimensional perspective on reputation as an intangible asset. In: Barnett, M., & Pollock, A. (Eds.), *Oxford Handbook of Corporate Reputation*. Oxford University Press, pp. 16–22.

Robertson, C. 2008. Kola Real's low-cost international expansion strategy. *Thunderbird International Business Review*, 50(1): 59–70.

Robson, F. 2012. Empire of the sun: Havaianas' march to the top. *Sydney Morning Herald*, December 17. www.smh.com.au/small-business/entrepreneur/empire-of-the-sun-havaianas-march-to-the-top-20121216-2bia8.html (accessed October 20, 2015).

Sabharwal, S. 2007. Titan stops ticking in Europe. *Rediff*, July 5. www.rediff.com/money/2007/jul/05tit.htm.

Saleem, N. 2010. Emirates sells SriLankan stake. Gulfnews.com, July 9. http://gulfnews.com/business/aviation/emirates-sells-srilankan-stake-1.652115 (accessed February 25, 2015).

Santiso, J. 2013. *The Decade of the Multilatinas*. Cambridge University Press.

Sany Group Co., Ltd. Company profile, p. 17, February 2012. http://down.sanygroup.com/files/20120410170630471.pdf (accessed October 19, 2015).

Sauvant, K. P. 2008. *The Rise of Transnational Corporations from Emerging Markets: Threat or Opportunity?* Cheltenham, UK: Edward Elgar.

Sauvant, K. P., Maschek, W. A., & McAllister, G. A. 2010. *Foreign Direct Investments from Emerging Markets: The Challenges Ahead*. London: Palgrave Macmillan.

Schein, E. H. 2010. *Organizational Culture and Leadership* (4 ed.). San Francisco: Jossey-Bass.

Scully, C. Z. 2014. 2014 Global Top 100: Candy Industry's exclusive list of the top 100 confectionery companies in the world! *Candy Industry*, January 31. www.candyindustry.com/articles/86039-global-top-100-candy-industrys-exclusive-list-of-the-top-100-confectionery-companies-in-the-world?page=5 (accessed December 27, 2014).

Shankarmahesh, M. N. 2006. Consumer ethnocentrism: An integrative review of its antecedents and consequences. *International Marketing Review*, 23(2): 146–172.

Shaver, J. M., & Flyer, F. 2000. Agglomeration economies, firm heterogeneity, and foreign direct investment in the United States. *Strategic Management Journal*, 21 (12): 1175–1193.

Shaw, A. 2014. Lenovo to hand out $100 refunds, $250 vouchers to settle IdeaPad suit. *ComputerWorld*, September 22. Accessed at: www.computerworld.com/article/2686571/lenovo-to-hand-out-100-refunds-250-vouchers-to-settle-ideapad-suit.html.

Shenkar, O., & Zeira, Y. 1992. Role conflict and role ambiguity of chief executive officers. *Journal of International Business Studies*, 23(1): 55–75 (p. 57).

Shleifer, A., & Vishny, R. W. 1997. A survey of corporate governance. *Journal of Finance*, 52(2): 737–783 (p. 737).

Sidhva, S. 1997a. Foreign foray. *Far Eastern Economic Review*, July 10: 64.

Sidhva, S. 1997b. Review 200: Asia's leading companies. *Far Eastern Economic Review*, December 25.

Siegel, J. 2009. *Grupo Bimbo*. Harvard Business School Case 9–707-521, revised August 28.

Siekierska, A. 2013. Fraud investigation into Chilean retail giant Cencosud continues. *Santiago Times*, January 19. http://santiagotimes.cl/fraud-investigation-into-chilean-retail-giant-cencosud-continues/ (accessed December 31, 2014).

Singh, M. 2009. India's top automaker, Tata Motors, hits a rough patch. *Time*, February 24. http://content.time.com/time/world/article/0,8599,1881404,00.html (accessed December 13, 2014).

Sinochem. 2012. http://english.sinochem.com/g1007/s1771/t7798.aspx December 17 (accessed December 28, 2014).

Sinochem 2012. Annual Report, p. 48.

Sinochem. 2013. www.sinochem.com/g440/s1033/t9536.aspx December 27 (accessed September 13, 2014).

Sinochem Group. 2012. Sinochem Group: Actively fulfilling social responsibilities and promoting local development in "going global" process. http://www.sinochem.com/g1007/s1771/t7798.aspx. (accessed September 13, 2014).

Skolkovo. 2009. *Operational Challenges Facing Emerging Multinationals from Russia and China*. Skolkovo Monthly Briefing. Skolkovo Institute for Emerging Markets Studies, June. https://iems.skolkovo.ru/downloads/documents/SKOLKOVO_IEMS/Research_Reports/SKOLKOVO_IEMS_Research_2009-06-10_en.pdf (accessed September 13, 2014).

Smith, P. B. S., Torres, C., Leong, C. -H., Budhwar, P., Achoui, M., & Lebedeva, N. 2012. Are indigenous approaches to achieving influence in business organizations distinctive? A comparative study of guanxi, wasta, jeitinho, svyazi and pulling strings. *International Journal of Human Resource Management*, 23(2): 333–348.

Song, J. A. 2007. SAIC finetunes Korean strategy. *Financial Times*, May 2. www.ft.com/intl/cms/s/0/b0e478c8-f8e9-11db-a940-000b5df10621.html#axzz3KUiNWsIy.

Sousa, D. 2014. Ambev estuda expansão das franquias Nosso Bar (Ambev studies the expansion of the franchise Nosso Bar). *Exame*, August 11. http://exame.abril.com.br/pme/noticias/ambev-estuda-expansao-das-franquias-nosso-bar.

Statista. 2014. Global net sales by leading home appliance manufacturers in 2013 (in million U.S. dollars). www.statista.com/statistics/266689/net-sales-of-leading-home-appliance-manufacturers-worlwide/ (accessed December 7, 2014).

Stahl, G. K., & Koster, K. 2013. Lenovo-IBM: Bridging cultures, languages, and time zones. Integration challenges (B). Case number 0005/2013, Vienna University of Economics and Business.

Stopford, J., & Strange, S., 1992. *Rival States, Rival Firms: Competition for World Market Shares*. New York: Cambridge University Press.

Stopford, J. M., & Wells, L. T. Jr. 1972. *Managing the Multinational Enterprise: Organization of the Firm and Ownership of the Subsidiary*. New York: Basic Books.

Sun, J. X. 2012. ZTE's losses in oversea expansion exceed expectations. *National Business Daily*, November 28. http://tech.163.com/12/1128/02/8HC5GVR9000915BE.html (accessed October 19, 2015).

Tabakman, M. 2010. Who's the Bimbo here? Another class action focusing on independent contractor. Fox Rothschild LLP. July 7. http://wagehourlaw.foxrothschild.com/2010/07/articles/class-actions/whos-the-bimbo-here-another-class-action-focusing-on-independent-contractor/ (accessed January 1, 2016).

Tabliabue, J. 2003. Thomson and TCL to join TV units. *New York Times*, November 4. www.nytimes.com/2003/11/04/business/thomson-and-tcl-to-join-tv-units.html (accessed September 13, 2014).

Thunderbird. 2014. Thunderbird Global Mindset Inventory. http://globalmindset.thunderbird.edu/home/global-mindset-inventory (accessed December 27, 2014).

Tse., T., & Couturier, J., 2009. Lenovo's acquisition of IBM's PC division: A short-cut to be a world player or a lemon that leads to nowhere? London: ESCP Europe Business School.

Turpin, D. 2013. How Havaianas built a global brand: Flip-flop maker excelled at planning and marketing. *Financial Times*, September 3. www.ft.com/cms/s/0/230b83b0-1166-11e3-8321-00144feabdc0.html.

UNCTAD. 2014. Annex table 29 – The top 100 non-financial TNCs from developing and transition economies, ranked by foreign assets, 2012a, UNCTAD. http://unctad.org/en/Pages/DIAE/World%20Investment%20Report/Annex-Tables.aspx (accessed September 13, 2014).

UNCTAD. 2015. Foreign Direct Investment Database. http://unctadstat.unctad.org/wds/ReportFolders/reportFolders.aspx (accessed October 09, 2015).

Union Advocate. 2014. Steel mill's expansion leaves St. Paul Pipefitters out in the cold, January 10. http://advocate.stpaulunions.org/2014/01/10/steel-mills-expansion-leaves-st-paul-pipefitters-out-in-the-cold/.

United Steelworkers. 2006. Steelworkers ratify agreement with Gerdau in Canada; Gerard Slams Company's Behavior in U.S., August 1. www.usw.ca/media/news/releases?id=0194.

Uranga, R. 2011. Timeline: Mexico's Cemex shares hit multi-year low. *Reuters*, October 4. www.reuters.com/article/2011/10/04/us-cemex-timeline-idUSTRE7937HI20111004 (accessed November 27, 2014).

Van Voris, B., & Riseborough, J. 2014. Rio Tinto sues Vale, BSGR claiming conspiracy over mine. *Bloomberg*, May 1. www.bloomberg.com/news/2014–04-30/rio-tinto-sues-vale-bsgr-claiming-conspiracy-over-mine.html (accessed November 27, 2014).

Vernon, R. 1966. International investment and international trade in the product cycle. *Quarterly Journal of Economics*, 80: 190–207.

Vernon, R. 1977. *Storm over the Multinationals: The Real Issues*. Boston, MA: Harvard University Press.

Wang, Z. 2008. TCL's Liang Yaorong: Analyzing the profitability for every TV we are selling. *China Business News*, February 14. http://tech.qq.com/a/20080214/000154.htm (accessed October 19, 2015).

Wang, Z. B. 2010. Who is suppressing Huawei. *China Economy & Informatization*, December 8, 2010. http://finance.sina.com.cn/chanjing/gsnews/20101208/07309072389.shtml (accessed October 19, 2015).

Webber, J. 2012. Argentina: Sweet success is achieved in different packs. *Financial Times*, June 20. www.ft.com/intl/cms/s/0/1befcf4e-b480-11e1-bb2e-00144feabdc0.html#axzz38oMNlb00 (accessed July 29, 2014).

WEG. 2014. Timeline. http://weg50.weg.net/50/en/timeline/ (accessed December 3, 2014).

Wembridge, M., Milne, R., & Catherine Belton, C. 2012. VimpelCom shareholders feud on hold. *Financial Times*, August 16. http://www.ft.com/intl/cms/s/0/afd1261c-e7ad-11e1-8686-00144feab49a.html. (accessed September 13, 2014).

Wides-Munoz, L. 2014. Infosys whistleblower taking on company again. *ABC News*, October 7. Accessed online at: http://abcnews.go.com/US/wireStory/infosys-whistleblower-taking-company-26020131. (accessed September 13, 2014).

Wildau, G. 2014. New Silk Road raises hopes for increased China–Arab trade. *Financial Times*, June 30. www.ft.com/intl/cms/s/0/11190312-f874-11e3-815f-00144feabdc0.html#axzz390Cftd6c.

Wilson, J., Burgis, T., & Leahy, J. 2014. Rio Tinto sues Vale and BSGR over Guinea mine controversy. *Financial Times*, April 30. www.ft.com/intl/cms/s/0/8ef9c710-d06c-11e3-af2b-00144feabdc0.html#axzz3b413EpNf (accessed September 13, 2014).

Wright, R. 2006a. DP World gains strategic advantage. *Financial Times*, February 10. www.ft.com/intl/cms/s/0/9364c838-9a68-11da-8b63-0000779e2340.html#axzz3pf1Tpavl (accessed October 26, 2015).

Wright, R. 2006b. DP World expects $750m from US ports sale. *Financial Times*, March 21. www.ft.com/cms/s/0/ee7ab3b4-b8fd-11da-b57d-0000779e2340.html#ixzz3pf33KRcJ (accessed October 26, 2015).

Xie, Chunfang., & Meng, lin. 2008. The experience and insight of Gree international operation. *Market Modernization*, 561(December): 87–88.

Yan, Y. L. 2005. Huawei in Russia. *Telecom World*, 6. http://tech.sina.com .cn/t/2005-06-06/1903628119.shtml (accessed October 19, 2015).

Yergin, D., & Stanislaw, J. 1998. *The Commanding Heights: The Battle for the World Economy*. New York: Touchstone.

Yeung, A., Xin, K., Pfoertsch, W., & Liu, S. J. 2011. *The Globalization of Chinese Companies: Strategies for Conquering International Markets*. Singapore: Wiley.

Zaheer, S. 1995. Overcoming the liability of foreignness. *Academy of Management Journal*, 38: 341–363.

Zeng, M., & Williamson, P. 2007. *Dragons at Your Door*. Boston, MA: Harvard Business Press.

Zhang, L. 2007. TCL got Mckinsey's top manager for TTE. *Shanghai Youth Daily*, March 22. http://tech.sina.com.cn/e/2007-03-22/14341428835.shtml (accessed October 19, 2015).

Zheng, X. 2013. A study on the marketing strategy of GREE Oversea Sales Company in American Region. Master's thesis, Huazhong University of Science & Technology, April.

Zhiguo, J. 2012. Tsingtao's chairman on jump-starting a sluggish company. *Harvard Business Review*, April. https://hbr.org/2012/04/tsingtaos-chairman-on-jump-starting-a-sluggish-company (accessed December 14, 2014).

Zhou, N., Park, S. H., & Ungson, G. R. 2013. Profitable growth: Avoiding the "growth fetish" in emerging markets. *Business Horizons*, 56: 473–481.

Ziyan, C. 2013. Gree denies Soleus accusations. *ChinaDaily USA*, June 21. http://usa.chinadaily.com.cn/business/2013–06/21/content_16645175.htm (accessed December 30, 2014).

Zoomlion. 2013a. Zoomlion Heavy Industries annual report, p. 18.

Zoomlion. 2013b. Another important overseas M&A by Zoomlion – Acquisition of M-TEC, No. 1 dry-mixed mortar equipment brand in the world. Press release, December 26. http://en.zoomlion.com/news/20131226103431539.htm. (accessed September 13, 2014).

ZTE. 2013. ZTE faces Mongolia corruption probe. *Financial Times*, April 12. www.ft.com/intl/cms/s/0/94ced06e-a362-11e2-ac00-00144feabdc0.html#axzz3nzUDgoxs (accessed September 13, 2014).

ZTE. 2014. About ZTE. www.en.zte.com.cn/en/about/corporate_information/vision/ (accessed 30 December 2014).

Index

Note: Page numbers in *italic* refer to tables.

Printed in the United States
By Bookmasters